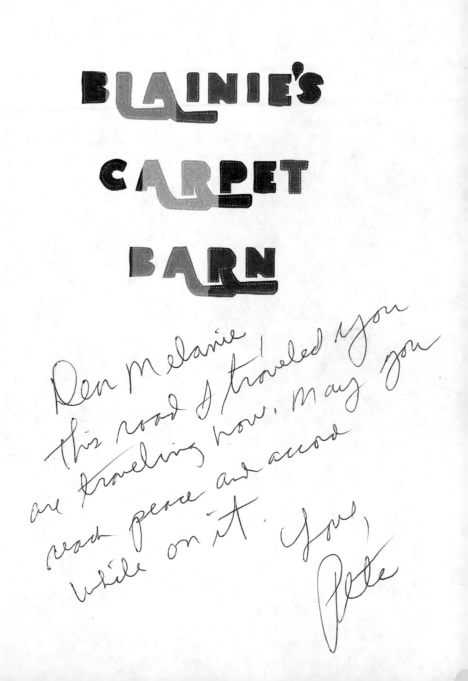

BLAINIE'S CARPET BARN

Dear Melanie,
this road I traveled you
are traveling now. May you
reach peace and accord
while on it.
Yours,
Pete

BLAINIE'S CARPET BARN

Becoming My Father's Father

Peter Gorham

TATE PUBLISHING
AND ENTERPRISES, LLC

Published by Tate Publishing & Enterprises, LLC
127 E. Trade Center Terrace | Mustang, Oklahoma 73064 USA
1.888.361.9473 | www.tatepublishing.com

Tate Publishing is committed to excellence in the publishing industry. The company reflects the philosophy established by the founders, based on Psalm 68:11,

"The Lord gave the word and great was the company of those who published it."

Book design copyright © 2012 by Peter Gorham. All rights reserved.
Cover design by Ashley Itenberg
Interior design by Ashley Itenberg

Published in the United States of America

ISBN: 978-1-62147-196-7
1. Family & Relationships / Eldercare
2. Family & Relationships / Aging
12.11.02

Dedication

To my parents, Blaine and Roberta Gorham, who taught us knowledge and wisdom, love and laughter.

Acknowledgments

I wish to thank:

Judith Ludwig Gorham, my wife, whose love and commitment to me and my parents helped to make this final journey we all traveled more endurable, more natural, and even humorous.

Judith Marquardt. Her faith in me and my book and her gentle but determined nudging made it possible to condense 300,000 words to 100,000 and still tell a resonant story. She patiently sat with me day after day, word after word, doing that.

Heidi Humes, author of *Oscar E., The Croissant King*, volunteered her fine sensibilities and considerable skills to my project. Her loyalty, style, and resolute work habits helped move me forward with hope.

Leigh and Bob Moberg. Their belief in my writing, and in me, in addition to the strength of their own faith, first convinced me that my story was worthy and needed to be read.

Will Gorham, our son, a fine writer and editor himself. We thank him not only for his literary skills but also for the unique love and humor he shared with his grandparents.

The many friends and relatives who walked lovingly and faithfully with Blaine and Roberta throughout their lives, until the end.

The countless unsung heroes and saints who humbly give care, love, and hope to the elderly, the sick, and the needy. We particularly thank those at Seminary Manor who gave our parents healing love and tender mercy.

Into my heart an air that kills

From yon far country blows:

What are those blue remembered hills,

What spires, what farms are those?

That is the land of lost content,

I see it shining plain,

The happy highways where I went

And cannot come again

—A Shropshire Lad, A.E. Housman

On Becoming
My Father's Father

Charles Blaine Gorham, my father, was a good man. He made people laugh, and he showered them with love, which was healing. He was attentive to each person he met in whatever situation he met them in, graciously offering them the time they needed to finish their business, discuss their lives, or open their hearts— or to listen to him. He made everyone seem special and believed that every person was worthy.

The most important and best thing that ever happened to my father was my mother, Roberta. She was lovely, intelligent, gentle, graceful, and level headed. She was my father's source of inspiration and his imperative for honesty.

My father's mentality was eccentric and like no one else's. As a boy, I was embarrassed by him. He did not have normal boundaries. Nor was he inhibited by false pride. He regarded pride as a detriment to moving ahead.

My father was confident and willful. He had an overpowering persuasive ability born of charm, humor, intuition, and superhuman persistence. But he instinctively knew when to be aggressive and when to surrender in order to gain an advantage to be used somewhere in the future, even the distant future, which he was constantly looking into and analyzing and re-configuring.

My father's ethical beliefs, which generally prescribed that he should harm no one and that everyone should win, benefitted both him and others at once. He was truly generous.

Blaine Gorham could outwit, out-talk, and out-charm most people. He loved the challenge of selling something to someone—carpet, his point of view, a plan, a direction, himself.

When Blaine was fifteen years old, the Great Depression began and lasted until his mid-twenties. He somehow escaped being branded forever by its ravages, but he talked about its ominous shadow often in my youth. So it was a great relief when my father proclaimed to me as a young man, "I know now that I will always be able to provide for us no matter how bad things might get." This had a deep positive impact upon my general sense of security.

By the time my father said to me late in his life, "I'm afraid of almost everything now," I had acquired a strength of my own—largely from him—with which to lessen his uncertainty.

At the end of his life, I would become my father's father. He would gladly give me authority over him, trusting absolutely that like a fiduciary I would hold his and my mother's interests above my own.

For Blaine, this reversal of roles was easy to make. Pride did not stand in his way. For me, though, it was like waking up in darkness and walking outside onto a different planet. At first it was a fascinating place to have landed. Eventually, though, I just wanted to go home.

But I stayed until the end.

This book begins where my father's mental decline has become evident and where the wide, rich lives of my father and my mother first begin to compress and then to unravel.

Part One

Fall 2004

What Blaine says he wants now is to be sitting on a back porch—as I see it, a farmhouse porch—rocking in the sun that's setting over a field of memories, having no responsibilities for anything or anyone, slipping away painlessly day by day, month by month, into some peaceful and passive place that's warm and undemanding where he can nap at will...eventually forever.

At lunch, Blaine and I talk about my mother. My father married a prize woman whose grace, honesty, and intelligence gave him power and legitimacy. The two of them have been together inseparably for sixty-four years. Looking after her is now my father's sole purpose in life. He is obsessed with her survival. "Pete," he says, "the theme song for this stage of your mother's and my life is 'Stayin' Alive.'"

My mother's lungs have been failing for years. She's had a heart valve replaced, a broken hip, mycobacterium avium complex, lifelong arthritis, deteriorating spine, countless cases of pneumonia, skin so thin that it rubs off with a washcloth, macular degeneration, recurring nausea and diarrhea, and increasing deafness. But she has stayed alive for eighty-eight years. She has been at the threshold of death so many times that it is no longer shocking to anyone but Blaine when she arrives at it again.

After lunch, I drop my father off at Seminary Estates, the assisted care center where he and my mother are living on a trial basis, for the winter. He looks calmer and released for an hour and a half from his war with worry, like a soldier resting on a nearby island between battles.

Today is a big day. Blaine and I are going to clean out the refrigerator at my parents' house and sort through the canned goods in the cupboards. My father's lifelong insistence upon peculiar and irrational methods and behaviors has morphed into a full-blown obsession. It is amusing in a way and sad in another. For a couple of years, Blaine has been fixated upon (among other things) food spoilage. The expiration dates stamped on packaged food items mean nothing to him. He throws food out when he feels it's been on the shelf too long. He tosses out meat and produce—even eggs, pickles, salad dressing, and mayonnaise—almost as soon as they've arrived from the store.

On the five-mile drive to their unoccupied house in the country, Blaine reads a note to me that my mother has written. "Do not touch the refrigerator today, only the canned goods."

He is not yet ready to deal with culling the good food from the bad food. I can see that he is comfortable wandering aimlessly around the house, remembering pleasant things that happened here, which satisfies his need to accomplish something today. But I know precisely what will satisfy mine. So I start taking the canned goods out of the cupboards and putting them on the counter neatly into categories. I find three empty bags: food for my mother and father, food for me and Judy, and food for the garbage can.

Blaine comes back, and I explain what I'm doing. He's excited by the prospect, and he begins to focus beside me. We consider each item one at a time. I linger at first with each verdict, but he knows without the slightest equivocation how to dispose of each of them. It is a marvel to behold my ninety-year-old father's stalwart and beefy discharge of duties.

"Artichoke hearts," I say.

"Throw 'em out!"

"But they don't expire until January."

"Throw 'em out!"

My father would never buy artichoke hearts and probably doesn't know what they are. However, if they were served to him in a dish, he would eat them without needing to know what he was eating. Don't ask, don't tell.

"I'll take them," I say, and I put them in the Pete and Judy bag.

"Good," he says.

Blaine and I speed through this decision-making process. He is amazed at what we've done—at what he's done, which is making perhaps fifty decisions in thirty minutes. Just like he used to do in his small carpet business in the halcyon days when he was "king." We hug each other. There are tears in my father's eyes.

"How about the refrigerator?" I ask him.

He's stunned and can't answer. He remembers the mantra he'd practiced on the drive to the house. "Roberta has told me not to deal with the refrigerator today." Blaine hands me the small piece of paper, which says in my mother's handwriting, "Do *not* clean out the refrigerator."

I know that it is the refrigerator that he wants to deal with most of all, but my mother has forbidden him from indiscriminately plundering its valuable items, most of which are still good, knowing that if he had his way, he would eradicate them all like a revolutionary getting rid of potential dissent. "My greatest fear," he says, "is that mold will develop in the refrigerator and that it will invade your mother's lungs and she'll die."

I put my arm around his shoulder. "Well, Dad, let's at least open the door."

I do, and I see that the refrigerator is jam-packed with food items. I say, "Well, I can see already that some things need to be thrown out."

"Pete, I am so glad you're here to make these decisions."

One Tupperware container has mold swimming in soup brine. I show it to Blaine, and he recoils in horror. "Ah," he says with new energy, "good thing we looked here, don't you think?"

We know to leave enough items on the door and the shelves so that it's hard to tell precisely what we've removed. My mother has an excellent memory.

"Do you think we took too much?" my father asks sheepishly at the end of our purge.

"No," I say. "We took just what we should have. I'll tell Mom it was my idea."

"Good, good, I like that," he says.

I gather the bags together and tie them off at the tops and carry them to my car's trunk. It is getting late, and I need to move on, for we still have to unload the garbage and the bag for me and Judy at my home before going to Seminary Estates with their bag.

I go back inside the house. Blaine is standing at the kitchen counter, looking intently at a piece of paper in his hand. I walk up to him. He is focused like a hawk, and his eyes are furrowed and squinting in an obvious effort to understand something. His hands are bony and purplish, and the veins are prominent.

"What's wrong, Dad?"

He doesn't answer but keeps staring down at the note my mother's written.

"I had a thought, Pete, but it's gone. It's like fishing. The fish comes by your line and nibbles, and you get excited. But then it goes on. But if you wait, sometimes it comes back and gets caught on the hook. Oh, I remember! Your mother said, 'Do not remove anything from the refrigerator.'"

"Well, Dad, that was my decision, not yours. I'm going to tell Mom that I forced you to throw stuff out and that you tried to stop me, but I overpowered you. Okay?"

"Good, I like that."

My mother is sitting on the couch reading as always. It is so hot inside that I feel sick for a minute and want to hurry back outside into the cool air. I say to my mother, "We did it. And I made an executive decision."

"What was that?" she asks suspiciously.

"I cleaned the refrigerator, too. Dad told me not to and showed me your note, but I did it anyway over his objection. And we found a number of items that were old and even moldy, so I'm glad we did."

I bring the rest of the food in, sit with my parents awhile and talk, and then get up to go home. My father walks me down the long corridor to the doorway and stops me before I leave and says, "Thanks, son. I could not have done this alone."

A few days later, I visit my parents. Blaine's distressed.

"What's wrong, Dad?"

"I forgot to call Dan to clean out the gutters at our house, and now the crawlspace has water in it, and the sump pump is running all the time."

"That's what a sump pump is supposed to do—run. It's been raining for days. It runs, Dad, when it rains."

"But the reason there's water in the crawlspace is because I didn't get the gutters cleaned out."

"No, that's not the reason. The reason is because it's been raining for days, and the level of the ground water has been rising, and it's asking your sump pump to run. That's why the sump pump is there—to pump out the water. It's been doing that for thirty-three years, Dad."

"But mold will form with all that moisture down there, and your mother will get sick."

"But Dad, Mom doesn't live there now. She lives at Seminary Estates."

"But she'll go back in the spring."

"That's six months away. Let's worry in six months."

We talk like this for thirty minutes with my mother joining in to help me try to convince him of the absurdity of his worries.

"Dad, finish your meal." He can't. He needs to continue to make his point over and over about the mold and the water and the sump pump and his culpability for not cleaning the gutters. We re-explain it all, but he still doesn't listen. He looks sad and vulnerable, crushed and blameworthy.

"I know we'll never return home for good again," my mother says. "I know we need to sell the house, but I just can't throw all of my things away. I'm not practical in that way like most people. I need time to sort through them. I need a time when all of the family is back together, and we can sit down and go through them one by one."

That will never happen. What my mother really needs, like all of us will eventually need, is for her health and her Golden Years to return. For the days to come back when she arose at six and made coffee and went for a walk in the woods and then came back and sat on the deck and watched the birds in the trees and the ducks on the lake and went for a ride in the boat and went fishing and cooked dinner and had family reunions.

Blaine says, "I can't understand all this anymore." I tell him I'll clean the gutters on Thursday. He won't let me because he is afraid I'll fall off the roof. Then, out of nowhere, he articulates his refrigerator worry again. The mold is creeping back into the food, and he needs to deal with it again. He remembers we went there and cleaned it out and were satisfied that it was safe, but the feeling of assurance has left him. He wants to turn the refrigerator off so it won't produce mold any longer. My mother says that my brother Bill is coming with his friend, and she has offered them the house. That is unacceptable to my father. He prefers that my brother stay in a motel. My mother won't have it.

He wants to turn the heat down low to kill the mold. And turn the water off. Good thing I didn't tell him that the water line to the toilet started leaking today and I had to fix it.

"Dad, do you want me to go out with you at the end of the week, and we'll look at all this stuff again and see how it looks?"

"Yes, I would *love* that."

We set a date for Thursday. I get up to leave and stand by the door and talk to them both.

"I never thought it would come to this," my mother says. "But I could be happy if Blaine was happy. If we sell the house, he'll find something else to worry about."

Blaine calls off our meeting for Thursday. The imaginary mold at his house has become secondary to my mother's cold, which has become worse. Besides, he got a good night's sleep, so things look better. In addition, Dan cleaned out the gutters. It stopped raining, so presumably the sump pump stopped running. And the sun came out again.

Winter 2004-2005

I arrive to pick up Blaine to go to the bank and deposit five thousand dollars, which is the earnest money from the prospective purchaser of their lake house in Minnesota.

I had told him I'd deposit the check myself, but he needs to go along, he thinks. I have done enough things like this with my father to know to be wary. I suggest we go to the drive-up and make the deposit. "Oh no," he says. "We need to go into the main bank downtown. I want to take my coat off and sit down awhile and talk to someone and sign the check in front of them."

I can envision us sitting in the bank president's office for an hour or two talking about Rotary and having this otherwise ordinary transaction take the entire morning. "No, Dad, we're going to the drive-up, and we'll go inside of the kiosk. I know the women there. That will be fine." He finds this suggestion unacceptable and makes lame excuses for why we must go to the main bank instead. I pull into the kiosk parking lot, and he reluctantly shuffles in with me.

My father is in the background and technically has surrendered authority to me, which he wants but instinctively resists. In no time the transaction is over. What would have taken my father at least three hours to do on his own has taken us ten minutes. Because I have known Blaine Gorham for fifty-nine years and have waited innumerable times for countless hours for him to transact something in his infinitely patient, inefficient, and mysterious but somehow ultimately successful style, I have preferred to do things in my own lean, efficient style in these later years where I've been involved. The richness he has gathered into his life from spending inordinate amounts of time with others in all situations with no sense of purpose or time or urgency has eluded me. I am less because of it. But my productivity rating is high.

Our roles have started to change. We're each trying to get accustomed to a new, hybrid one. Now I am the busy middle-aged man, and Blaine is the child with time on his hands who needs direction.

I decide to go into Seminary Estates to explain to my mother what we've done. The open dining room is just beyond the foyer. In front of it is a hallway that leads to another hallway that goes to their apartment— the last apartment on the left way down at the other end. It is quite a long walk and good exercise for both of my parents. Halfway to their room, there is a sitting area, which is wider than the rest of the hallway with comfortable chairs and a desk and tall lamps and carpet of a different, lighter color. My father insists upon stopping there to sit and rest, and I oblige.

"This is the oasis, Pete. The caravan of camels starts out down there," he says while pointing to the end of the hallway. "Its destination is the dining room. But along the way, the camels get thirsty, and the riders get weary and covered with sand. So they stop here for a rest at the oasis. See the palm trees?" he says, pointing at the tall lamps. They *do* look like palm trees with lampshades that bend up toward heaven like palm branches. "And these are chairs in the sand." The carpet is beige like sand. "And there's the sun," he says while pointing to the florescent lights above. "And you can feel the cool breeze blowing." He's right; there is a breeze coming from the open door at the end of the hallway. "We meet weary travelers here and sometimes go on with them after a rest."

I call my parents at eight thirty that night. Blaine answers it and says that my mother's gone to bed already. He thanks me profusely for helping him with the deposit and then asks what I'm doing. I tell him I'm trying to hook up Judy's wireless computer to mine, and it's exasperating. I tell him that it gives me fear to deal with electronic computer-age equipment. "How well I understand," he says. "That's how I felt as a boy when I was expected to harness Chester Walker's team. I could never get the bridle on the horses because I was so afraid that they were going to step on my foot."

My mother goes into the emergency room. She can't breathe and is dizzy and can't walk. The pulmonologist thinks she has a recurrence of what she's always called "bird disease," which she first got decades ago. Its actual name is Mycobacterium Avium Complex or MAC. In my research about it, I've discovered that it is often associated with AIDS patients, which I decide not to share with her. I also discovered that it is not transmitted by birds, as my mother has always believed, but is a disease that birds also get. I don't share that either, since she won't want to have been wrong.

Upon visiting Roberta later in the day, she tells me that the doctor now thinks her ailment is not pneumonia or MAC but is something else whose name she can't remember.

I call my father and ask how he's doing. He's confused by Roberta's hospitalization and seems lonely and yet scared he'll have to take care of her again when she gets home. He is conflicted by his own need and by his sense of obligation to take care of his wife at the end of her life, as his father and grandfather both did with their wives, and his waning ability to do so. I promise him she'll be all right and so will he—in the morning.

I talk to Judy and then call him back and ask if he wants to spend the night with us. He chuckles. "No, I'm okay now…after our talk. You must have known I needed to talk. But I'll take a rain check. There are nights when it just seems so lonely, and then I'll need it more. You remember the last time she went into the hospital when I came over that afternoon to talk? I wanted to stay with you all night, except it wasn't night yet!"

I call Blaine at nine the next morning. He's fine and has totally recovered from despair. The man has incredible powers of regeneration. Probably if he lost an arm, it would grow right back. We arrange to meet at the hospital at eleven. "Your mother is ready to bolt," he says.

I have been at Seminary Estates the entire morning, helping my father sort through scrapbooks and memorabilia to put together a letter of eulogy for the wife of his friend who's died. We are through for now, and I'm tired and ready to leave. But he picks up another document that has been copied so many times it looks like a cheap forgery. "Sit down," he begs me.

"I was never a good student, Pete, because all I wanted to do was to have fun. My mother was so worried that I wouldn't make something of myself that she went to see one of the teachers she knew for advice. Of course, they all knew each other in that little town of one hundred people. The teacher told my mother that there was a part in a play coming up, the part of a fast-talking comedian, and she thought I would be perfect for that part because I loved to talk and make people laugh. My mother was hoping for a more dignified role for me—a banker perhaps or a scientist—but this was better than nothing."

Blaine hands me the multi-page document. "I had to memorize this and stand in front of the entire school and perform it. I was scared for weeks. I practiced and practiced in front of a mirror. The moment came for me to be on stage, and I naturally started acting this part. Suddenly people began smiling who hadn't smiled for years, and then the audience started laughing, and I became energized and animated. That made them laugh more. At that moment, my life took a new direction, and I knew what I would be forever. I would be an entertainer, an actor. I would tell stories and make people laugh and make them happy. This right here," he says holding the document, "changed my life—forever."

Blaine was born in the small town of Winfield, Iowa. His family soon moved to Olds, Iowa, population 100, but Winfield is where my grandfather lived again later when I knew him with his second wife Nell who had Parkinson's disease.

When I was a boy in the fifties, we would visit this little town five or ten times a year and go to my grandparents' farm. It was a charming, little farmhouse on a small acreage. There were tall trees in the yard, a fruit orchard, old barns and barn lots with pigs and cows and chickens that walked around in sloppy mud. There were mysterious places with secret passageways and haymows dark and aromatic, which were only accessible by built-in wooden ladders. In the fruit orchard were many tall poles, and on the tops of the poles were bird houses for purple martins—birds my grandfather favored for their beauty and their grace. Visiting the farm was a fairyland adventure for me and my brothers.

After dinner in the summer, we went outside into the yard beneath the huge maple trees and sat in brightly colored, metal chairs. *My grandfather would whistle with the birds in the trees as the sun went down. He was a world-class whistler who was hired regularly to whistle at people's weddings in the area. He could literally whistle the birds into the trees above us and was able to whistle just like a robin or a cardinal. It was uncanny. The yard was like an aviary with birds landing in the trees, swallows perching on their birdhouse posts, birds buzzing around everywhere. They loved my grandfather and seemed to think he was one of them.*

The drive home was always dark and sad. We were leaving the peaceful farm and my gentle, lovely grandfather and returning to where our responsibilities were—school for us boys and work for my parents where the phone rang all the time with calls for my father about carpet problems.

The last event of freedom and happiness and solidarity that took place on these Sundays was at the Mississippi River, crossing that great bridge that spans the no-man's land between Iowa and Illinois. At nighttime you could still view dark islands in the river and barges moving slowly. It was somewhere near here at dusk that my father would start singing and the rest of us joined in. He always sang a song that I learned just a few years ago called "In the Garden." It goes like this:

> *I come to the garden alone while the dew is still on the roses, and the voices I hear falling on my ear, the son of God discloses. And he walks with me and he talks with me and he tells me I am his own, and the joy we share as we tarry there, none other has ever known.*

I didn't know what the song meant, but I could feel its poignancy. The word "tarry" felt like a great word.

It seems truly amazing to me now—in that mythical, yearning yet helpless way the past seems to be—that I could have lived that experience and the ones I do today in the same lifetime and be the same person.

Spring 2005

I return to Seminary Estates to see how my parents are doing. They're fine. My mother looks lovely and happy. My father's back is much better. I fill the bird feeder outside their window as I usually do. I don't stay long.

My father walks me down to the oasis. His gait is sprightly, considering the condition of his spine. I know that the prednisone the doctor injected into his spine will wear off in a week or two, and the pain will return, but for now life is good.

We walk past the oasis. The day is beautiful. Sun is pouring into the halls from every window. The residents are prowling around still after dinner and before bed. One old lady passes us in a wheelchair. She has the most lovely smile on her face. She's very thin and old but still beautiful. One of her legs is gone. Blaine stops her, and they talk, and he holds her hand and jokes around. They laugh and part.

"That's Mrs. Hendricks. Her husband was my first patient at hospice. He died years ago. She has diabetes. They took her leg not long ago."

We walk together to the front door and stand in the foyer in the early evening sun. Blaine thanks me for taking him to the pain clinic. I hug him. He says something, but I don't listen because I'm thinking of that smile on Mrs. Hendricks's face—even right after she's lost her leg. It was radiant, joyous, and enlightened.

In one of the Seminary Estate's smaller dining rooms, a group of card players sits intently around a table. It's an odd-looking group of ninety-year-old gamblers. They still look pretty ferocious even after almost a century. One old lady in a motorized wheel chair is so blind that her head is almost touching the table, trying to see what's been played. They never notice me or wave because this is *very serious* stuff and demands their complete attention.

I hear various TV programs from apartments I pass on either side of the hallway; some are extremely loud because the listener is deaf. A few doors are open, and inside are people sitting talking or watching the news—or just alone in silence, staring. Invariably, their apartments are spotless and attractively decorated but not crowded.

I like being around these old people. They are predictable and orderly and believe things like, "Cleanliness is next to godliness" and "The Lord helps him who helps himself." These old people are not into being politically correct; they are simply into being correct. They aren't confused about what's the right way to do things or wonder if their notions accommodate everyone's particular plight. They are ninety, and their bodies are falling apart. They're on walkers and in wheel chairs, and they've lost their memories, their spouses, their homes, and their eligibility to drive a car. But they still keep their apartments immaculate. They're polite and deferential and don't cut ahead in line or take more than their share or knowingly play their music too loudly.

Blaine joined hospice in the early 1990s and was in it for almost eight years. He would sit for hours with old people who were dying and talk to them. "Usher them into eternity," he would say. My father has always been a compassionate and caring person, but I was surprised that he took on these assignments that put him face to face with death. I ask him why he did it.

"Well, son, it's like this. I was in my middle seventies, and your mother and I were leading the life of Riley. We owned two houses, spent the summers at the lake, and sometimes spent the winters in Florida. But I was no fool. I could see what was coming next. One by one, all my older friends and relatives were falling in the line of fire and being dragged off to the hospital and the nursing home, breaking their hips, and losing their memories. Big strong men were becoming faint, old codgers with broken hearts and iron lungs. It became pretty clear to me that one day soon I was going to be among them. And I thought I'd better find out what it's like. And I did…for seven and a half years. And now I'm one of them."

"Your dad was very effective," my mother says, "because he was able to talk to these people about what was important to them at this critical moment at the end of their life."

"What I was not effective at, Pete, was taking them to the bathroom, which was part of our duty. It was because I was horrified I'd drop one of them."

I knock on Room 142 at Seminary Estates. My mother is happy to see me. She turns the television off and tells me that Blaine is not here. "I don't know where he is," she says, "and I don't think he ever knows anymore himself. He might go to get something and not be back for two hours, and then he'll come back with bags of things he hadn't intended to buy. He gets mad at me because I won't go with him to the doctor, but it makes my blood pressure go up to sit there with him while he talks to the doctor and nurses about totally irrelevant things. He has no interest in their diagnosis or their explanations. When he gets back and I ask him what the doctor said, he hands me a piece of paper the doctor wrote on in incomprehensible handwriting and says, 'There, I told Dr. Carl to write it all down because I knew you'd ask.' He doesn't remember anything but worries about everything, about nothing. He drives me crazy. He complains all the time about how all of the responsibility is just too much for him and that he can't take it anymore. Pete, he has *no* responsibility. He sleeps all day long. If he has to mail a letter or pick up a prescription the next day, he can't sleep at night for worrying about it. When the cleaning lady comes for an hour on Thursdays, he worries before she comes about what he'll do while she's here."

Then my mother says something that I will think about for days, and the poignancy of which grows deeper and wider each time I ponder it. She says, "I feel like I've lost my best friend. He used to have such broad vision and never worried about small stuff. He always saw the *big picture*. But now he is continuously mired in pettiness and obsession." She sounds lonely.

On my way home, I think about how being with my mother is easy because she is logical, calm, soft-spoken, predictable, reasonable, unequivocal, instrumental, mechanical, practical, cooperative, and usually sweet. She is open-minded, but she also sees things as being proper and improper, doable and not-doable. Her world has an orderliness that maintains that there is a best way to do things. It makes sense. I learned these things from her. From my father, I learned that the world is a mystery, that it can be changed by one's will, that there are many ways to do things and that none of them is absolutely correct; that to provide an answer or an explanation is to put boundaries around the world, and that every style and every behavior is proper if done in a spirit of love.

My mother and I are returning from their house in the country. At the city limits is a beautiful, old farmhouse with an interesting weathered barn behind it. I comment upon the farmhouse to my mother. "That's where a teacher of mine lived. I want to tell you something I've never told anyone. This woman was the only teacher who ever sent me to detention, and it was a horrifying, humiliating experience for me. She was very strict and was in charge of our study hall. Various boys had been talking, and she warned us that the next student who talked would be sent to detention. The boy behind me started playing with the back of my head, and when I turned around to stop him, the teacher looked up and assumed I was disobeying her, and she sent me to detention. In those days, good girls were never sent to detention. Only boys were. It was awful for me. I never got over it."

Judy and I pick Blaine up to go to the hospital for an MRI.

"How're you doing, Blaine?" she asks.

"Piss poor," he says. She asks him if he's taking his pain pills. "Yes," he says. And his anxiety pills? "Yes."

"Do you have anxiety?"

"Yes," he says. "The first time they told me I did was when I was two years old. But at last I can admit it."

At the hospital we find a check-in desk. The woman there seems to know Blaine. Her name is Debbie.

"Wait until I put my steed away," Blaine says, parking his walker and finding a chair. "Your name's Debbie, right?"

She's impressed. "Yes! What a good memory!"

"That and the note on your shirt that says 'Debbie,'" he says. She laughs. Debbie directs us to the MRI area through a door and down a hallway. We check in at the MRI desk, and as we are walking down the hallway to the waiting room, Blaine says something to me that appears to be profound and/or prophetic but cryptic. "Pete, this is the day that the walrus made." His voice breaks. I repeat it as a question. "Right," he says almost in tears. "This is the day that the walrus made." I tell him I don't know what he means.

"I'll tell you some time," he says.

I would like to get it cleared up for my own sake, but it doesn't seem to be the right time. To have my father explain the meaning of *day of the walrus* just before going into a mine shaft full of cascading electrons designed to map out the inside of his body seems inappropriate, but I hope he'll remember to bring it up again.

We sit down in a small waiting room next to the MRI room. A strong-looking nurse, whom I like immediately, comes up to us at once. She has a quick smile and lots of compassion, which is perfect for this situation. Blaine asks her name, and she introduces herself as "Tammi with an *i*." She explains a few preliminary things to us and tells us she'll be back in a minute when the MRI machine is ready.

"Debbie?" Blaine says.

"Tammi," she corrects.

"I'm sorry. Tammi. Are you going to be with me?"

"Yes, I will be in constant contact with you."

"So you'll be with me at all times?"

"Yes, I'll be in constant contact with you."

"What I mean is, you'll never leave me, will you?"

Tammi evidently senses that Blaine could go on repeating the same thing for hours (which he could) without blinking until it elicits the response he wants. "I won't be with you all the time, but I'll be in constant contact."

"Thanks, Debbie."

"Tammi."

"I'm sorry. Tammi. I have one more question to ask. You ready? What if I have to pee?"

"Well, you should pee now, Mr. Gorham."

"I will, Debbie."

"Tammi," I say.

"Sorry. Tammi. I will pee now, Tammi. But what if I have to pee again in there?"

"We'll stop."

"So I shouldn't just pee right there?"

"No, we'll come out."

"You mean you'll have a bedpan?"

"No, I mean we'll come out and go to the bathroom again. But then we'll have to start all over."

"That's fine. I'm just trying to get the ground rules straight."

Tammi laughs. Thank God.

"But you'll be with me all the time, right?"

"I'll be in constant contact with you, Mr. Gorham, that's right."

"She can't be with you, Dad, since there's only two inches of space between your body and the machine."

Tammi laughs. "But I'll be in constant contact."

She leaves and comes back in a couple of minutes and says, "Are you ready?"

"I have to pee first," Blaine says. He goes into the bathroom. While he's there, Tammi and I discuss the MRI procedure. She explains that after the first images are taken, she'll bring Blaine out and inject him with a substance that will highlight areas that have had previous cancers or surgeries and then put him back through again and compare the images for new cancers. She says it is extremely important that he not move, or else the images will not line up. I emphasize that she must repeat that to him over and over because he is mainly concentrating upon having to pee during the MRI procedure.

At least ten minutes have passed, and Blaine is still in the bathroom. Tammi knocks on the bathroom door.

"Come in," Blaine says in a voice loud enough for me to hear across the waiting room. Tammi goes in, closes the door behind her, and is in the bathroom for five minutes. She comes out with a distressed look on her face. "He's very concerned about having to pee during the MRI. He can't seem to get beyond that." I offer to retrieve him myself. I knock on the bathroom door.

"Come in," Blaine yells. He is sitting on the toilet with his pants down.

"Are you done, Dad?"

"I don't want to pee in the MRI," he says.

"You won't. Just pull up your pants, and let's go do it." He does without hesitation.

Tammi looks relieved when we both come out. She puts her arm around Blaine, and the three of us start toward the MRI room. Blaine stops her and says, "Debbie, this just proves one thing. You can lead a horse to drink, but you can't make him water. You promised to stay with me all the time, didn't you?"

"I'll be in constant contact, Mr. Gorham."

Blaine and Tammi go together into the dressing room. I wait outside by the door and try to hear what they're saying. She tells him to put on a gown and to take off everything metal and put it all in a little locker provided, which has its own key, which I can keep. But Blaine insists that I keep his wallet and his rings myself—one from his father and one that my mother gave him to commemorate being free of prostate cancer for five years, therefore cured.

Most of the discussion they're having has to do with Blaine peeing during the MRI and Tammi staying with him at all times. I think what he wants to hear is that if he happens to pee during the procedure he won't be electrocuted.

They open the dressing room door. Blaine is now in a gown. He hands me his rings and his wallet, and she hands me the key to the locker. Before the pee discussion can start again, I say, "Blaine, Tammi has told me that the most important thing to remember is don't move during the MRI because if you do they'll have to start over." I repeat that several more times before they go together across the MRI threshold, over which she has instructed me not to go.

The MRI room is very bright and is almost visionary. I think this will please Blaine. Tammi is gently nudging him down onto the table at the mouth of the MRI machine, which I must say is intimidating. However, Blaine has not even noticed this feature and never once comments about it. He is still going through the various possibilities of what might happen if he has to pee. Tammi is patiently explaining it over and over like a saint. I think to myself, watching and listening to her, that she, along with most other nurses, should get a medal—the Medal of Compassion and Caring. It should be the highest honor available to medical personnel and should confer upon the recipients lifetime health benefits or something like that and should include a day of recognition each year…perhaps in a parade through the downtown with bands playing and floats and an honor guard and a speech by the mayor and prayers from various church leaders.

Blaine is cold. Tammi puts a blanket on him. He's still cold. She puts another one on him and then another one. He is done talking about peeing, but then a man in a white coat comes in while carrying a clipboard. He says hello to me. He's very friendly for a doctor. I ask him if he's a doctor. No, he's Tammi's helper, he says. He greets Blaine. Within a minute, Blaine is recasting for the man the possibilities of peeing on himself during the MRI and promising to do it if he can't be extricated from the machine in time. Tammi intervenes, and the man in the white coat leaves the room. She calms Blaine again. He lies back down. Now all is calm, and all is bright.

It feels to me for an instant, standing just outside of the MRI room looking at my ninety-year-old father who is about to be fed into the mouth of a frighteningly space-age cylinder in an overly bright room in a modern hospital, as if I am sending my father to Heaven—that we have convinced him that this will take him there and that he is ready to go.

"Okay, Mr. Gorham. Now don't move."

Tammi comes out of the room, closes the door, looks at me, puts her thumbs up, and says "We got him! Now go rest and come back in an hour."

I walk home, which is four blocks away, and have a cup of tea. When I return, I notice that the waiting room, which was previously empty, is now completely full of others waiting for an MRI, which is not a good sign, even though, thank God, the bathroom is unoccupied. The moment that I arrive at the door of the MRI room, I hear Tammi say, "We're finished, Mr. Gorham. You did great." Blaine is being wheeled out of the room. He looks dazed, his spirit drained. He's cold.

I finally get my father dressed and ready, and I wheel him out to the main door. We've been there for almost four hours.

Roberta meets us at the front door of Seminary Estates. It's lunch time, and the residents are milling about. Blaine sees his wife waiting and says to me, "When she asks me what took so long, I'll tell her to ask you."

"Tell her how you remember it, Dad. That's what she wants to hear."

"I remember Cindy and Debbi and Barbara and Paul. That's how I remember it."

"You mean Tammi."

"Right. Tammi."

We take the elevator to the third floor—Dr. Strauch's office. Before entering the office, Blaine asks me to sit down next to him. "We need to talk about the plan." He pulls several pages of notes from a folder he's been carrying. One page is a list of medicines, and another is a list of questions my mother wants us to ask.

"You'll ask these questions because I can't remember them. Now here's what I'm going to say. First, I have no pain when I'm in bed. When I get up, I have constant pain. Second, I'm going to tell Dr. Carl that I must continue walking in order to take a crap. And third, we want to see Dr. Dinh early if we can, but we don't want to take anyone's place. That's not fair because everyone's hurting. But if someone stops hurting and cancels, we want Dr. Dinh to know we can jump out of bed at any time and drive to Peoria for the operation."

Dr. Dinh is the surgeon who will, we hope, perform the same kyphoplasty operation on Blaine's fractured vertebrae that he performed two years ago on his other fractured vertebrae—with 100-percent success. Blaine repeats for emphasis, "Everyone is hurting, and I don't want to take anyone's place who's hurting. I'm not brave, and I'm not a baby. I'm somewhere in between. When I went in the box, they found big trouble." The "box" is the MRI chamber.

"Loretta, honey," Blaine says to Dr. Strauch's nurse after she sits down, taking her wrist tenderly. "I don't want you to just stand by the phone all day long, waiting for Dr. Dinh to call about me because I know he's got other patients, and so do you, but if you could call him every fifteen minutes or so until he gets an earlier appointment, that would be great." Loretta laughs and starts asking all the prefatory questions.

When she leaves, Blaine says to me, "Now Loretta will make up notes about what I told her, for Dr. Carl to see, and he'll say, 'We don't have to go over these things again, Blaine, because Loretta made notes about them.' But I'll tell him all of the things again anyway."

"I know, Dad, you were always the great repeater."

Dr. Carl Strauch finally comes in. He's holding a file he's received from the hospital with the MRI readings, and he says, "Your back's a mess, Blaine."

"He's so honest, isn't he, Pete?"

Strauch ignores that. "Are you groggy at all, Blaine?"

"Groggy is my middle name. I think I'm missing a few links upstairs. I'm ninety."

Blaine's swollen legs are a concern to the doctor. After offering several suggestions to relieve them, Dr. Strauch says to me finally, "And if those don't work, we need to increase the diuretics. Of course, then he'll be going to the bathroom all the time."

"That's all right," Blaine says. "I don't mind. I'll just go from the bed to the bath and beyond."

Carl gets up to leave. He's been patient and attentive while Blaine has been cryptic and evasive. But somehow they understand and love each other. Blaine shakes Carl's hand and says, "My help in ages past."

I take Blaine back to Seminary Estates and let him off, but I return at four to translate for my mother the notes I've scribbled down this morning.

Roberta is alone. She is clear-headed and rational and reasonable. Without my father's overpowering personality there, she and I will be able to quietly go through the questions. Blaine's asleep in his bedroom.

"Do you understand the notes?" I ask her.

"No, and your father was no help. He couldn't tell me anything the doctor said. How can you spend two hours talking to the doctor and not remember one thing he said?"

"Dad does most of the talking."

"Yes, that's the trouble. And why does he have all of these copies of the same thing? My God, the man is crazy about making copies. He makes copies of everything, and then he loses them. He's like a tribesman with a camera."

Blaine has fallen out of bed and is being taken to the hospital in an ambulance. My mother calls and would like me to go as soon as possible to check up on him. I call Judy for her assistance, and we go to the emergency room where Blaine, whose face is bloodied from the fall, is trying to convince the doctors and nurses that he needs to spend the night there. "I want to be taken care of," he says. They disagree and after repeated attempts, Blaine accepts that he must go home. Judy and I drive him. It is nine o'clock and dark and silent in the car as we drive back to Seminary Estates. We're all tired, and Judy and I are hungry. I'm sitting in the back seat, Judy's driving, and Blaine's riding shotgun. He puts his hand on the back of hers and says, "Judy, it's the *Day of the Walrus*." Judy doesn't comment. Then he says it again and this time his voice cracks. "It's the *Day of the Walrus*."

At Seminary Estates, Judy walks ahead to talk to Roberta, and Blaine and I move ever so slowly down the hallway. He must stop at the oasis and rest. He sits down, tired, and closes his eyes.

It is nighttime, and the camels are kneeling in the cool desert sand. The stars are the only light except the moon, but they are penetrating the unique night in a surreal way that makes the heavens shine like black oil. There is an adrenaline silence coming from the stillness of this resting place so purely that it seems ironically almost corporeal, but its purity is precisely commensurate with its total lack of life's movement.

Sometimes my father and I can be silent together in an almost holy way. I look at Blaine's face, and he is looking back at me in a childlike way as if he's alert to all of these things going on, all of these currents of manipulation and leverage designed from an incredibly complex blueprint for survival's power somewhere in his head that was there when he was born, which he had no choice but to embrace and to follow and is what has energized him for almost a hundred years. And even though he is all of these fronts he portrays—the old, doddering man, the forgetful octogenarian, the cagey salesman, the Christian mystic—he will always be, in addition to those things, a very wise and profound human being who contains within himself some strange and uncanny mixture of utter selfishness and practicality along with unearthly, idealistic, sacrificial concern for the whole of humanity. His power is directed always toward achieving, often unconsciously, both contradictory ends—sometimes at once.

"Let's go, Blaine."

He rises dutifully, and we continue our last slow steps toward home. Halfway there, I can see there is a bed in the middle of the hallway that is blocking most of its width. As we get close to it, I say, "Oh, oh, I hope you can get through there, Blaine."

He says, "If I can't get through it, I'm going to get up on it and go to sleep."

He deftly moves the walker through the narrow passageway, and shortly after that we arrive at their apartment. Inside it is warm and cozy and Roberta is talking to Judy. My mother is moved to see my father's bandaged face. I note the compassion on her face and hear the caring tone in her voice. It is clear to me why they have stayed together for sixty-five years.

I talk Judy into climbing aboard the walker, and I push her back to the foyer where two old men are still talking. When they see her, it pleases them, and they laugh at us. I park the walker under the stairway, and we walk out together, saying good night to the old men.

In the morning as we get dressed to go to lunch, Judy says to me, "What was all that about a walrus last night?"

It was the winter of 1958. I was thirteen years old. Our family was to spend Christmas at the YMCA camp at Estes Park, Colorado. We drove there from Illinois in our Buick. The YMCA camp was a magical place with log cabins throughout the mountains that surrounded the base camp administration buildings and common gathering places.

My father's business was struggling, and his partnership was dissolving. Ahead of him was the unknown. He had had a nervous breakdown and had been hospitalized.

At the YMCA camp, Blaine met Dr. Frank Laubach, a Presbyterian missionary known throughout the world for his teachings, his writings, and his missions. Dr. Laubach was dignified and gray-haired and charismatic. His message was "Each One Teach One."

Blaine had an epiphany there with Dr. Laubach and instantly was converted into someone else. Even to a cynical teenager like me, it was apparent that the earth underneath my father's feet had moved and had moved him to a different spot, and he would never be the same. Although he had always been church-going and religious, at the Y Camp he was stricken, one might say, with the light. On our drive back to Illinois, late at night as everyone slept but my father, who was driving, and me, who was listening raptly to this man who used to be my father, I became an exclusive witness to the power of transformation and saw firsthand that it is possible to change ourselves if we must or if we want, not just over time but instantly.

Unfortunately, Blaine, being the eccentric person he always was, became converted not just to a form of hybrid Christian mysticism, but he tried to imbue us all with it. Every day for years, he prayed long prayers at each meal and had Bible studies before and sometimes after or even during the meals. His favorite phrase was, "A spirit is over the land." He still says that. "It is an estrangement against the Lord," was another, which fortunately he doesn't say anymore. All of Sunday was spent in church. The church became the focus of our lives throughout the week, not because any of us three boys wanted that but because my father had the fever of conversion.

In addition to being ponderous, it could also be funny and sometimes hilarious. And from it came a man, my father, who never again deviated from his plan to apply the principles of Christianity—the good principles, the Ten Commandments—to every aspect of his life. He applied them to his new carpet business, which flourished; to his employees, who prospered; to his customers, who got good deals and a head full of teachings and laughter. Eventually, my father learned that one teaches best by teaching indirectly— through example. He applied his principles humbly and in like measure to the most exalted of men and to the most common, of which he considered himself one.

My father hired people at his store that no one else would hire—an illiterate black man, a mentally challenged, partially blind midget, drunkards, the old, the lame, the young, women, the dispossessed, and the lonely. He gave them a home and a place to go and be accepted and loved equally.

Even though my mother would not let my father name the ten-thousand-square-foot, red warehouse he bought, "Blainie's Carpet Barn," that's how I always thought of it—Blainie's Carpet Barn.

Summer 2005

My father leans over toward her like a boy saying good-bye to his mother, and Roberta kisses him tenderly on the forehead. We walk slowly out the back door to where I have parked the car. The appointment with Dr. Dinh is at one thirty. It's twelve o'clock.

Peoria is an hour away. When he's finally comfortable, Blaine speaks his first words. "Now is the time of the Walrus."

"What does that *mean*, Dad?"

"Well, it means we're going to see Dr. Dinh. And it means sister's gone." (Blaine's only sister died last month.)

My father has not been outside of Seminary Estates for weeks, and he's not been on a long ride like this for months. His senses are so glutted with stimuli that stuff is pouring out of his subconscious, mixing with his memory.

"I knew very early in my life, Pete, that I didn't know shit from Shinola. And furthermore, I didn't care. And so I've surrounded myself my whole life with people who do. That has been my complete success in life—finding people who know and who know how."

About ten minutes from Peoria, the shape and color and bounteousness of the land is impressive—hilly and densely wooded, not far from Edgar Lee Masters' beloved Spoon River. "This is wonderful, Pete. I haven't been out like this for so long that the blue sky and all of the green are startling to me."

We find Dr. Dinh's office. The parking lot is empty. It has a favorable appeal. Inside, there are almost no people waiting, and we go right up to the tall, dark-haired, middle-aged receptionist. She looks serious, but when she smiles, at the edge of her officiousness, she's youthful and pretty. She immediately starts pulling out insurance forms for us to sign and asks me what my relationship is to Charles (my father's given name). "Are you power of attorney?"

"Wait just a minute," Blaine says, fumbling for his glasses.

"Oh, I'm sorry. You need to find your glasses first?"

"Honey, let me tell you who we are."

A look crosses her face which is fear and contempt at once. She has probably heard this before—that it's the mayor's son or the archbishop or some other luminary standing in front of her who thinks he deserves special dispensation.

"He's the brains," Blaine says, pointing to me, "the power of attorney, and every other power. I'm just the body. These glasses are a foil. They don't have *anything* to do with understanding."

The receptionist sends us to the waiting area, armed with medical history forms and pictures to identify degrees of pain. We've been through this before. We'll do it with dispatch. I start Blaine filling out the medical history form, the first few lines being his name and age and height and so forth, while I use the restroom. When I return, he is distressed that he has "screwed it up already." I take the forms back and start filling them out and ask him a few questions, and in no time we're done. We are called soon after that into the waiting room.

"The time has come, the Walrus said."

Dr. Dinh is a young, handsome Chinese-American surgeon who is serious and intellectual and never quite understands what Blaine is talking about. Who does? He treated Blaine three years ago for this same problem—fractured vertebrae—and completely restored his mobility within two weeks. It was miraculous. I remember him telling us at the time that the problem may happen again.

Basically, Dr. Dinh shot cement into the vertebral cavities to support the vertebrae and the spine. It is the hope of all of us that he can do it again. I remember one time in Minnesota, shortly after Blaine's first back operation, when my mother was in the hospital. We were going to visit her, and Blaine had to tell her something he didn't want to tell her. He was agonizing over it and trying to make up lies about it. My brother and I coached him about how to tell the truth, and he wrote it down on crib notes, which he held in his baseball cap.

As he was telling it to my mother (reading it, actually), she said "Blaine, are you *reading* this?" He told her no. She said "Yes, I can see that you're *reading* this."

Discussing the incident later in the hallway, Blaine said to us, "I've always been a spineless dope except for that little place where Dr. Dinh shot cement into my back."

Dr. Dinh and I communicate very well. I act as a translator, a mediator between him and my father, explaining them both to each other. I've always refused to believe that my father cannot understand things and have preferred to think that he has no curiosity, but really it would be easier to accept that he *couldn't* understand explanations. As he said just an hour before, "I realized early in my life that I didn't know shit from Shinola, and I didn't care." The problem is that even though Blaine will not listen to explanations of how things work or what precisely is wrong, he will continue to dominate the conversation. So I feel it's my job to be the interpreter. Actually, Dr. Dinh and I don't need Blaine at all; in fact, our understanding would be facilitated if he weren't there.

Dr. Dinh explains to us (to me) that Blaine's bones in the lower back area have been compromised by the radiation he received after the surgery he obviously once had in that area (prostate surgery twenty-five years ago). Even though Blaine and I can't remember if he *did* have radiation therapy, Dr. Dinh says he can tell that he did from the MRI.

Then he says this, which is rather shocking, "I am inclined to just wait and let the bone heal itself." I didn't know that was possible, but he explains that it is. That's hopeful. Still, my understanding is muddled. If his bones are deteriorating from aging and from radiation and fracturing one after another, how can they be mending at the same time? Dr. Dinh says they do. Then I ask him why they don't just perform the same operation and cure his problem immediately rather than have a ninety-year-old man wait somewhere between six months and forever for his bones to heal? "Because," he says, "there's a much higher risk now of not surviving surgery, that is, anesthesia. In three years, your father has become much frailer. He might not be able to stand it. We rarely give anesthesia to someone ninety years of age."

Like all doctors, Dr. Dinh's goal appears to be to get out of the room and on to the next room, not wasting time on irrelevant or emotional issues. He explains that he needs Blaine to take a bone scan before he can make a final determination.

Before Dr. Dinh can leave, my father, who is perfectly content to spend time on nothing *but* irrelevant and emotional issues, takes his hand and says, "Dr. Dinh, I have to tell you something now because I have to tell these things to people while they live…or while I live. Thank you for giving me three good years of life." His voice is cracking. "I am grateful to you for this no matter what happens next." Dr. Dinh, a man who probably steels himself against emotional intrusions that always try to assault his objectivity, is touched. His face softens for a moment into a boy's face.

On the way back home, we are quiet for a long time. About twenty miles from home, Blaine starts to ramble in a stream of consciousness, thanking God for his long and fascinating life and talking about his business and how he never judged anyone who worked for him because he figured whatever they did had to be better than what he could have done. Then he says to me, "Pete, I want you to know that I am at peace, and I am ready for my end. My entire life, I have been a negotiator. And I have negotiated with the Lord, as well. I have said, 'Lord, give me a good wife, and I shall serve you. Give me a good family, and I shall teach them your ways correctly. Give me a prosperous business, and I shall be fair and just to those who work for me.' I said, 'Lord, save me from prostate cancer, and I shall spend the last days of my life dedicated to you.' I am ready now. I have nothing left to bargain for and nothing to bargain with. I have no vitality or strength. My memory is fading, and so is my will. And I am at peace."

Blaine started his business in the 1940s. My mother had an uncle who had become a successful businessman and sold Venetian blinds. So that's what Blaine decided to do. He had tried various jobs working for others and hated them all. He'd just wanted to have fun in life, and a real job wasn't fun.

He opened a store next to the town's bowery in a spooky, old, three-story brick building. He never paid any attention to the first axiom of real estate—location. His type of success would have been possible in any venue.

After some years, he took on a partner—a man who knew the carpet business. So eventually Blaine sold not only Venetian blinds but also window shades and draperies and carpet. After eighteen years of partnership, the two men split up. Blaine had a nervous breakdown, got saved and healed, and bought a building on Main Street that became an estimable carpet store. Always drawn to an auction house-type of life, however, he later bought an abandoned, red warehouse next to the railroad tracks, sold the building on Main Street, and started his real dream: Blainie's Carpet Barn. It was a healthy compromise between my mother's need for respectability and his own flim-flam, junk-dealer, rag-man nature. He became a respectable rug man. "I was a person who hated order and loved chaos. So the carpet business and the carpet warehouse were perfect for me— total confusion all of the time!"

One of Blaine's primary business mantras was, "If you buy it right, it's half sold." And what a mantra it was. We heard it a thousand times. "If you buy it right, it's half sold." This and a handful of other didactic aphorisms sacred to my father (such as, "A spirit is over the land," or, "Everyone needs to win") schooled us boys unwittingly in the fundamentals of business and mysticism.

It was up to my mother to school us in everything else.

✳ ✳ ✳ ✳ ✳

Today is my birthday. It could be possible for me to feel resentful on this day of mine, for having to take a nearly ninety-one-year-old man to a city fifty miles away at seven in the morning to have a bone scan and x-rays, which will take nine hours. But I don't, for some reason.

It's going to be a hot day—in the nineties.

Immediately upon entering the Interstate at the edge of town, Blaine begins talking about being a boy on a farm in Olds, Iowa, and having an easy-going father like his. "While the other boys were leaning against a plow all summer, I was sitting on our porch, listening to the St. Louis Browns, and playing games. That's all I ever really wanted to do—have fun."

My grandfather was a chicken culler. In those days, every farmer had scores of chickens that ran around the farm freely. My grandfather traveled to farms in the area each morning very early (before sunrise) in his old truck with steel cages on the back. He culled out the sick and non-producing chickens from the rest so that they would not infect the other chickens or waste the farmers' money. He would kill the sick ones, wring their necks right there in front of me. He took the farmers' non-laying but healthy chickens to the market and sold them. People paid him for this. He was a lovely, funny man. He entertained these farmers. He was like a vaudevillian but a dignified one. He created a job, and then everyone needed him because he was charming and gave humor and lightness to their otherwise grim days.

His job was to make people feel better, and he did it with chickens. He was honest, and they trusted his decisions and knew he'd properly broker their livestock.

It's a long hallway to Imaging, our destination. Blaine wants to walk it. After spending a befuddling, long hour checking in at various stops, he is eventually given a cocktail to drink, which will show up in the imaging procedure. He must wait for an hour and a half for the solution to circulate around his body. He chooses to nap on a gurney, which the nurses lovingly prepare for him.

I leave the hospital and go downtown by the river to a small café and get a sandwich and sit outside. It is very hot, and the air is heavy with humidity. The hospital was cold and dry. My body is feeling delirious from the sudden radical temperature and humidity changes.

I watch the water move constantly onward, never stopping for a second but still retaining its definite unchanging identity. I contemplate that each rich, individual life, like each drop of water in the river, is part of the total volume that is humanity itself, which follows a course to the sea. Who long remembers any single person who has lived and loved, except for a few names of those who've made a lasting mark upon the world's history? The rest of us disappear into oblivion.

I remember Blaine saying to me many times during the years when he was most prominent and most energetic that he was the king of the world—his world: the carpet business in Galesburg, Illinois. It was his metaphor for everything else and tied together his competitive spirit and his artistry and his need to be an entertainer and a provider and a small source of compassion and understanding and humility in this vast world of neediness...the king of the world.

At that time, he never ran out of energy. He was never cold or hot or aware that it was snowing or raining. Every day was a good day and a chapter of an adventure story that never ended. He was the one that everyone wanted. Earl, Bob, Delma, Dobbie, Louis, Dick, Jerry, Francis, the bankers, the advertisers, the carpet salesmen, the truckers, the customers—everyone sought out "the king of the world." He had all of the answers. The little farm boy from Olds, Iowa, which had a population of one hundred fifty, was the king of the world.

At the height of his carpet business, Blaine had some twenty employees and an unbelievable number of customers streaming into his store every day. He was a master businessman with an uncanny instinct for selling. He thought of his everlasting sales as carnivals with balloons and prizes and carpet giveaways—things which appealed to the basic desires of humankind. He thought of himself as an honorable flim-flam man of excellence.

"Pete, I thought of my business as a pirate ship. The carpet layers—a crew of tough, local characters who were independent contractors—I regarded as buccaneers with black eye patches and peg legs who you needed and had to work with but who you had to keep your eyes on at all times or else they'd steal off and leave the job half completed and go to a bar. I was the captain of the pirate ship," he said, which was a distinction he regaled in. "As long as I could provide work and gold doubloons to the shipmates, I was safe, but mutiny was always nearby, and I had to sleep with one eye open and a dagger by my side.

"My primary goal was to keep the men busy. If I didn't, they would betray me and go to another ship and maybe never return. So there were weeks during the winter when I had to sell carpet below the price I had paid for it in order to keep the employees busy. People often asked me how I could sell carpet so cheaply. 'I lose on every deal,' I told them, 'but I make it up in volume.'"

Finally at 12:45, I go through the "Nuclear Medicine" door and back to the area where I was before lunch. It's quiet and dark, and I can see Blaine who is lying like a stiff on a tray in the room that is lighted only by control lights on the machines. There is a huge, nuclear donut that is suspended in midair like a halo, and it is passing slowly around my father's body. He is staring up at the ceiling and is completely robed from head to toe in white blankets with a white towel over his eyes. It's spooky. Sitting in the corner of the room watching over my father is a compassionate-looking nurse named Jill. She tells me to go to the waiting room. "Your dad asked me to stay with him the whole time."

In twenty minutes, Jill comes and gets me. The scan is over. Blaine hears me and says, "Pete, this is Jill. She's been watching over me, haven't you, honey?" Jill tenderly repositions the blankets to cover Blaine more thoroughly and pats him gently on the chest. "Jill has to leave soon for an appointment with her eleven-week-old daughter, but she's arranged for me to see the doctor so I can ask him some questions." I shudder to think what questions my father, who never knew shit from Shinola and never cared, might ask a busy nuclear medicine doctor.

Jill pats him gently again and says tenderly, "We need to get you up now and in a wheelchair." She gathers up all of his things he's given her—belt, wallet, keys, pocket change, watch, socks—and puts them in a bag. Blaine mentions again that he needs to talk to the doctor, Dr. Carter Young. Before he can get up, another nurse comes into the room and tells Jill that Dr. Young needs more x-rays so that he can see a certain area of Blaine's spine more clearly. So Jill gets him off the slab and into the wheelchair and covers him again with white blankets from his toes to his chin. He looks like a mummy. Not one inch of his body is un-blanketed except between his mouth and his eyebrows. Jill puts my father's baseball cap back on, which says, "The New Millennium," and she says "Here, this will give you a little color."

When the wheelchair pushes the double doors open, every face in the big waiting room turns to see Blaine, who is completely robed in white like a dangerous prisoner in a straightjacket while wearing a dark blue baseball hat. It feels like a loony Mel Brooks movie with Blaine starring as a deformed, old gunslinger who's arrived to clean up the bar if he can just stand up first.

There are no empty seats, so Jill pushes the wheelchair into a corner. Blaine takes her hand again and says, "Thank you, honey, for watching over me. I guess Saint Peter didn't need me yet. I know you have to go to your daughter. I'll just wait here."

Blaine and Jill hug each other, and he whispers, "I love you, honey. Take care of the little one."

I find a chair in a makeshift waiting area across from the only other person waiting—an old man who has fallen asleep while reading. I pick up a *People* magazine with forty-two-year old Tom Cruise smiling halfway across the cover. Eventually I get to the article about his upcoming third marriage to Katie Holmes who is twenty-six years of age. There is a picture of the Eiffel Tower and Cruise standing beside it with that huge grin on his face. Underneath the picture, there is a quote from him saying, "Today is my favorite day in my entire life. I'll never forget this day. Ever." I wonder if he said something similar to his first wife, Mimi Rogers, or his second wife, Nicole Kidman. Apparently Cruise was able to persuade the Paris City Hall to allow him to have a private viewing at the Eiffel Tower after it closed to visitors late one night. After that, he and Katie retired to their $4,200-a-night Coco Chanel suite.

"I've just never met anyone like her," Cruise says.

What about Nicole Kidman? Or Mimi Rogers?

The nurse brings Blaine back to the waiting room. He takes her hand and holds on to it. "Honey, what should I ask the doctor?"

"What do you want to know?"

"I don't know. What *do* I want to know?"

"Dad, you need to formulate these questions and have them ready. This man won't have a lot of time."

"Neither do I. Okay, here's what I want to know. I'm going to get right to the heart of the matter. Are you ready?" He looks at Dr. Young's nurse and says, "Is Dr. Young a nice man?"

"Yes, he is," she says.

"Good, then I'm not going to waste his time with all this casual talk like I usually do because both Dr. Young and I are busy men. I'm going to see him, shake his hand, look him in the eye, and say, 'Doc, how am I doin'?' How's that?" Blaine is still holding the nurse's hand and looking her in the eye, unblinking. She smiles.

"You're doing fine. You remember that question now, and I'll go see where the doctor is."

Blaine looks at me and says, 'Dr. Young, how am I doing?' How does that sound, Pete?"

"I think it sounds perfect. Don't say anything else. Let's rehearse it. One, two, three, go."

"Dr. Young, how am I doing?"

"You got it. That's all you need to say."

I am very worried that Dr. Young is a formidable nuclear medicine scientist who likes tiny, subatomic things and not people, but he found when he became a doctor that occasionally he had to talk to the people he was taking pictures of, like Blaine. And he has very little aptitude or interest in doing it and almost no people skills or any sense of humor. I am fearing that Dr. Young will be a rigid man of a few well-chosen words, leading crisply to a well-defined point, about to engage with a man of thousands of arbitrarily chosen ones who admits to using words as smokescreens and whose relevance can only be understood if one is willing to listen to a monologue of interminable length.

I just hope that my father can remember the six words and the six words only. "Dr. Young, how am I doing?"

Dr. Carter Young enters the relatively dark room behind his nurse. "Blaine, this is Dr. Young," she says.

The doctor reaches out to shake Blaine's hand, and Blaine says, "Let me stand up," and starts to push himself up laboriously from the wheelchair. Dr. Young says that's not necessary and begs him to sit down again, but Blaine insists upon rising up, saying, "Dr. Young, my mother (who's dead now, bless her soul) always taught me to stand up when my superiors come into the room. That way she figured I'd get a lot of exercise."

Eventually Blaine makes it to a quasi-standing position and puts his hand out to Dr. Young. "My pleasure, Doctor, thank you so much for coming to talk to us. I have just one question, if I can remember it. But first let me sit down again." Then he introduces me to Dr. Young as his son and counselor.

I can see instantly that Dr. Young is a very kind and warm man. He has been smiling the whole time since entering the room. In addition, he has voluntarily sat down on the side of the bed beside Blaine, indicating by that body language that he's prepared to listen. To my dismay, however, he seems to be looking at *me* for something, like approval or confirmation or even direction. His eyes dart back and forth from Blaine to me. Maybe the word has reached the corners of the hospital that it is I who speaks a language they can understand and that I, the quiet one, know the meaning of the sorcerer's riddles.

"I'm getting to my one question. Be patient. Please. I grew up on a little farm in a little town in Iowa. My father had pigs. All day long the pigs would root around in the slop and the mud for the few kernels of corn that had fallen off the wagon or for an acorn that had fallen from a tree that was buried deep in the mud and the manure. My father used to say, 'Even a blind sow finds an acorn now and then,' which for me means that eventually if I just keep talking I'll say something meaningful. That's always been my philosophy. But since I know you're a busy man and don't have time to root around in the manure with me, I'm going to cut right to the chase. I have just one question. Are you ready?"

Dr. Young's face is aglow in delight, listening to my bizarre father. I know I can relax now for a while.

"I have tried to reduce all of my questions, whatever they were, to just one because you're a busy man. Are you ready?" Dr. Young says he's ready.

Blaine reaches over and takes the good doctor's hand and says, "Okay, Dr. Carter Young, here's what I want to know. How am I doing?"

With barely a moment's hesitation, Dr. Young says, "Well, do you mean, 'Do I have any more bones left to break?'" and smiles a robust smile. We all laugh at this joke, which unfortunately turns out not to be a joke.

"You have twenty fractures in your ribs alone and of course problems with your spine, too. That's why I needed more x-rays. Usually such widespread deterioration of the bones indicates cancer. However, all of these fractures in your ribs are in the same place. They are lined up like soldiers. Cancer doesn't look like that."

"Is it cancer?" Blaine asks, not having listened beyond the word *cancer*.

"I'm ninety percent sure it's not cancer and that what is showing up is the result of the fractures. However, that's not good, either. It means your bones are so brittle that they're breaking from the least concussion."

"What's causing that, doctor?"

"The fact that your bones are almost ninety-one years old, Blaine. That's what's causing it. I tell people that every day they live beyond the age of seventy-five is a gift."

"You're right, doctor. I've been given a lot of gifts, haven't I? What should I do?"

"Here's what you should do, Blaine. Do nothing. Do not fall again. Your sole purpose in life should become fall management. If you fall again, you will end up in the hospital permanently. Then you'll get pneumonia, and then you'll die. Do *not* fall." Dr. Young says that after a patient is ninety he thinks no invasive procedure of any type should be used for any reason.

As sobering as this news is, it's what Dr. Dinh said, too.

The four of us spend another ten minutes together, the doctor fully present and not eyeing his watch or edging toward the door. He tells us about his ninety-two year old grandfather. "I believe that the attitude of the patient is just as important as his physical condition," he says. "It is rare to see a man ninety years old so alive and entertaining with such a young and frolicsome character as you, sir."

We enter the streets of Peoria and then the interstate back to Galesburg. We hardly say a word. When we are finally out of Peoria into the inspirational rolling hills of the Spoon River's geology I say to Blaine, "Well, Dad, what have you got to say about everything that's happened today?"

He is quiet for a long time. He says, "I'm thinking. It takes me a little longer than it used to." His eyes are furrowed in thought. "Here's what I think, 'The times, they are a changin', the Walrus said."

"I don't think the Walrus said that, Dad."

"No?"

"No, Bob Dylan said that."

"Well, then, maybe Bob Dylan is the Walrus."

"Maybe so."

It's still extremely hot. Not a good day to move the last items from my parents' house to Seminary Estates. Bit by bit, my mother is letting go. We will probably sell their house within six months.

I pick up Blaine and take him to St. Mary's hospital to be fitted for a back brace. "Well, Dad, another medical adventure, eh?"

"And that's good because when they're over, then they play a dirge."

I park the car and go into the building to find my father. He's wandered up to the emergency desk and the women behind it look confused. He introduces me, and they ask if my father was supposed to go to the emergency room. "Not yet," I say. I read the instructions on the paper Roberta gave us. "They told us to come here and then go to Health and Rehabilitation."

They explain that Health and Rehabilitation is clear at the opposite end of the building on the floor above and tell us how to get there.

There is a Bible lying on the desk and Blaine puts his hand on it and says, "See, honey, we were in the right church but the wrong pew." They laugh.

It's a long walk. The last part is up an incline. The way is fairly steep and Blaine is slowing down. When he stops to take a rest, saying, "It's hard," I mention to him that Lance Armstrong just two days ago won yet another Tour de France, logging a career total of over 21,000 miles of bicycle racing in the Pyrenees mountains after having overcome testicular, brain, and lung cancer to come back and win the 2,200-mile, three week-long race (some say the most grueling endurance sport ever devised by man) for the seventh time in a row. Blaine is inspired to go on.

I announce to the desk that Blaine Gorham is here for his appointment to see Dr. Bhanti. As we are sitting recovering from the Tour de St. Mary's, we watch various people of all ages and in all stages of crippledom arrive at the Department of Health and Rehabilitation. Blaine nudges me. "We're all here—the halt and the lame."

It is very quiet in the waiting room. Suddenly, Blaine quotes from the Bible in a loud voice, "And He said, 'Get up and walk,' and they threw down their canes and their crutches and followed Him." People are staring at us.

An old man wearing a wide-brimmed fishing hat walks in and sits down with his wife right across from us. He is skinny and toothless and tanned very dark and hasn't shaved for days. He is wearing white socks with dark polyester trousers and a short-sleeved Sears and Roebuck style shirt—dressed up for the doctor. Blaine nudges me and whispers, "Look at this old geezer in the sombrero. He's been in the field."

"Charles?" inquires a doctor in a white smock who's come from the back. He is holding a clipboard and smiling a gentle uncertain smile. He is dark-skinned, Indian or Middle Eastern, and is young. Roberta has written on the piece of paper that his name is Amit Bhanti.

I acknowledge him by pointing to my father. I mouth the words, "Right here!"

Dr. Bhanti comes up to us and introduces himself as Amit.

"Dr. Amit," Blaine says, "Let me stand up and shake your hand."

"I'm not a doctor. I'm an orthodist."

"Well, Dr. Amit, you're *my* doctor, and I intend to treat you like a doctor by transferring all of my worries onto your shoulders." Blaine touches his fingertips together and bows and says, "Allah be praised."

"Which kind of brace are you looking to get?" Amit asks. "The one which goes clear up the back and chest and down to the pelvis, which I'd recommend, or the shorter one? You must have someone who can help you put the long brace on in the morning and take it off at bedtime…"

Blaine interrupts. "Doctor Amit, do you remember in the Middle Ages when the men left for the Crusades on horseback, and they rode their horses for days and days wearing heavy chain-metal vests and armor from their ankles to their chin to help parry enemy spears? I don't want that kind of brace. I want the shorter one."

Amit has Blaine lie on his stomach and takes measurements.

The three of us talk quite a while longer about returning next week to fit the brace, and then Blaine shakes Amit's hand and holds onto it, saying, "I like you, Amit. And you're able to tolerate me, and I'm grateful for that. If this brace doesn't work, would you be willing to try the other one later? You could consider me a noble experiment."

"Of course," Amit says. "That's exactly what we'll do." And then we all shake hands again, and Amit says, "I hope I'm like you when I'm ninety."

At Seminary Estates, we choose to go in the back door, and I ask Blaine if he has his key. He fumbles around and finds it finally. "I forget everything now, Pete."

"I think your memory is still pretty good. You just remember what you want."

"Roberta accuses me of all sorts of skullduggery like that, which, of course, I'm guilty of, but it's also true I can't quite sort it all out anymore, Pete."

"You can still fool 'em, Dad. Who cares if you got it right—just so you can still fool them into believing you do."

"Isn't that the truth, Pete? I've been doing that my *whole* life."

I am now not only my father's father and my father's son and my father's closest friend and my father's counselor, but I have also become one of his team of doctors—in my case, a pseudo-doctor. I'm not sure that I like that. My roles are getting more and more comprehensive and onerous and mystifying as my parents are starting to surrender, bit by bit, their independence and authority to the person next in line—me. The role of caretaker does not necessarily fall upon the relative most compassionate but upon the one closest geographically.

I feel strong and capable of leading and inspiring troops. I feel as if I am on top and am full of wisdom and power, capable of exercising it with dispatch and decisiveness—even with abandon. No one is standing in my way anymore to being king of the world, as it were—the same king of a similar small fiefdom that my father was king of only thirty years ago.

But look at him now—full of fractured bones, bent over like a coolie from pain, four inches shorter than he once was, weighing 115 pounds, being without confidence in his memory or his direction, and living in a cantonment of old people.

Be prepared to change from king to pauper.

Every Wednesday morning, my father had a staff meeting at Blainie's Carpet Barn. He often would start the meeting this way. "Okay, folks, the most important thing to do before we can make any headway at all is to determine who was to blame for any and all of the mistakes that have taken place in the last week. Until we determine that, I won't have your undivided attention. I'll only have you ready to pounce upon one another or to defend yourselves. So I want everyone to hear me out. Is everyone listening? Are you listening, Bob? Are you listening, Delma? Are you listening, Earl? Are you listening, Dick?

"It's me. I'm to blame for everything. The door that got jammed. That was me. The wrong price. That was me. The wrong carpet installed in the wrong house. That was my fault. Running the carpet prod through the roll of carpet. I did it. I'm to blame for everything that happened wrong since our last meeting. Now let's not talk anymore about who was to blame. It was me."

The air has cooled. Summer is breaking.

There to greet me as I open the door to Seminary Estates apartment number 142 is my mother, sitting at the same place at the end of the couch where she always sits. It is hot and stuffy. I ask to open the windows and sit across from her.

My mother at eighty-eight has lost nothing mentally. She is curious and contemporary yet lives in the present or the future, rarely contemplating the past. Her memory is still better than mine, and her sense of organization into the future is uncanny. Even her body has improved in the last six months, and she looks lovely. She still has the smile of a girl without guile.

The roles have reversed. My father, who just a year ago was healthy and strong, repeating over and over that his only purpose now on earth was to care for my mother, has declined both physically and mentally to the point where he prefers to be taken care of. And because there is no one to do it but my mother, she has improved commensurate to his decline.

Blaine waddles into the room. He is in his undershorts and T-shirt. He struggles with where to sit, where I, his pseudo-doctor, will want him to be in order to be examined. As soon as I bring up the subject I am here for—his swollen stomach—he stands up and shuffles over toward me. His legs are so thin that I wonder how they can propel him at all. Only the edemic water retention in his calves gives them definition. For some reason, he takes off his T-shirt before pulling his undershorts down, probably because my father has always believed, here in the most literal sense, that one is better off to reveal everything; that is, unless one must conceal everything.

It is quite a sight, a nearly ninety-one-year old naked body, and I try not to appear over-curious about it. His skin is grayish yellow and wrinkled in long, small folds of flesh despite the fact that there is no excess poundage to his scrawny body. His chest is sunken, and there is no pectoral definition anymore, not even really any flesh, just some evidence of a shape that's gone. The body is absent of hair like a hairless terrier. There is a tiny, little potbelly at his lower stomach, which is perfectly rounded. He asks me to touch it, and I do. It feels like a stout but not fully inflated basketball. I keep pushing on it, and it gives remarkably obstinate resistance. I think of the myriad of commercials on television, touting their product as being able to transform obesity into abs of steel. These abs of my father's would be envied by many.

"Like I told you on the phone last night, I just noticed this tightness in the last week." I've speculated since he called me in a panic last night that it could be related to his edema or that it could simply be his abdominal muscles, which are now totally uncovered without softening flesh upon them. I tell him they seem tight.

"See, what I said!"

I'm not concerned, though, since he is having no adverse symptoms. He is even more preoccupied with his belly button, which is now hidden in a fold of flesh, and he can't get at it. "I'm worried about infection," he says.

My mother, who tells him perpetually to stand up straight, says again, "Blaine, your posture is so terrible anymore that it's probably causing a realignment of your abdomen and a withdrawal of your navel." She doesn't seem concerned, either. In fact, she says, "My stomach is hard, too," and she stands up and pulls her pants down below her navel and walks over to have me feel her stomach.

I must say that even though both of them now consider me a member of their physician staff, I am not at all comfortable with examining the stomachs of my naked and almost-naked parents. There is something too clearly ontological about standing so close to the nexus of my existence where it all began for me—and I am beginning to worry that the experience will catapult me into an even higher, more bizarre realm of relationship than the one of being the parent of my parents. It is raising in me a slight sense of panic, which, like any good doctor, I am trying to conceal.

I feel my mother's stomach, and to my astonishment, it is nearly as hard as my father's. They are both normal, or else they are both sick. I wonder if they're suffering from malnutrition. I am glad, though, that my mother's stomach is just as hard as my father's because it means I can more forcefully resist his arguments for going immediately to see the doctor since my mother is not the least bit concerned about her own distended abdomen.

I am only relieved for a second though because my father is now concentrating fiercely upon his hidden navel and the possibility that it will get infected. He approaches me, carrying a huge, yellow flashlight (he has four or five of them placed strategically throughout his 600-square-foot apartment). "Pete," he says, handing me the flashlight, "see if you can see the inside of my navel." I refuse. There are some things even a pseudo-doctor won't do.

He sits down again and begins reeling off a list of maladies he is plagued by, and I say to him, "Dad, you need to get busy with other things besides thinking about your health all day long."

"How can I? There is no time for anything. I have so many other responsibilities."

My mother sighs. "What do you have to do, Blaine? Nothing. You just worry about every little thing. Tell me, what do you have to do?"

Blaine looks like a guilty dog. My mother continues. "Blaine, the main thing you do all day long is look after yourself."

A Google search by my friend, which entered the words, "Gorham Carpets" yielded a small biography written by a guy named Carl Rader, which is just a blurb about himself and his life to perhaps immortalize himself in a small way. Mr. Rader's piece is about Galesburg, Illinois, and growing up there.

In one and one half pages, he sets down his life and says, basically, what a nice town Galesburg was to grow up in. He lists a number of landmarks in town and mentions "Gorham's Carpets." It's not much. I almost deleted it. However, I copied it for Blaine, mainly to show him how incredible the Internet is.

In my car, on our way to breakfast as Judy and Roberta are talking in the back seat, I hand these pages to Blaine, who is sitting next to me, and say, "This is taken from the Internet. Some guy mentions Gorham's Carpets."

I join the conversation with the women, and by the time we're a couple of blocks from the restaurant, I notice Blaine is still reading these two pages I've given him over and over. He is holding them in his hands very tenderly.

"What do you think of that, Dad?"

He doesn't quite understand where it came from, and I explain it to him again. "You're famous now, Dad. The entire world knows about Blainie's Carpet Barn." He doesn't understand who wrote it, and I point to the name at the bottom, Carl Rader, and ask if he remembers him. By this time, my mother is listening to us and says, "You remember him, Blaine. He worked for us during the late '60s. Didn't he go to prison?"

Now my father's light comes on. He says, "This is just amazing," and thanks me over and over for bringing it to him. "He was a poor boy from the south side of town," my mother says. "His mother worked at a diner down the street. You got to know her and hired her son to work for us just doing menial tasks." In the piece, Carl Rader refers to this experience at Blaine's carpet store as "where I learned my first trade."

Roberta remembers that Carl Rader was drafted right out of high school and was sent immediately into the Vietnam War. "He was a gentle boy and shy and had no confidence. It was a tragedy for him. Remember, he was put under the command of Lieutenant William Calley?"

Calley was an unemployed college dropout who had managed to graduate from Officers' Training School at Fort Benning, Georgia. On March 16, 1968, the men of Charlie Company, 11th Brigade—Carl Rader's company—were ordered by their commanding officer, William Calley, to enter the village of My Lai on a search-and-destroy mission. They entered firing and ended up massacring the entire unarmed village of some three hundred residents—many of whom were women, young children, and old people. Journalist Seymour Hersh found out about it and exposed it in the media. It was called "The My Lai Massacre" and was front-page news for months. There was a Pentagon investigation which resulted in Calley being charged with murder. Calley and the other members of his company were sent to prison. One of them was Carl Rader. He was sent to Leavenworth Federal Penitentiary.

As I am looking for a place to park at the crowded New Friendly Café Restaurant, Blaine says, "If ever there was a person who did not deserve to go to Leavenworth, it was Carl Rader." Blaine has tears in his eyes as he once again reads the piece and once again says, "I don't know how to thank you for bringing me this."

"Don't you remember, Blaine? You visited Carl Rader at Leavenworth one time when we went to visit your sister in Tulsa."

I can picture my father talking Leavenworth Federal Penitentiary officials into letting him visit a boy who used to work at his carpet store and who was in prison for participating in one of the most publicized and notorious military scandals of the century. Even for my father, who used to drive us two hundred miles to the state basketball tournaments in March, having no tickets and being completely confident that he could get us into this coveted event by buying tickets from scalpers for a reasonable price, even for my father, getting into Leavenworth Federal Penitentiary under these circumstances must have been a daunting task. But just as he always got us tickets to the state tournament, even though we all sat in entirely different sections of the stadium, sometimes next to our opponents' fans whom we couldn't clap around without being beat up, Blaine also talked his way into Leavenworth Federal Prison to visit Carl Rader, a former employee of his who was a gentle boy from the poor side of town.

"I remember I tried to hold his hand, but I couldn't because there was glass separating us, so we put our fingertips as close to each other as we could, and we said a prayer. The guards listened to us."

Whatever he did that day with Carl Rader at Leavenworth Federal Prison must have been poignant because my father cannot stop reading this piece written by the boy, and he can't stop thanking me for bringing it to him or stop the tears from going down his cheeks at various times during the meal at the New Friendly Café.

Finally, I ask Blaine for the piece of writing and read it myself. It is well written for a boy who might not even have graduated from high school and who spent many years in federal prison. Indeed, it is touching. He refers to how he was teased by the other kids at school for being so small and for having such an ill-shaped body, but he says this was good because it taught him early how to survive. He refers to his mother working at the diner and mentions that they were poor. He talks about Gorham's Carpets and various other places in Galesburg that meant something to him and says what a nice town Galesburg was to grow up in. He is traveling back to who he was before he knew how to know himself—before the torrent of weirdness happened in his life.

I hand the paper back to Blaine and tell him to write something back to Carl Rader and that I'll send it to him by way of the e-mail address underneath his name.

Fall 2005

It's a family reunion.

My brothers are here from Colorado and Cleveland. So are two of my nephews and their wives and children—thirteen people in all. It's my younger brother Bill's birthday, and so we're having a party. Roberta has not been in our house for over two years, and Blaine hasn't been for over a year. My brothers are big and strong, and their sons are even bigger, so they'll just pick Blaine and Roberta up and carry them up the stairs into the house. If they have to go to the bathroom later, they'll carry them up another flight of stairs.

Four generations together.

Blaine is strangely silent throughout the dinner. I ask him several times if he's feeling okay. He says he is, but I can tell that something's amiss. Then I notice what appears to be a small handwritten note that is sitting to the right of his plate. He keeps looking down at it. It's hidden under his napkin, so I can't tell what it says. His plate is an assortment of half-eaten foods. I encourage him to eat up.

At the end of this raucous meal of good eaters eating good food and laughing heartily, in a rare instance of silence, my father makes a pronouncement, "I want to read something."

He uncovers the note. "I don't trust my memory anymore, so I have to write everything down. I also don't trust I'll understand what I've written down." My brother Mike, across the table from us, has taken out a manila envelope and is removing a poem from it. "Mike's going to read to you something about the Walrus."

My brother explains that Blaine had talked to him on the phone a while back and had asked him if he'd ever heard, "The time has come, the Walrus said." Mike had quoted from memory a stanza from Lewis Carroll's poem *The Walrus and the Carpenter* and had said, "This is the only reference to the Walrus I know, Dad." Blaine had been thrilled. He has asked Mike to read the poem, which Mike does now.

At the eleventh stanza, my brother stops and interjects, "This is probably the part Dad is referring to."

> *"The time has come," the Walrus said,*
>
> *"To talk of many things:*
>
> *Of shoes, and ships, and sealing-wax,*
>
> *Of cabbages, and kings,*
>
> *And why the sea is boiling hot,*
>
> *And whether pigs have wings."*

Most of the group has no idea what this is all about. They look at each other for direction. Someone snickers uncomfortably. No one except my father seems to want to talk of shoes (the legacy for the living) and ships (the afterlife) or sealing wax (death) or cabbages or kings— all of the tender and profound issues that should be but never are discussed prior to one's death with all of those people dear to one's heart. Mike makes a valiant effort to gently convey to everyone Blaine's need to discuss his own impending death. But the silent consensus apparently is that now is *not* the time to talk of these many things.

"Well, folks, this is important to me that you understand—that now's the time to talk about these things—and I don't think I'm capable of doing it." After another awkward silence, the group becomes loud again. Their much more prosaic desire is to eat the dessert of homemade birthday cake and ice cream. Blaine looks disappointed. But he'll bring it up again. He can wait.

Winter 2005-2006

The Jewish salesmen in Chicago that Blaine befriended first inspired him to find out about the South. It was his association with them that led to his traveling to the carpet mills in Georgia and the Carolinas, making friends there with people in the carpet warehouses and secretaries in the offices who could steer him to good deals. "Those warehouses," Blaine said, "all had rooms in the back full of carpet that was discontinued or flawed in some small imperceptible way or just too ugly for most people to buy. I would sneak through the back doors and get to know the forklift drivers and the warehousemen. It was as important to know them as it was to know the president of the company. But not just them, the traveling salesmen, too. These people knew what could be bought right, which pieces weren't selling or were discontinued or damaged in some way. They knew where all the dogs and skins were that were just taking up warehouse space. And to me, those were nuggets of gold because I could turn them into pedigrees and fur coats. Before I accosted the people up front, I knew every reject they had in the back better than they did, and I'd offer to take it off their hands for nothing." These were my friends—these forklift drivers and secretaries and laborers. They knew I was a junk man and where the junk was. I treated them right." (Traveling salesmen were always showing up at our house for dinner and would sometimes spend their otherwise lonely nights at our house.)

"I'd buy up everything in the warehouse they didn't want—entire semi-truck loads full of castoffs and discards—and have them shipped back to Galesburg. The companies would give me ninety days' credit. And in that ninety days, I'd run a huge blow-out sale, saying, 'Overstocked! Must pay off the merchandise! Selling below suggested retail prices!' I would have bought the carpet so cheap that I could sell it cheaper than anyone else around and still make a good profit.

"I eventually eliminated custom ordering because I couldn't handle the vagaries of customers' perceptions and behaviors. If people ordered from a sample book, they were invariably disappointed with the roll that came in. I loved the finality of the huge sales where I'd say to the people, 'Now, let's roll out this piece and make sure it's exactly what you want and that there are no problems with it because I have a cash and carry policy here that says that once you take it, it's yours! I don't want you to bring it back and say you don't like it or that it's got a tiny flaw. So we'll go over it right here and now, and when you say, "I'm satisfied," we'll roll it up, put it in your truck, you'll pay me, and it's yours forever until you come back to buy another one.' I'd have the men roll the remnant out under the florescent lights, and everyone would crawl all over it until they were satisfied that they wanted it.

"Eventually I even got out of arranging for the carpet to be laid since that was another thing that could go wrong. I said, 'I never want to hear this statement again: "The installers aren't here yet, and the party's tonight."'

Blaine began buying *seconds* from the mills in the south. They had various flaws that repeated themselves at certain intervals, missed yarns, or inconsistent patterns. "I'd buy these rolls for practically nothing and then we'd bring them back to the warehouse and cut out the flaws and make perfectly good remnants. I'd say to the customer, 'This piece of carpet has an extra shot of yarn in it, but I'm not going to charge you anything extra for it!'"

I remember an ugly carpet style called "Candy Stripe" with all of the colors running together in a Jackson Pollack-like cacophony. Blaine often returned with this style of carpet when he came back from his trips to Georgia. Candy Stripe carpet was a way for the manufacturer to use up batches of yarn left over from various other rolls of carpet. But "Candy Stripe" made it sound as if someone actually designed it that way instead of just sweeping the floor. And what did people in a small Midwestern town know about style? Blaine would sell Candy Stripe for two dollars and fifty cents a square yard, having bought it for fifty cents a square yard. No other carpet company in the entire Midwest had prices that low.

People would flock into Blaine's sales from several counties. For the two or three days of the sale, my father would be gone all the time, practically living at the Carpet Barn, attending to the hundreds of people that streamed into his warehouse until finally the whole semi-truck full of carpet was gone in addition to most of the other inventory in his store, which my father naturally included in the sale. He'd prepare for these sales for days. People would ask him how he could sell so low, and he'd say, "I lose on every deal, but I make it up on the volume."

But what Blaine understood was, "If you buy it right, it's half sold."

Spring 2006

Blaine and Roberta have finally sold their primary house. However, no one wants to sort through the objects collected there for over thirty-five years. So Judy will assume the unenviable task of being the listing broker and the moving coordinator, thus making her life inestimably complex both physically and emotionally. As moving coordinator, she must contact all of the relatives, equitably distribute the belongings among them, and arrange for everyone to remove these items from the house in time for the auctioneer to haul away the remainder as well as contact and arrange with the cleaning and repair crews and make sure the trash man will have the trash removed before the new owners take possession. On top of that, of course, she has to attend to all of the ordinary details of the real estate closing.

Each time relatives come back—they all seem to come at different times—they wallow with my parents on memory lane while Judy and I must keep pushing them forward. Judy is skilled enough at such delicate negotiations that she is able somehow to move the herd constantly toward the goal. But that job has taken its toll on her peace of mind and mine, too.

Today we have made some executive decisions about what is garbage, what is going to the auctioneer, and finally what things only Blaine and Roberta can decide about—the very personal stuff, which contains nuggets of nostalgia, which are things my parents cannot hold onto any longer and must finally let go.

For my father, this includes the hundreds of ads he wrote forty to sixty years ago. These ads, which he cherishes and could never part with, he artistically and painstakingly designed himself. They contained effective psychology that was dredged from his own intuitive wisdom about human nature. They were able to draw carpet buyers from all around the county, from the hills and the draws of every rural hamlet within twenty-five miles of Galesburg, to Blainie's Carpet Barn. These buyers were often crusty, old sodbusters with eighth grade educations who had just sold their grain and who had wads of cash in their wallets, manure on their boots, and loam under their fingernails. They were towed in, kicking and screaming, by their wives who desperately wanted to change the carpet that had been in their house for so many generations that it had changed colors—fearful wives who had finally persuaded their cheapskate husbands to "at least go to Blainie's Carpet Barn, even if you don't buy anything, just to see what he's got." These rugged farmers were itching for a fight with any city slicker like Blaine who might try to get their grain money away from them. They were ready for a battle, and so was Blaine.

These ads, because of the fundamental power which my father invested them with, put food on our table, sent us boys to college, and allowed us to reach a higher socio-economic status, which some in the community probably regarded as enviable, and which certainly had not been the birthright of either my mother or my father.

We lived with these ads. Blaine discussed them constantly. If he wasn't talking about God and religion or quoting from the Bible, he was talking about his newest AD. His pride was uncontainable and also not understandable to us. We just thought that an AD was an AD. But how many dinners started with a prayer long enough to chill the food and ended with a dissertation about ads? It wasn't until after I'd left home before I realized that others simply ate their meals and left the table without once discussing either God or the carpet business or analyzing their relative indebtedness to either.

The reason Blaine was so good at writing ads and so proud of what he wrote (and even knew that there was a difference between a good AD and a bad AD) was because he had gone to advertising school. And also, he was a naturally good artist—a skill which he never developed in any way except by drawing ads.

Going to advertising school had been at the end of a long series of other career moves. Blaine had studied the psychology behind writing an AD that would influence the behavior of its readers. Now, of course, the entire country is organized by advertising. Then, however, advertising was not well developed or very sophisticated, especially in a place like Galesburg. There were few national or international franchises that marketed themselves in the same way throughout the country and the world. For the most part, advertising was local—whatever the local businessman dreamed up. And often it was not effective because it was simply a product of his ego needs.

So Blaine had a leg up on other local businessmen, and he was daring and willing to be the first to try new advertising techniques—many of which he had learned in Chicago and on the road, traveling to the carpet mills in the southeast to get good deals on carpet, reading the newspapers and billboards in other towns and cities along the way. He was a world traveler in the world of rug men.

From all of the items in the house, the only thing Blaine is concerned about passing on to us are these ads. He has stored them in the garage for years and years. The paper they are written upon has yellowed and is brittle and covered with dust. The ads in the boxes are tall and wide and extend beyond the heavy cardboard booklets in the garage that contain them. He wants my older brother and me to go through them all.

I am not in the mood to do this. I have seen them all before; in fact, I was there at their creation. Eventually, I do sit down and thumb through twenty-five ads or so. I remember these sales, which he ran countless times and that brought hundreds of people through the doors. I wouldn't see my father for days. Even though by this time Blaine had hired several other carpet salesmen, and during these sales he even recruited some of the workmen to sell carpet, most of the people who came into the store wanted to see Blainie. They thought that only Blainie could give you the best deal, which was only partly true. As a matter of fact, all of the salesmen were paid a salary plus a commission based not simply upon how much they sold but upon how much they sold the carpet above the price that he'd paid for it. But the only one who knew what that price was, was Blaine, and he wouldn't tell anyone. Each piece of carpet was coded in a way that told the salesmen it could be reduced to a price no lower than "X" amount, and if they could not make a sale without going below that, they needed to see Blaine. If they got to this point, they knew they would not only have to negotiate with the customer on the price but that they would also have to negotiate with Blaine for a commission. So not only were customers constantly looking for Blaine to slash prices, the salesmen were also looking for him to cut the price below the coded limits and still give them a commission.

Of course, no one could ever find Blaine. During these sales, the phone rang at our house all the time with people asking, "Do you know where Blaine is?"

The liability of my father's style was that the most hardened, inveterate hagglers wanted Blainie because they knew when it came to the real crunch time that somehow or another Blaine would have to be recruited. Everyone wanted Blaine, including us, his family, who were waiting for him to come home so we could eat dinner.

Winter 2006-2007

I make a routine visit to my parents. My mother answers the door. Blaine is in the back somewhere in the midst of his long and complex daily after-shower ritual. I sit down and ask my mother how she's doing. "Oh, okay, I guess," she says without conviction.

"What's wrong?" I ask her.

She puts her hand to the side of her mouth and whispers loudly, "He's driving me *crazy!*" I ask her what he's doing. "Oh my goodness, he is just obsessing almost more than I've *ever* seen him do."

Just then, Blaine comes down the hall and immediately after greeting me in a worried and distressed tone of his own, he says, "Pete, come here. Let me show you something." He takes me into the bathroom and shows me the special dressing chair from the medical supply store that my mother uses to sit on in front of the mirror. "Can you get another one of these?" he asks. "It's broken and wobbly, and I don't want it fixed. I want a new one because I'm afraid Roberta's going to fall." I pick it up and see that the wing nut holding the legs together is loose. I start to tighten it. "I don't want you to fix it," he insists, "I want a new one." I tighten it anyway, but I can see that it will never tighten like a new chair. I take it into the living room. He follows me, and we sit down. "Roberta, Pete's going to get you a new chair."

My mother sighs loudly and says, "Blaine, if you don't stop talking about that chair, I'm going to scream." He keeps talking about the chair. Then he takes me back to the bathroom and shows me how my mother pulls the chair up to the sink and sits on it and looks in the mirror. He wonders what she'll sit in now that the old chair is gone and they're waiting for me to bring back a new one. He asks her that.

"I don't need a chair. I'll just stand at the sink."

He ignores that. "How about one of these folding chairs? Can you use that until Pete gets back with the new chair?" She doesn't answer. "Roberta?"

She looks up and scowls, "I told you, I'm tired of talking about this chair. Pete, he's been talking about it all morning long, and I'm not going to talk about it anymore."

"Pete, come here," Blaine says and goes back into the bathroom.

I stay where I am, and my mother says, "See what I mean? He's just crazy." I ask her if she can sit in a folding chair until I get a new one. "Of course," she says, "but he won't accept that." I take a folding chair into the bathroom, unfold it, and put it where the other one was.

"Okay, Dad, that's the one we're going to use until I can get another one." He asks me if I think it's strong enough. Then he pulls it up to the sink and asks me to sit in it. I do and tell him it's strong enough. "What about Roberta? Is it strong enough for her?" I don't answer but put it back where it was—five feet away from the sink. "This is how it will be, Dad, until I get another one."

"When will that be?"

"I don't know," I tell him. "I'm on a job and working all day long, and it might be a few days."

"Oh, no. We need it now."

My mother yells from the living room that she does *not* need the chair now and that she'll just stand at the sink. Then he goes back into the living room and says, "Roberta, I want you to come into the bathroom and sit at the folding chair at the sink and see if it will work while we wait for Pete to get a chair as soon as he's off work." My mother literally screams in a tone of anger I have never heard her use before, "Blaine, I will not discuss this chair again. I am *sick* of talking about it. You don't care about me at all. You just always want to get your way."

For a few seconds, my father looks crestfallen, but I believe it is only an act, for within an instant he has returned to the bathroom and is pulling the folding chair up to the sink again and calls for me. It is truly pathetic. I am in a mood, mercifully, to feel sorrow rather than anger (as my mother feels, who is with him all day long). I go back into the bathroom. "Sit in the chair, will you, Pete?" I tell him I won't. "This is where we should leave it, in front of the sink, pushed over here to the right side because if she has to drag it from back there she might fall, and I just could not live with myself if she fell."

It feels as if my father is having a hallucination, and he has to do something to make the hallucination stop. He has made my mother his mother now, and she clearly resents it. She is the only one who understands the extent to which my father's mind has begun to deteriorate. She cannot accept this. She is angry—angry because, I suspect, the man she married and loved and admired and who was once in his own words (not that long ago) the "king of the world," who could conquer almost any situation or problem by his amazing determination and perseverance and ability to win over anyone in any situation, is now a scared and obsessed, frail, old man who doesn't make much sense. He still has a charming sense of humor and ability to bedazzle folks for short bursts of time and has the wisdom to know when to walk away while the crowd is still laughing. But beyond that, he is unbelievably frustrating and compulsive and repetitive and incapable and forgetful and, most of all, scared.

I say to my father in front of my mother, "Dad, is there something else that's bothering you?"

He ponders my question as if I might be on to something, and either he knows what it is and is not willing to expose himself, or he knows that there is something else but is not able to grasp it. Then he gives a canned answer, which I don't accept. I say, "It seems to me, Dad, that something else is bothering you. Do you know what it is?"

Finally, he says, "Yes, I don't have any control over anything anymore."

I have considered many times how awful it must be for someone in need of controlling everything and everyone to lose their ability and their power to control even their own body. I say, "Dad, you can't control everything. You'll just go crazy trying. You have to let go. Remember, the concept of faith that you spoke about a million times? Well, you have to have a large measure of that now in your life."

He nods in agreement but says, "You know when I lost control? When I had to stop driving. Up until then, I could just get in the car and solve these problems myself."

"You know what else, Dad? You and Mom are now together all day long and all night long in your little apartment, and you can't just get in the car alone and go for a drive."

My mother agrees. "Even though I've accepted my limited life now, I miss driving terribly."

I see the vista out ahead of me. It is the best time of my life. I am healthy. I have peace and quiet and solitude and money. I have freedom to a measure I only dreamed of as a young man, which I deliberately engineered to happen. For a while, I'll be in a greater and greater near-total freedom in regard to what I want to be and what I still want to accomplish and experience. But I can see clearly the end of this where the light of this life recedes into the darkness my parents have stepped into and out of which they will never step completely again. And this much is hauntingly clear to me because I have heard so many people in my parents' situation repeat it so often; it is coming, and it is a mean and cruel and irreversible real ending. Suddenly one is walking along in light, and the very next step he takes is into the darkness. The only things he can do from then on are to regret that the light is gone, embrace its memory, or somehow with wisdom and graciousness, accept the darkness.

My mother gets up and says, "I'm going to dinner, Blaine. Do you want to come along?" Yes, of course he does, but he is psychologically not ever able, for some debilitating reason too complex to understand, to leave as planned or to make a decision or even answer a question. She goes ahead. We come later. Halfway to the dining room, Blaine remembers he forgot something. I go back to get it and leave him at the oasis.

When I come back, Blaine is sitting in a chair, staring at the wall in front of him with a celestial look on his face as if somewhere inside of him he has, as I have seen him do so many times before in moments of stress, accessed a powerful lake of repose and has dived into it to be washed completely and instantly in some sacred water that is capable of restoring his integrity and his grace and placing him back at the center of the deep and unfathomable peace he always has been able to have. He looks at me with that look I've seen so many times that says, "Okay, I went astray as I always go astray, but I have found my way again, or rather it has found me. I am ready to go forward again, son."

We walk together to the dining room, which I know closes at five thirty. It is five thirty. Blaine starts to walk me to the door, and I say, "You'd better go eat, Dad. They close right now."

And he says, "Oh, I think they'll wait. And if not, I'll just go sit with Roberta. She's all the nourishment I need."

We walk to the door, and at the door, my father puts his arms around my neck and says, "Pete, no one knows this, and I don't tell your mother even, but my mental processes don't work right anymore." Then he looks up at me and says, "Do you know who you are now, Pete? You are now my friend. Thank you, my friend."

I knock on my parents' door on Sunday morning. My mother answers. She looks good. She has put on nearly twenty pounds in a year, and her color is healthy. She has a radiance that had been gone too long. Blaine comes into the room and is still in his robe, and he shakes my hand and sits down.

"Let me tell you the wonderful thing that happened to me this week," my mother says, reaching for a letter on the coffee table.

She starts explaining what it is, and Blaine and I grow silent. The letter is from a woman who was my mother's favorite student when she taught, when she was just out of college, at a one-room country school in rural Illinois called Frog Pond in the 1930s. Apparently, my mother was also her favorite teacher—ever. The woman went on to get a master's degree from Northwestern and work for the Federal Reserve Bank of Chicago. She later moved to Florida and eventually became the vice president of a corporation with 140 stores that is listed on the New York Stock Exchange. She now lives in Peoria.

My mother reads the letter. It is one entire page— typewritten and single-spaced. On the back of it is a long, handwritten postscript, which she reads, as well.

The letter starts out congratulating my mother on becoming ninety, which her sister had told her about. She notes that this fact has led her to reflect upon "those days long ago at Frog Pond." Then she says, "I don't think it would hurt you to know that, in my mind, I have always thought of you as being my favorite teacher among all those I had along the way. I never felt deprived (because of you) for having gone to a one-room school."

This is the dream of every teacher—to be told by a former student whose life became a success that the teacher was the reason that life got better and that because of the teacher, the Frog Pond where the student was born got transformed into a sea of possibilities.

The woman, whose name is Eileen, closes her letter by saying, "I just wanted you to know that I was thinking of you. I have good, if fading, memories of those early days. I am fortunate that our paths crossed along that country road—I know I owe you a lot in pointing me in the right direction. With my love, Eileen."

I can't stop thinking about this letter all the way down the deserted Seminary Estates Sunday hallway and into the blue-sky, yellow, sunlit winter, soon to be spring, and then into my car and all the way home. I think of Eileen writing to her teacher, my mother, seventy-five years later, about their one-room school house out in the country, somewhere just after the turn of the century, full of backward, innocent farm kids, some, maybe Eileen herself, meeting for the first time a teacher from the big city of Galesburg. My mother would unknowingly catapult Eileen's life onto a new planet, from which she would look down in wonder from another galaxy three-quarters of a century later and think, *Who* were *you? And who was I? I need to find these things out before it is too late.*

My mother is going *stone* deaf. For years she's gotten appointments wrong and has heard information incorrectly. Once she showed up for a Christmas dinner at a friend's house only to be told that the dinner she was invited to was for New Year's Eve. We have witnessed enough of these anomalies to be certain that she simply heard things wrong. Unfortunately, Roberta was a teacher with a very good memory who prided herself upon being accurate. She has a need to be correct, and so it would usually not occur to her, nor would she ever accept someone else's casual undocumented observation, especially if she couldn't hear it, that *she* had made a mistake.

This is a pattern that I am tempted to believe has a possible psychosomatic origin as well as the original organic one, which she inherited from her father. Is my mother needing attention or needing to make a foray out into the world more regularly than she is allowed to do? Or, how shall I say it, after sixty-six years of listening to my father's B.S. and now having no way to escape it by telling him to go somewhere else or by going somewhere else herself—because they are now not able to drive and are confined together to a few hundred square feet in an old people's complex—is her body doing what bodies do in such situations… shutting down?

All of this, of course, makes me feel guilty since I am the main gate to her freedom. If I were to take her on constant meandering rides or take her out to lunch or to the doctor any time she felt like going, I could assuage some of her discontent at life's final paltry offerings.

For the last two weeks, my mother has experienced something that scares her. When she takes her hearing aides out, she can't hear a thing; she is completely deaf. And now, even with the hearing aides in, she can barely hear anything. Her worry, of course, is that like every other machine that has ever moved and done work over time and miles, the parts of her body that make it up are reaching the point of being beyond repair. At the very top of this is probably the worry that she will spend the last years of her life like her deaf father did—unable to hear or communicate with anyone. No more telephone conversations, no more family group discussions, no more television or radio, no more spoken words heard—nothing but lonely solitude with an occasional irrelevant conversation-stopping interjection thrown in by her from the mute sidelines where the deaf must reside most of the time. But even worse, she is also going blind, so she can't read, which was her favorite pastime.

I will pick up my parents this morning at ten a.m. and take them for a long ride and probably somewhere to lunch. And maybe, like long rides do for children who are crying, it will calm their souls and make them right again for some brief moment. Roberta has said that she and my father need to get out more and that they might just have to hire someone to drive them places whenever they feel like going.

My mother is sitting in the front foyer diligently, on time as she always is and always was and always will be, addressing her responsibility *not* to inconvenience others. My father is not there. He is rarely on time and never clogs the free flow of his mind and of his world with onerous things like responsibility. I am like my mother. I arrive five minutes before an appointment and wait…eventually in anger and resentment.

I say something to my mother. She asks me to repeat it. I say it again, only louder and more crisply.

She cups her hand behind her right ear and smiles sadly and says, "I just can't hear you, Pete," so I walk up close and condense my statement into a few common words, hoping she can read my lips at least, and I scream it. She finally understands or at least pretends to.

We sit there beside each other, communicating in this primitive way or in silence, which is easier, for nearly twenty minutes, waiting for my father. Finally, we both react to his tardiness with soliloquies about his chronic lateness and his selfishness and about how he charms everyone in order to get his way.

"Why don't we just get in the car and go for a ride ourselves?" I say.

"*WHAT?*" I'm not sure if she can't hear what I said or if she's appalled by it. I repeat it loud and close and simply, and she says, "Well, he'd wonder where we are."

Whatever consequences my mother has used to alter my father's behavior over the sixty-six years of their marriage, they have not been severe enough to stop him. He's much too cunning for someone as guileless as her.

I insist that we get in the car, and I drive away. When I complete a circuit of a few miles and arrive again at the door ten minutes later, there is Kristy, helping Blaine through the door.

"See," my mother says, "He always gets someone to help him."

I am angry when Blaine gets in the car. Even though he is ninety-two years old, losing his memory, frail, and weighs only about 130 pounds, I tell him he's selfish and self-centered and uses everyone else's good will and their desire to please and their generosity and sense of responsibility in order to conduct the merry life of a child and to play and do whatever he wants to do all day long. I go on and on about this for a long time, and he falls into silence. "What did you say?" my mother yells from the back seat, indicating she hasn't heard one word of what I've said.

My father says sheepishly, "She doesn't hear a word you're saying, Pete." I change the tone of my conversation and make it lighter. "You're in trouble now, Dad, because now you have to answer for *both* of you, and you don't want to answer even for yourself."

He laughs. "I'm way ahead of you, Pete. I have already considered the many dire consequences of her deafness."

"Well now, in a way, it's perfect for you. You never needed anyone to talk, anyway. Now that she can't hear and can't listen, she probably won't talk, either, so you can talk all the time and will never have to listen." My father laughs like a little kid.

"Let's go to Rio," my mother says.

We continue to drive through beautiful, rolling farm country that is just starting to green again with the miracle of spring. There are cows and goats and horses everywhere, grazing contentedly on hillsides. There are old, weathered barns and foursquare farm houses and corn cribs and machinery getting ready to plow the earth for another planting. I drive on. They are both enthralled by the modest glory of the land and the springtime and the uncanny way that a Midwesterner can drive two miles from his house and be out in a countryside, which is still the way it was a hundred years ago, and can feel the present turn into the past instantly and evoke old memories.

The old memories churned up for Blaine are memories of the carpet business when he was in partnership with Dale Johnson. "We would load my station wagon with carpet and drapery sample books and head out to farmers' homes after work when they'd come in from the fields, and we'd have evangelistic sessions with the people. These were hours-long sessions in the homes where we all eventually would get to the truth, and the truth was finally revealed: that the people wanted and were willing to buy something. I was the missionary who showed how the truth could be made real.

"I knew these farmers. I had been one of them and had been formed by them. Here's what I knew. I knew that even though the woman was the one who wanted the carpet and who might have a sense of color and taste—maybe even an artistic sense that never got developed in the few years of school that she'd attended before becoming indentured to the farm—it was the man who would decide what to buy because all he cared about was how much it cost. So it was my mission to find the right piece of carpet for her at the right price for him.

"Dale and I covered this territory like the Dixie dew," my father says as we approach the town of North

Henderson, having missed somewhere the turn to Rio. But no one cares. Everyone is happy—joyous, even. I drive along and only half-listen to the constant banter of my father who is talking about the carpet business sixty years ago with Dale Johnson and about this house and that house where they had Evangelistic Sessions. I wonder if he's just making it up as we go along or if he truly remembers particular houses he points to in these villages and lands of so long ago. And mostly I wonder why I have never heard the saying, "We covered this territory *like the Dixie dew.*" I keep repeating it to myself so I won't forget it because it is so beautiful and old and so evocative and has come out of the mouth of my ninety-two-year-old father to my sixty-one-year-old ears for the first time ever.

"Look at that old schoolhouse over there," my mother says with excitement in her voice. "That's what Frog Pond looked like," where she taught Eileen, her finest pupil, to whom she is now writing regularly.

My father starts singing, "Those were the days, my friend. We thought they'd never end. But they did."

At Seminary Estates, my mother, as usual, is already out of the car only seconds after I park and is waiting for me to bring her walker to her. When I return from ushering her into the building, Blaine is still in the car. I open the door, and he slowly turns toward me and struggles to get out of the car seat and up to his walker. Then he stops and sits back down in the seat and starts singing, "I wandered down the hill, Maggie."

When I get home and do a Google search on "I wandered down the hill, Maggie," this is what I find:

I wandered to the hill, Maggie,

To watch the scene below,

The creek and the creaking old mill, Maggie,

Where you and I used to go.

Oh, the green grove is gone from the hill, Maggie,

Where once the daisies sprung,

But I love you, and I always will, Maggie,

Since you and I were young.

Although we have grown old and gray, Maggie,

As spray by the white breakers flung;

But to me you're as fair as you were, Maggie,

When you and I were young!

Spring 2007

Today Blaine looks morose, in fact, almost comatose. Two days ago, he went to his doctor because he was still feeling anxiety. He went alone without anyone telling me, driven by Mary, their helper. He returned to Seminary Estates with a prescription to double his dosage of anti-depressants and an instruction to see a psychiatrist. My mother had asked him to explain these things, and Blaine couldn't do it. He had no recollection of what had taken place.

My mother says, "If only I had gone with him!" which I interpret to mean, "If only *Pete* had gone with him!"

I question Blaine about his feelings, a thing which is, as my brother once described, "Like trying to catch a greased sea eel with your bare hands." Blaine ponders awhile and then says, "In the carpet business, my mission was always to find out what the customer was thinking without letting them know what I was thinking. I was an actor on a stage, hiding who I really was behind who I needed to be. I guess now I'm supposed to be the real me, whoever that is."

Whoever my father really is, a double dose of anti-depressants has made him someone different.

Perhaps it's the real Blaine who has emerged from the doubled dosage and is sitting before me depressed, quiet, emotionally flat, relatively uninteresting, and withdrawn, smiling inwardly to himself like a slightly deranged Buddha.

We leave a message for Dr. Strauch's nurse to call us with instructions about the added anti-depressant. My mother repeats, "I wish someone had gone with him."

As we are waiting for the doctor to call, I ask them if they'd like to go for a ride on Saturday, and then I'll take them to dinner after that. They love the idea. But when I say, "Judy and I are going to see her parents on Sunday (Mother's Day), so I thought we could celebrate it with you on Saturday," my mother says, "Ah ha! So that's the reason you want to take us out to dinner on Saturday," and falls silent. I feel so uncomfortable after a few minutes of the three of us staring vacantly in different directions in their tiny apartment that I say, "Well, I need to go," and get up to leave.

"I'll pick you up around five on Saturday, okay?"

"That's sounds fine," my mother says, "but not as nice as Mother's Day would have been." My father, for the first time that I can remember in months, makes no effort to say good-bye or to follow me to the door or the oasis or to calm the rippled waters. My mother bids me a cool good-bye.

The next day, I call my parents. My mother answers. She sounds distant. I ask if the doctor called. Yes, he did. He said that Blaine had sounded uncertain and frightened and that that's why he'd wanted him to see a psychiatrist—which Blaine hadn't mentioned—and why he'd increased his medication.

I have trouble imagining how even a psychiatrist who is highly trained in eliciting motives and forces and repressed emotions can break through my father's impenetrable psyche.

My mother calls me two days later. Blaine has an appointment to see the psychiatrist next Thursday, and she'd like me to go with him.

Never in my life could I have envisioned accompanying my father to see a psychiatrist, although I have envisioned going to a psychiatrist *because* of my father.

It's Mother's Day. I have decided to stay home and take my parents for a ride and then to dinner. Judy is going alone to her parents' house.

I assemble a small, wooden basket of delectable snacks and add a few lilacs from our backyard to the Mother's Day basket Judy got at the flower shop. It's four in the afternoon. The day is perfect—sunny, warm but cool, and quiet. It is a day that evokes memories.

The door to my parents' apartment is ajar, as I knew it would be, because my mother is thoughtful. I open it and see her sitting on the couch. She looks at me and smiles. Whatever I have done wrong in my life has been forgiven and cancelled by *mother-love*, that great phenomenon probably borrowed by Christianity itself that allows one to achieve redemption from any crime through absolute forgiveness.

My mother looks gorgeous. I hand her the flowers and the basket and a Mother's Day card, which she opens and reads immediately. Her face melts into the shape of appreciation, and she leans forward and takes my hand and pulls me into her and kisses me.

Blaine makes his entrance from the hallway. He is completely dressed and ready to go. How rare that is.

"Okay, where shall we go?" I always ask before pulling out onto the main road.

My mother always says, "Blaine, where do you want to go today?"

He always says, "I don't care." Then my mother always mentions the exact destination she has been thinking of since the moment I offered to take them for a ride. "Let's see if we can find where Lucille Lovely used to live."

Lucille Lovely was my grandmother's friend who lived in the country on a small, lovely acreage in a house that her husband Fred built.

My mother has a clear idea where the Lovely's house was, but we cannot find it. After driving for an hour in the beautiful Illinois countryside on the edge of the woods with the corn stalks just starting to grow, we wonder if the Lovely's estate is no longer there, although my mother keeps suggesting it is over there in those trees. But there is no way to get "over there" since those trees are in the center of a farmer's land. So we finally give up. We drive back to Galesburg and to a Perkins restaurant—their chosen eatery.

Blaine has come to life again. I ask him if his stomach feels better. "I think so," he says. "That one pill that I take—what do I take that for anyway, Roberta?— Whatever it is, it's the one that gives me a stomach ache."

"Anxiety," my mother says.

"Oh, is that it? Anxiety?"

After dinner, we decide to drive to the hospital to see Mary Lynne, a fellow Seminary Estates resident who fell in the beauty shop Friday and broke her hip. She is the sister of my father's former partner in his early carpet business. My mother says that Mary Lynne is quiet and doesn't have many friends, and so they want to look in on her.

I let my parents out at the entrance to the hospital and first set up their walkers, open their doors, close their doors, and then open the door to the hospital. My father says, "Pete, this is the infirm paying a hospital visit to the more infirm."

We wander alone through the halls of the empty Sunday hospital—two slow, frail, and underweight old people on walkers and their caretaker, searching for Mary Lynne.

We find her room at the very end of the second-floor hallway. Mary Lynne is happy to see my parents. My mother holds her hand and consoles her. She is a lovely woman and is the same age as Roberta and was in her class from grade school through college. She seems quite stoic about her predicament, and I watch in awe from a chair on the other side of the room, listening to these three old people who were clearly once children and who are still children underneath ninety-year-old faces and bodies. Their genuine concern for one another is touching, and I feel healed by it in some tangible way.

That night, I sleep an uninterrupted dreamless sleep, which is a rare luxury, and in the morning I feel wonderful, as if cured in the darkness of some malady I didn't even know I had.

I knock on Room 142 at 1:35 p.m. It seems unusually quiet inside. Finally Blaine opens the door slowly and says he's almost ready and hands me a wad of papers, saying, "Your mother says to read these," and he scurries away down the hallway. The door to my mother's room is shut because it's naptime.

"That's where I'd like to be," he says while pointing to her door.

I look at the papers. They seem to be various information-gathering papers, but the last one, which my mother has highlighted, is a privacy statement from the psychiatrist's office. It is standard boilerplate language—typical lawyer overkill. I don't know why I need to read these unless it's to understand Roberta's concern, which was voiced earlier, that Seminary Estates might be getting papers from the psychiatrist's office (whose name seems harmless), and she is afraid those papers might precipitate an investigation by Seminary

Estates itself into my father's sanity, which would result in the two of them being thrown out on the streets. I've tried to assure her that this is an ungrounded fear and that even if Blaine is judged to be insane, he will still be able to charm them all into keeping him.

Finally Blaine is ready—almost on time. He takes a few tissues. "I might need these in case I start crying," he says and stuffs a few more into his pockets.

His body language seems dismally frightened and unsure. He is walking slowly with his walker, moving gently from side to side in the hallway and his head bowed way down as if in prayer. I ask him how he's doing.

"I just want to lie down and be fed. I'd rather it not be intravenously, but if that's all there is, that's okay, too. Sooner or later, that'll be the only way left."

I caution Blaine that we are late, and we need to keep going. "I won't talk to anyone even if they start talking to me," he says.

Once in the car, he remembers what Roberta coached him to ask me, "Did you read the papers your mother wanted you to read?"

"Yes, I did, but I have no idea why she wanted me to read them."

"Because she's still sane, and she wrote them."

"Okay, yes, I read them."

"Good, then my part's over."

I let Blaine out near the entrance to the psychiatrist's office and tell him to wait while I park the car. When I come back, he's sitting in the sun with his head bowed down again. His eyes are closed, and he's praying out loud. "Dear Lord, you know that I've always been insane, and you've helped me hide it from the world for ninety-two years. Please, dear Lord, let me hide it today, as well. Thank you for all of the gifts that you have given me."

I study the list of doctors beside the elevator. "What's the doctor's name?" I ask Blaine. He has no idea. I look at the papers Roberta gave me, which has the psychiatrist's card in it. "Heidi Sauer," I say.

"I'd prefer it to be Heidi *Sweet.*"

As we are waiting for the elevator, Blaine fumbles with his pockets, which are heavy-laden. He pulls out a pair of glasses from one pocket and looks at them bewildered. Then he pulls out another pair from his other pocket. And then he removes the pair he's wearing and hands them all to me and says, "Would you take these back to the car?"

"No, we have to get to the doctor's office. Why did you bring three pairs of glasses?"

"I don't know. Why do I do anything?"

We ride the elevator to the second floor. Blaine gets out and goes immediately to the bench in front of the elevator and says, "I'll sit down now."

I grab his elbow and pull him back up and say, "Come on, Dad, you can sit in the office."

No one is in the psychiatrist's office except a receptionist who looks rather serious. I tell Blaine to sit down, and I tell her who we are and hand her the papers my mother gave me. She seems unhappy to deal with me rather than the patient himself, who is already sitting comfortably across the room. Her first question is, of course, "Did you bring your insurance cards?" I look to Blaine and ask him if he brought his insurance cards. He struggles to get out of the chair and then struggles to get his wallet out of his pocket and then walks ever so slowly to the receptionist's desk, still fumbling with his wallet that it is now caught somehow on his pocket. He says to the receptionist, "What is your name?" She says it's Carol. He shakes her hand and holds on to it and says, "Carol, the pace will have to slow down really slow now because I ain't very fast." She laughs.

Carol gets the necessary information from his insurance and Medicare cards and hands them back, and Blaine puts the cards back meticulously into his wallet into certain slots. Carol tells us to have a seat.

I sit down at right angles to the chair Blaine finds. I look around the room while Blaine studies a little three-by-five notebook he has brought with him and on which he has written all over.

There are pamphlets hanging on the wall about various things that don't seem very interesting for a psychiatrist's office, but I do see one about depression. I pick it up and read the ten questions to ask oneself to determine if one is depressed or not. Even though I do answer a few of them affirmatively, I don't feel strongly enough about my answers to feel alarmed that I am clinically depressed yet.

Blaine is still studying his notes with amazing focus. I ask him what he's reading.

"Well, Pete, your mother said that I am not to speak first, that the psychiatrist will be the first to speak. When she asks me the first question, then I am allowed to answer, and then I'm going to read this. Otherwise, if I start talking first, I'll end up twisting and turning furtively in the wind. But this way I'll be clean as a hound's tooth."

"What have you written there?"

"I've written the story of my life, at least the way I want it to be known. I'm going to read it all as soon as she asks the first question."

I ask Blaine if I can read what he's written. He hands it to me.

"Worried a good deal—angst—worried about what? Who knows? Can't tolerate change. Can't handle change or the thought of change. No will to do anything! Read very little—used to read all the time. My thoughts flutter. They come like birds, and then they fly away. I anticipate trouble—it doesn't come. Hard to remember. Dishes daily—routine things. Can't handle change—upsets me. Flighty—thoughts depart. I'm against change—any change!"

Just then, the door opens, and Ms. Sauer comes out and asks for Mr. Blaine Gorham. She is a big woman with intense eyes and is dressed casually. She goes to Blaine, and they shake hands, and he asks her name. We both stand up, and I say to her, "I'm his son. Is it okay if I come in, too?" I think I detect an instant of disapproval followed immediately by consent.

Blaine says, "He's my right bower."

"How are you?" she asks.

"I'm here."

In Ms. Sauer's office, we take three separate seats with Blaine sitting on a small couch all by himself.

"It says here you worry a lot. What do you worry about?"

Blaine remains silent, staring peacefully at space. Heidi waits. I observe them both. Blaine looks over at the business card the psychiatrist handed him in the hallway, which he's placed beside himself on the couch. "Well, Heidi, it's like this. Roberta—that's my wife—Roberta said don't talk until the doctor asks you what you worry about, which you just did. So now I can talk, right?"

Heidi replies, "Right."

"I've written some notes that I'm going to read now to you." He puts on his glasses and pulls out his little note card and reads.

Heidi takes notes furiously.

When he's finished reading, she looks to me and says, "Change is a big theme, isn't it?" She asks Blaine, "What kind of change don't you like?"

"I hate all change because I can't handle it anymore. I don't like anything to happen that I don't know is going to happen beforehand."

"You mean like if someone comes to the door and you didn't expect them?"

"Exactly."

"But if you know they're coming, it's okay then."

"It is as long as they're someone I want to see."

"So do you avoid people now? Do you avoid crowds?"

"Crowds are okay because I don't have to do anything. I can just look at them. I don't have to talk to them."

"You don't like talking to people now?"

"I'm no spring chicken anymore, Heidi. I'm not complaining. I'm happy to be alive. But my characteristics are drifting away. I had to talk incessantly in the carpet business—the business I had for forty or fifty years. I had to continuously talk so no one would have a chance to think about anything other than buying carpet. I had to provide for my family, and the only tool I knew how to use was talk. So I talked and talked all day long every day. I was an actor, an entertainer. I just kept people there in the store, buying things. And now I'm tired of talking." He keeps on talking.

Blaine is beginning already, I can see, to capture the leadership of the group by the force of his expression, by his thespian meanderings, his power to amuse and entertain total strangers and make them love and cherish and need him. I've seen him do it a thousand times, and I know its form well. He continues to carry on in his inimitable style, which will ultimately yield an apparently loose but actually highly integrated overall meaning, if one can pay attention long enough, as I assume a psychiatrist should know how to do. Blaine talks non-stop for five more minutes.

"You say you have no will to do anything. Are you sad?"

"Very interesting question. May I think?" Heidi indicates he may think. "I was in hospice for many years. I lament. I know I'm sorry for a multitude of things."

"Do you have guilt?"

"Guilt is my middle name, and my other middle name is worry. Yes, I have guilt. I have more than my share of guilt. When I was born and they were passing out guilt, they said, 'I think we should give two portions to this guy.'"

"Have you always been a worrier?"

"Yes, always. I had my first worry when I was two years old."

"Do you know what that was about?"

"No, I have no idea. It was probably earlier, maybe the day I was born. But no, I don't feel less worry when I know someone is coming because then I have to get prepared, and that causes me to worry. And my thoughts depart me now, then return later dressed in different clothes." Blaine talks on and on. I watch them both, Heidi watching Blaine, and Blaine freely associating. Blaine is at ease with the therapist, willing immediately to talk about himself in the deepest way with the most uncanny humility and humor while at the same time dodging and avoiding any mention or recognition of the psychic forces that have woven him together into the ninety-two-year-old tapestry that he has become.

Finally after Blaine's lecture is finished temporarily, he says "I like our meeting here because we're cozy, and there is no change until I quit talking—which is *now*!"

Heidi smiles and takes over again. "Would you be willing to come back for therapy? I think it would help you."

"Let's see." He seems to be calculating in his head.

"I think, Blaine, you need to learn how to stop these thoughts of anxiety. It is a pattern that you can work on. Anxiety is a necessary thing, but a lot of your anxiety is not necessary to have. Do you worry about losing your memory? About Alzheimer's?"

"Yes, I suppose I do."

Let me give you a memory test. Heidi reaches over on a cabinet next to her and picks up a piece of paper.

"I want you to answer these questions as quickly as you can." She asks him twenty-one simple questions. Then she asks him more questions on another test. She quickly grades the tests.

"You answered eighteen of twenty-one questions correctly on the first test. That's very good. If you had Alzheimer's or severe memory loss, you might be able to answer three. On the other test, you scored 25 of 30 right. That's normal memory function for a man your age." Blaine seems pleased with this.

"How do you sleep, Blaine?"

"I sleep like a baby, all night."

"You don't worry at night?"

"There is no time to worry at night, Heidi, because I've worried all day."

"How do you shut it off?"

"My lamps go out."

"That's wonderful. Maybe you can learn to shut your lamps off during the day, too, when you start to have pointless worry."

She asks him if he has trouble concentrating. "Bingo! That's why I can't read." She asks him if he's grumpy. "I'm not sure, but Roberta thinks so." She asks him if he was nervous about coming in today. "I'm always nervous about revealing myself." He answers all her questions with lengthy anecdotes, and some are irrelevant.

Heidi reaches up on the cabinet and pulls down a thick book and opens it to a page and reads a description of Blaine's condition and asks if that describes him. He agrees that it does. "Generalized Anxiety Disorder," it's called, which means anxiety that doesn't have a reasonable object but just occurs as a reaction.

Blaine brings up Roberta's name again and again throughout the session. Their relationship after sixty-seven years of marriage is so complex and interdependent with love and anger and manipulation and need and renunciation and control and fear that it is probably not possible to understand my father without understanding who my mother is and what she represents to him.

Heidi asks Blaine if he's afraid of death. He smiles and begins to hum and sings in a shaky falsetto the poignant line from "Old Man River" that goes, "I'm tired of livin' and scared of dying." Heidi asks him if he's tired of living, and he answers emphatically, "Oh, no, dear Lord. I ain't tired of living yet. Don't take me yet, please, dear Lord. You see, Heidi, I'm a salesman. I was always making deals. I've made deals with the Lord all my life. I never wanted to die." Tears come to my father's eyes. "When I was forty, I asked the Lord if He could just let me live until I was fifty. And then when I was fifty, I just wanted to live to be sixty. And then seventy. And then eighty. And then ninety. And now I'm ninety-two. No, I'm not tired of livin', but how much longer can I expect the Lord to give me preferential treatment? No, I'm not afraid of dying, but I don't want to." Heidi is on the edge of her seat, leaning toward him.

"Are you afraid of Roberta dying? And leaving you all alone?"

In a rare, non-reflective moment, Blaine answers immediately, "Yes!"

She says to me, "I see you've been taking notes the whole time. Is there anything you want to say here?"

"The only thing I want to say, which I'm sure you already know, is that after being married for sixty-seven years to one another, my mother and my father have some issues that need to be dealt with, if that's possible."

Heidi turns to Blaine. "How do you feel about coming back for therapy? What do you envision happening from more therapy?"

Blaine smiles and thinks and then says, "I think you would ask me one buckeye question after another, and

I'd attempt to avoid them like a swordsman deflecting life-threatening blows. I'd feel obliged to tell you all the things I'd fend you off from asking on your own."

"Does that mean you'll come back? In two weeks?"

Blaine's at a watershed. If he consents to come back, he'll have given power back to Heidi. My father is a master at controlling the possession of power without seeming powerful. She'll probe him more, and what she finds may not set him free. It may confuse him more. He's still thinking.

Finally Blaine puts his hand out to Heidi. She takes it in a handshake. "Yes," he says. I feel that I should no longer be a part of Blaine's self-discovery, and I mention this to Heidi. She sounds neutral, but then she says, "Usually no one else is present." But later on, I'll wonder if I'll be missing an opportunity to understand myself better, too, by understanding my father better.

We have been with Heidi almost two hours. The session was supposed to be an hour long. Her next patients file into her office just as soon as we leave it, and I hear her apologize profusely to them for being so late. She doesn't even have time to say good-bye to us.

Blaine and I stand at the receptionist's desk, and Blaine asks her to please make an appointment for him in two weeks.

"I'll do anything for you, sir."

"Bless you."

We ride the elevator back down to the first floor. Blaine looks tired. He's crumpled over as if his back is overburdened and as if he is facing something grave. His tiny body is all bones, which shuffle and seem to rattle behind his walker. We get off the elevator at the first floor, and an old cleaning lady is standing there with a bucket and a mop. She looks at Blaine and asks blankly, "How are you today?"

He stops and looks at her and then takes both of her hands in his and says, "Honey, I feel like a buck on a mountain."

Summer 2007

It's eight p.m. Judy and I are at a party in the countryside. I didn't want to go, but Judy is being honored for raising funds for a local charity. It is a peaceful, hilly setting near the woods. We are swinging together in the back yard in a tree swing that smells delightfully like an old cedar closet, and I'm petting a smelly but very affectionate, overweight golden retriever.

I only know about five people here. I've changed, though, and am glad we've come since I feel comfortable around these salt-of-the-earth people whom I don't know. We have just discovered the home-cooked dishes of chicken and salads and desserts in the attached open garage.

Within a half-hour, the ceremony will start, and Judy will be duly recognized as the one whose volunteer efforts created a most impressive financial windfall for this organization. Two people have already come up to her with tears of gratitude.

Judy's cell phone rings. It's my mother. She tells Judy that my father's hand has turned totally blue and is swollen like a softball and that they're scared and think he needs to go to the emergency room. "Can you take him?"

Instead of saying, "No, because I am about to be honored at a party of two hundred people fifteen miles from where you are," Judy says, "Yes, we'll be there as soon as we can."

I am silently annoyed even though Judy, who deserves to be annoyed, isn't. Having accompanied my father numerous other times to the emergency room of the hospital, I know that we are in for a long and a weird night.

It's almost eight-thirty by the time we get to the apartment. Roberta is alone in the living room. Blaine is in the bedroom. I walk down the hallway and find him sitting on the side of his bed in the dark. I turn the light on and look at his hand. The entire back of it, and creeping up the wrist, is dark blue. The blueness is spreading, he says, and has been spreading since this morning when he discovered it.

"How did it happen?"

"That's what worries me the most, Pete. I don't know. I must have hit it on something when I awoke in the night when the alarm went off at two a.m. to awaken me to avoid peeing in the bed."

My mother yells at me from the living room, "You remember what happened to Shirley, don't you?" I tell her I don't. "Last year, Shirley, who lives right down the hall and is married to Jasper, had a similar situation with her leg—it turned blue. By the time they got her to the hospital, her whole leg was blue, and they told her she would have died if she hadn't come into the hospital just then."

With that chilling admonition, Judy, who by now is examining my father's blue hand tenderly but with a look of deep and almost professional concern, decides that we should go to the emergency room now.

I feel selfish and ashamed of myself for thinking that it's not serious at all and for wishing that I could just go home and have an hour or two of solitude before going to bed by ten thirty. I now have seen big, blue shadows on the bodies of countless old people, and I know that their skin is so thin and transparent from age and blood thinners that the slightest impact will create ghastly bruises from hematomas, all of which look like serious stuff but few of which really are. I cannot sort out my own selfish desire to be alone at this hour of Saturday night from the demands incumbent upon me as my father's primary pseudo-physician to objectively evaluate the requirements of his medical condition. So I acquiesce reluctantly and agree that we should go to the emergency room. Judy, a mere daughter-in-law, seems absolutely sure that that's what we should do. She does not give a single thought to that decision's power to ruin the rest of our Saturday night.

"Well, let's go," I say.

"I have to pee first," Blaine says.

I am struck ten minutes later in the living room, talking with my mother and Judy, that the object of the emergency, Blaine, is still peeing. "Blaine, let's go! This is an emergency, remember?"

Finally, the three of us amble slowly out the back door into the dusky evening and down the curved pathway to Judy's car. I sit in the back seat with Blaine in front.

We are quiet the first half of the way there, but then Blaine sings some old church hymn in a falsetto voice.

There are only three people waiting in the emergency room, and they are together. We walk up to the desk, and I tell the woman what's wrong. She is more officious than compassionate, and she gives us papers to fill out as Blaine plops his hand on the desk in front of her and leaves it there for her to see without saying a word. She never says anything about it or even glances at his hand that is placed two feet from her eyes. I have Blaine's wallet, and I fish through it for the proper numbers identifying him as a legitimate emergency room candidate. We sit down, and Judy joins us from the parking lot.

The only thing available to read while we wait is a hardcover book on the chair next to me about music theory. It is a strange book, first of all, for being a book on music theory in an emergency room but also because its organization is, well, disorganized. It seems as if someone who knew a lot about music wrote whatever came into his head without ever editing it again. But at least the book allows me to distance myself from what is happening—to enter a quasi-private zone which I need to be in during this Saturday night interlude between attending a party of strangers I didn't want to go to and being thrown into the hospital emergency room with my ninety-two-year-old father.

Judy asks me what I'm reading. I hand it to her. She is sitting next to Blaine, and together they look at it. The three others in the room are talking and are oblivious to us. The woman is on a cell phone, or else her ear hurts, and she's holding it while she talks.

Blaine asks Judy if she knows that he used to play the clarinet. "If I had done as my mother wanted me to do," he points out regretfully, "and practice, practice, practice, I would have become a famous clarinetist like Pete Fountain. But when my mother sent me to my room to practice, all I did was open my bedroom window and blow high notes as loud as I could so that my dog Peggy would start howling."

Three more people come into the emergency waiting room: a woman and her husband, carrying their little girl who is holding her ear, too, and crying sadly. They sit across the room. The mood of the room changes with this new group's claim upon part of it, and silence prevails until Blaine resumes his discussion of the clarinet. "Did you know, honey, that I went to the Chicago World's Fair with my high school band?" He is talking in a voice loud enough for everyone to hear. "There were five hundred kids from all over Iowa. There were ones who knew how to play, and then there were kids like me who just blew their clarinets out the window so the dog would howl. They told kids like me that if we were going to play, we could not play during the rests as kids like us were wont to do to get a laugh. In fact, they were so scared that we would do it anyway that they made us remove our reeds and just pretend to be playing. Which I gladly did, because then I could appear to be running glissandos up and down the scale like Liberace, and the audience would watch me."

The little girl is in her father's lap and is glued to him with her arms around his neck and her cheek on his chest. They all seem to be furtively listening to my father. She has stopped crying.

The entire emergency room is quiet now, even the nurse, listening to Blaine. He looks over at the people with the little girl and says, "She's stopped crying now."

"Yes," they whisper.

"Maybe I should climb up on Judy's lap like that, so I'll stop crying, too." The whole room laughs.

Suddenly the door from the parking lot swings open, and in come three ragged-looking people. They are all drunk, but the younger man without a shirt on whose forehead is bleeding is the drunkest. It's hard to understand them, but it sounds as if they want to get the young man stitched up so that he can go back and finish the fight. The woman is pregnant.

We have been waiting thirty minutes in the emergency room, and no patient has yet been called back for emergency treatment. But finally the obese man of the three people who were there when we arrived, who has been sighing a lot, is called back to the treatment area by a nurse. He is in a wheelchair.

Thirty minutes later, Blaine is still rattling on about something to Judy who is graciously comforting him by listening to him endlessly. My own mood has changed from feeling somewhat guilty to being slightly annoyed at the deterioration of my weekend to feeling totally justified in wishing I were alone at home, perhaps in bed, rather than enduring a late Saturday night with drunks and my father drunk with the opportunity to perform for a captive audience. He is going on and on about the carpet business, telling stories to Judy and all others within earshot.

Finally the nurse comes in and addresses Blaine's blue hand. "How did this happen?"

"I've been worried all night someone would ask me this," he says. "I've been afraid that a person who is in the emergency room with a totally blue hand would, by not remembering how it happened, expose himself as a doddering old man."

"He thinks he hit it on something when he woke up in the middle of the night and was groggy," I say. "It was blue when he got up this morning and has gotten worse and worse all day, and Judy and I thought he should come here." I am tempted to say, "Because Shirley almost died from waiting too long," but I don't.

The nurse looks at Blaine's hand and pushes on it here and there and asks him if it hurts. He tells her it doesn't. I ask her if she thinks it's broken. Without revealing anything more, she says, "The doctor will be in to look at it in a few minutes." Whatever nurses know, which is plenty, they can't say because of lawsuits. The doctor, who often doesn't know as much as his nurse, must be the one to say even though he may not know.

Thirty minutes later, we have not yet seen the doctor, and now the drunks are next to us in their own little, curtained area. They keep going outside to smoke and have befriended themselves to the fat man in the wheelchair in curtained area number one, so there is constant movement in the makeshift hallway that separates the curtained rooms. They are not very intelligent, and so it seems futile and pointless when the doctor does finally arrive and begins trying to explain to the drunk with the bloody forehead why the state of Illinois requires that the hospital disclose to him the potential dangers, although extremely remote, of electing to have a tetanus shot. The doctor notes that vaccines may use thiomerisol, which is believed by some to cause mercury poisoning, especially in infants, although that is still unproven. The drunken man's original kneejerk response of, "Yeah, give me a Tetanus shot," changes to, "Ah, hell, I don't need one."

It's now ten thirty p.m. We have been waiting in the emergency room for nearly two hours. Blaine is freezing and has called for blanket reinforcements. He is lying supine on the hospital gurney encased in blankets that the nurse keeps warming in the blanket warmer. I can tell from my father's behavior and from his general happiness with his current situation that he wants to spend the night in the hospital. I'm sure at some point he will advocate strongly for it. This is where he wants to be now—in total-care facilities where nurses and attendants come up and look after him all day long and talk to him and let him perform for them. He can be loved by complete strangers here and become instant friends with them and surrender all responsibility.

Another nurse comes in. Her name is Starla. Blaine wants it to be "Stella" and keeps making reference to "Stella by Starlight" and singing the first line of Ella Fitzgerald's song in a falsetto voice; "The song a robin sings, through years of endless springs…"

Starla recommends an x-ray, of course, but says only the doctor can really recommend anything, and he'll be in soon. Soon? That word has no relevance now. It's ten thirty.

The drunk next door wants a cigarette. The physician explains why he should quit smoking. I can see when the doctor finally comes through our curtain why he is naive enough to waste his time trying to convince a drunk with a low IQ to quit smoking. The doctor is very young and innocent and is one of the sweetest doctors I have ever met. He is a perfect match for my father.

Finally, the doctor tells Blaine to put ice on his hand and hold it above his head as much as possible and says it's just a bruise. Blaine asks him to write it down.

We are free to go. It is almost midnight. Blaine has to pee. We get him into the bathroom just across the hall and stand in the hallway and wait. As the doctor walks by, the drunks come out from behind their curtains and say, "Doc, we're going outside for one more cigarette."

My mother calls and says that Blaine went to see his doctor yesterday to ask about his stomach and that the doctor felt a mass there. Dr. Strauch has ordered an immediate MRI. "Will you take your father to the hospital and stay with him the whole time?"

I arrive two minutes early at Seminary Estates' front door. Blaine is waiting in a chair in the foyer. The first thing he asks me is, "Will you be with me *generally* today?"

"I'll be with you as I have to be and won't be with you if it's pointless."

"Oh, wonderful! You've become *just* the boy I raised to manhood."

A nice-looking, humorous nurse greets us, and we immediately establish a rapport. Upon hearing my father's name, she says, "Are you the Blaine Gorham from the carpet store? You made a big impression on my folks years ago by climbing around on the floor with me when I was just a toddler and saying, 'Okay folks, are you ready for the Double Rabbi low?'"

When we're done with the MRI, I wheel my father out the door and up the ramp and across the street and into the parking lot and load him into the car and drive home. We walk up the back walkway to Seminary Estates. Blaine stops and takes my arm. "Pete, I want to tell you something before we get to Roberta." He looks me in the eye with that unfaltering salesman look, which is placid now and easy to fix upon.

"I know where I am now."

"You do? Where?"

"I'm waiting for *Godot*."

My mother calls me after dinner and says that the doctor called, and the results of the tests showed abnormalities in the liver and the gall bladder, which perplexed him. She said he suspected the gall bladder, but he wants Blaine to have another more sophisticated MRI Monday morning to find out for sure.

Blaine is early.

As he walks through the front door of Seminary Estates, his pants fall down all the way to his knees. I can't believe my eyes. He is wearing white boxer shorts, and his tiny, little legs are white as snow. It seems like a joke. He is nonchalant and doesn't panic at all but calmly sets down in my arms the yellow folder that he is carrying, and says, "Hold this a minute," and he struggles to pull his pants up.

He pats his pockets, feeling for his house keys as he always does. "Have I forgotten anything?" he asks generically as he starts to get in the car. Then he turns to me and says, "Isn't that something—that a guy asks if he's forgotten anything whose pants just fell down?"

Blaine is quiet all the way to the hospital. No energy. I've never seen him so tired. We walk together into the hospital and to the admittance area where we've been so many times before. Now and then he stops and leans over as if he's praying.

Blaine must have breathed.

The MRI pictures are too blurry to be definitive. He has to go back tomorrow morning at nine thirty—this time for an ultrasound procedure. I am not happy. From the waiting room last week, I had heard the assistant say many times, "Now hold your breath," and then, "Great! You're doing terrific!" How much more of this can a frail ninety-two-year-old man take? How much more can I take?

I call the assistant. He returns my call two hours later. He is aware that the pictures came out blurry and is sorry. He says that he and another technician had tried and tried to enhance them so that the affected area was discernible, but it didn't work. I tell him Dr. Boydstun has ordered an ultrasound procedure next, and I ask him if that is an effective tool, wondering why, if it is, they didn't do it in the first place rather than sending a body born almost a century ago into a terrifying, dark cacophonous tunnel with instructions not to breathe. His answer is not what I want to hear. "If it were my father, I would try whatever I could."

Blaine's pain is getting worse. What will happen if no procedure works and they don't know which area of his stomach is causing the problem? Will they just start removing organs until he gets better or dies? Or will they do nothing, and he'll die of whatever he has?

When my mother called, telling me the bad news about the blurry MRCP results, she had said Blaine wanted to go to the emergency room and wanted to know if I'd take him. "No, I won't, Mom. We'll just go there and sit for hours and hours and finally have to come back home because they won't admit him without a doctor's order. I know Dad's ways. He'll intend to sit there like Gandhi until they have no choice but to carry him onto a hospital bed."

My mother agrees with me, but I can tell he's beating her down with his pressure. I agree to go out to Seminary Estates to talk to him after my mother says, "He will calm down if he talks to you."

It's four p.m. My mother is sitting on the couch, reading. She looks worried. She whispers, "Don't lose your temper with him, please. He can't take it." Blaine finally comes into the room on his walker. He is distant. He's still a shrewd guy with an uncanny ability to get what he wants. But I'm a stubborn guy with an uncanny ability to resist giving in. I know he wants to go to the emergency room, but I can see already that he doesn't need to go. What I think he wants is to gain admittance to the hospital and never return – to die in the arms of people caring for him, adoring him and adorning him with medicine and health care, feeding him through IVs so that he doesn't have to bother ever again even going to the dining room or lifting the food to his mouth.

My father hasn't eaten for two days. I talk to him about that. He is uncharacteristically negative and downright unpleasant about everything. "You have to eat, Dad, even if it doesn't taste good." I cook him a meal and literally feed him, which amuses him and restores his appetite.

As I leave, I remind him I'll pick him up at 9:10 in the morning. I walk to my truck. I turn the ignition key. It won't start. It's dead. It's a good truck with a good heart. I stand beside it for a minute and wonder if it sacrificed itself so that my father can live a little longer.

I walk back to room 142 and get the keys to my parents' car and drive it home with the windows down in the hot, sweltering heat of an early August evening.

It's still hot. Summer is gasping its last power before it surrenders to the fall and fall into the winter.

Just before I get Blaine out of the car underneath the hospital's canopy, he refers again to *Waiting for Godot*. "But I want *Godot* to know, I'm waiting patiently."

We go into the admittance area. The receptionist's desk is clear, so we walk right up to it, and I say, "Here we are again," thinking she might remember us since we were here just two days ago, but she doesn't. With each soul who clamors to her desk in its own unique pain and grief, she sees before her just another number and another task throughout her day—like all of us would eventually, I suppose. Even pain and anguish can become ordinary and expected when experienced in an assembly line of suffering.

Suddenly a woman enters the locker room where they've directed us to put on a gown. She looks kind and compassionate and smart—all of the things my father needs at this time. Her name is Sandy. She helps me remove Blaine's wool sweater, his winter shirt, his long-sleeve T-shirt, and his brace, and put the gown on over his distressingly formless, yellow, scrawny body. I remember my father teaching me at the age of thirteen how to lift weights, from which I learned one of the most important lessons of my life—that one can sculpt one's own destiny.

Blaine insists upon putting his winter sweater on over his gown and asks for a blanket over that. Sandy complies and then calls for a wheel chair. "It's a long way, and why should you walk?" Blaine agrees. The wheelchair comes, and she pushes Blaine to the ultrasound room. It's actually not a very long way, which is further evidence that Sandy is the angel we need right now.

The ultrasound department is like a proctor's room in a college dormitory. It's a big, comfortable space with low-lumen reading lamps and a desk with books on it and pictures of Sandy's cat on the wall. I like it immediately and feel as if Sandy has taken us into her home to make us feel at ease. In the middle of the room off to one side is a hospital bed, and next to it an elaborate computer keyboard with a big screen. She pulls a chair over to the other side of the bed for me to sit in and watch the screen.

Blaine keeps asking me if his hair is wet because it feels cold. I feel it, and it's not, and I tell him. He asks me if I'd get a towel and rub it dry anyway, which I do. He keeps insisting that it's wet, so I finally just cover it with the towel. Sandy sees this and goes and warms up a huge towel and drapes it over his head, and he lies back down and sighs, totally covered with blankets and warmed towels and a wool sweater except for a slot for his nose and eyes.

She prepares Blaine's stomach by smearing it with a warm, translucent jelly, presumably for receiving the sound waves bouncing back from his organs to the instrument connected to the computer screen, which she drags across the slimy jelly and which immediately forms a fairly accurate picture of my father's insides.

All the while, Blaine is charming Sandy with various compliments, and she is chuckling at him. Finally she's ready and starts systematically uncovering the goings on in my father's entrails, which I am privileged to observe—a thing about which most sons would not be able to boast.

"See that black circle? That's a gallstone. And *that's* the gall bladder. It's distended, as you can see." I can't see that, but I wonder why medical people prefer the word *distended* to *swollen*. However, I believe her, especially after discovering she's been doing this for thirty years. I believe her because my father taught me that people like Sandy probably know as much, maybe more, than the chief radiologist who will ultimately see the pictures Sandy takes and make a judgment of them and whom Dr. Boydstun will consult. But I know from my father that by going into thc back door where the forklift drivers unload the carpet, or by waiting in the waiting room and befriending the secretary, that I will learn as much from the Sandys of life as I could ever hope to learn from the Chief, whom I will probably never be allowed to see.

Blaine immediately falls asleep for the entire hour of the examination except when we have to turn him over to find his kidneys. At the end of the hour, I know who Sandy is, and she knows me, too. She is a good, compassionate caregiver.

I return Blaine to Seminary Estates. I remember my dead Ford Ranger, and I optimistically park my parents' car in its permanent spot and go back to my truck, open the door, and put the key in the ignition and turn it.

It starts right up!

By giving up its life, my truck has been reborn.

My mother calls me. She's heard from Dr. Strauch who's heard from Dr. Boydstun, who said, "Blaine needs to have his gall bladder removed." She says, "Dr. Strauch also said that at Blaine's age, an operation is risky. I'll call you when we have an appointment scheduled with the surgeon."

"I can't do it Monday," I tell her.

On Monday, my cell phone vibrates in my pocket while I'm roofing a garage. It's my mother who tells me they have an appointment this afternoon at 1:45 to see Dr. Davis, the surgeon who will remove Blaine's gall bladder and look around inside his viscera for other abnormalities. I sigh and decide not to remind her that I had told her Monday's a bad day for me.

I am becoming increasingly battle weary. My natural strength to withstand unlimited duress has never been superhuman. I consent to pick my parents up at one thirty, however.

My brother Mike arrived from Denver yesterday. Tonight, the night before surgery, we all go to Seminary Estates for the last dinner together before Blaine's surgery. We have pizza delivered and make a salad.

Blaine looks terrible. His color is wan, and he has no energy. When he talks, which is infrequently, he slurs his words and makes even less sense than usual. As we are all sitting around the living room talking, my mother whispers to me, "I'm nervous."

The food comes, and we all launch into it—except Blaine, who slowly and without any conviction or passion eats a small bowl of Campbell's soup we have prepared for him. I had thought he would say prayers and tell us all he loved us all evening, but he doesn't. My father asks my mother to say a prayer, and he lies on her lap like a little boy, and she strokes his head. The prayer she says sounds alarmingly final. The room becomes silent. Not wanting to experience what might issue forth if we stay much longer, I suggest to Mike and Judy that we leave. We all get up. By this time, my father is sitting up again. He looks lost and scared. I walk up to him, and he bows over like a horse asking to be stroked. I put my hand on the back of his shoulders. I am shocked how bony he is. The bones do not invite me to comfort them, but I leave my hands there and speak. "Dad, I know you. And I know you're thinking that tomorrow will be a perfect opportunity for you to drift off into Heaven. If ever anyone deserved to go to Heaven, it's you. And you *will* sometime. But not tomorrow. You've got responsibilities here still."

It's extremely hot and humid by five thirty a.m. when I wake up. My mother calls at eight and talks to Mike and says the hospital just called and the doctor is going to be early, and they can take Blaine right away.

Mike drives out to get them at eight, and I walk to the hospital ten minutes later, afraid I won't get there in time. At the hospital, there is no sign of them. I go into the waiting room by the front door where they will eventually have to come.

A half hour later, my brother drives up with our parents. I can see from the window that my father, who is sitting in the back seat, looks lost and yellow and even more frail than usual. So I get the only available wheelchair and push it outside under the canopy next to the car. It is a *huge* wheelchair that is designed for someone who weighs at least three hundred pounds.

Blaine looks like a tiny boy sitting in it with his legs dangling down among the metallic controls.

"What happened, Mike?"

"Oh, God, all of these people at Seminary Estates had to say good-bye to Dad and wish him luck. There was a stream of old people coming outside to the car and hugging him and talking to him like it was going to be his last day on Earth. One old guy raced up in a wheelchair and stood up just like he was throwing away his crutches at Lourdes. He hugged Dad and started to cry and said, 'You're my friend.' Even the manager came out and hugged him. It was touching, but we're late. Sorry."

I wheel Blaine to the elevator with my mother and brother right behind. We ride to the fifth floor and find our way to the surgery pre-op room, which is already bustling with nurses and patients ready to go under the knife. These stalwart nurses face this life and death chaos every day, I ponder, like firemen fighting a constant blaze.

Pre-op is like a MASH tent with temporary, curtained-off areas for patients about to undergo surgery. The overall impression that Pre-op gives is that life is not permanent but is extendable, although it is fast-moving and demanding and it can end quickly, so there is no sense in building elaborate structures to celebrate or support it.

By the time I arrive at Blaine's tent, he has already enlisted a nurse and has gained her assurance that she will "be with me the whole time." She has quickly seen, as surgical nurses must, I suppose, that the key to handling my father is with firm compassion. Both of them have each other—literally—in the palms of their hands. This, within sixty seconds! Blaine is already talking about blankets. "Not only that," she says, "but I'll warm them for you first."

She asks him if he'll put on his weird green surgery cap. "I'll put anything on that's warm," he says and dons it. He holds her hand.

"You'll never leave me, right?"

"Never."

The nurse says it's time to go and gets ready to wheel away the bed my father is lying on but waits a moment for my mother to kiss him. "I love you," he says to her tenderly with a tear in his eye. As the nurse wheels him out of the room, Blaine sings, "I'll see you after awhile."

My father has not told us all he loves us ten times as I'd thought he would. He seems scared as if he knows he'll finally see St. Peter and that St. Peter will know and recite each and every good and bad deed my father performed or was a part of in his long life, and that the sheet will tally up to a plus or a minus, and his eternal fate will be sealed accordingly. No doubt his biggest fear is that he will not have a chance to persuade the heartless, scientific, celestial determiners of each man's fate, who guard the Gate of Heaven, that perhaps they should re-figure my father's destiny according to a different, more favorable metric.

The nurse quickly pushes Blaine's gurney down the hall to the operating room. My brother and my mother and I go back to the waiting room to wait for the call to the family, instructing them that their loved one is out of surgery and the surgeon will see them in a private room and tell them how the operation went and that the patient will be okay. Or that the patient, sad to say, did not survive.

Two and one-half hours later, the telephone in the waiting room rings. Even though the room is full of people also waiting for calls, when the old woman volunteer answers it, I do not need to ask for whom the phone rings. I start to get up even before she nods at us and points.

It rings for us.

GALESBURG, ILLS.
Presbyterian
Church

He soars in the highs of creativity
And captures a world no one knows is there
Using adjectives as adverbs and verbs as nouns
And double entendres and verbal salchows
They sometimes wonder what he means
And sometimes he does too
But it doesn't matter because he is free
No one can ask him where he is going
Or why he is going there
Or when he is coming back
For there is no curfew upon his horizon.

Excerpt from Poetics
by Peter Gorham

She will marry a prince and they'll have lovely children,
They will live in a house on a lake
She will always be young and the house always pretty.
Of that there can be no mistake.

Excerpt from A Day at the Fair
by Peter Gorham

I feel the sun turn back today,
Head towards its journey seeking Day
The light upon the window sill
Remains a minute longer still
Ah, hope has been reborn anew
Today, a minute; tomorrow, two

In ninety days it will be spring
And next we'll hear the robins sing
The flowers will poke above the ground
Then Joy and Gladness will abound
A journey through a thousand miles
Begins with one step, single file

December Twenty Second
by Peter Gorham

My father's clock was not precise
The cord was frayed and it had no light.
I stored it high when he passed away
But I've just come back to it today.

My father's clock had a different time
It was slow and calm, not a thing like mine.
My clock's too fast and it moves too quick
So I'll replace my clock with his.

My Father's Clock
by Peter Gorham

Part Two

"In all that what truth will there be? Astride of a grave and a difficult birth. Down in the hole, lingeringly, the grave-digger puts on the forceps. We have time to grow old.

The air is full of our cries. (He listens.) But habit is a great deadener. But that is not the question. Why are we here, that is the question. And we are blessed in this, that we happen to know the answer. Yes, in this immense confusion one thing alone is clear. We are waiting for Godot to come."

—*Waiting for* Godot by Samuel Beckett

Fall 2007

Wild men who caught and sang the sun in flight

And learn, too late, they grieved it on its way,

Do not go gentle into that good night.

And you, my father, there on the sad height,

Curse, bless me now with your fierce tears, I pray.

Do not go gentle into that good night.

Rage, rage against the dying of the light.

—Dylan Thomas, at his father's deathbed

Blaine is in recovery. He has a roommate—a man who seems at once amused and bewildered by my father who is talking nonstop, already performing for his visitors. He is staring up at the ceiling while he talks, oblivious to his audience. He sounds as if he's drunk. "Thank you, Lord. I get to live a little longer." He is telling baldly anything that comes into his head.

"I worried for seventy-two years, and now they've operated the worry out of me." This is a reference to the *huge* ulcer the doctor discovered in Blaine's lower intestine after removing his "very ugly gall bladder."

"The ulcer," Dr. Davis said, "was probably caused by worrying about taking a crap every day." My father, of course, does not understand that an ulcer cannot simply be removed. But it's best that he doesn't know this, I think, because he has the power to heal himself with misconceptions alone.

"Don't you mean you worried for *ninety*-two years?" my brother asks him.

"Well, no, for the first twenty years I didn't worry about anything. I was at Parsons College, and I was still letting my Mama and Papa worry for me. And then one day I looked up, and everyone was fleeing! All of my mates were going off into their futures, and I was going to be all alone unless I found Roberta, which I finally did! And then I had to put my nose to the grinder. Three kids. And I had to shape up or ship out! And I've been worried ever since until now when Dr. Davis removed my ulcer. Oh, thank thee Lord!" Blaine bursts into singing "Everything Is Beautiful."

The nurse comes in. She is serious and is not amused by my father's behavior, especially his asking her over and over to repeat what he is to do and what the pills are for and when he can go to the bathroom again.

Another nurse comes in and tells Blaine she is going to walk him down to the restroom. This is a happy moment. Blaine asks her name. It's Rachel. She gingerly helps him out of bed and moves him toward the door and then the hallway. He sings to her, "Rachel, Rachel, I've been thinking, what a fine world it would be, if the men were all transported far beyond the Northern Sea."

"How long can I stay in the hospital?" he asks her.

"Have you asked your doctor?"

"No, I haven't. But I'd like to stay at least thirty days."

Blaine struggles to my car that is parked under the canopy at Seminary Estates. "Have a nice time," an old woman sitting in the foyer says to him.

"The people all say that any time you leave here, 'Have a nice time.'" He laughs. "They figure you must be going out on the town."

As a matter of fact, we're going to revisit Dr. Davis to have Blaine's stitches removed. And Roberta wants to know why Blaine's stomach still hurts just as bad and why his appetite hasn't returned, and so he's down to 100 pounds, and why his back is killing him, and especially why he's melancholy. The main thing my father wants to know is if I have the folder with the questions Roberta will ask him later.

The nurse calls us back to the examining room immediately. A young woman doctor enters the room. She is nice-looking, cheery, articulate, caring, and sharp. I like her immediately. "Are you Doctor Murphy?" my father asks her.

"Morrison. I'm the doctor's assistant. I was with you in surgery."

"Oh, you were? That's nice, bless you. Will Dr. Davis be in?"

"No, he's not here today. He asked me to meet with you."

"Oh? When will I see Dr. Davis?"

"Well, we could make an appointment for next week if you'd like."

"Okay."

I need to intervene here because I don't want to come back since I already believe that Ms. Morrison can answer any questions we have and will most likely give us more time and will tolerate Blaine's confusing line of thought. "Dad, let's just meet with Dr. Morrison. She was right there helping Dr. Davis in the operation. She probably knows things about you that you don't know about yourself." She laughs.

"What's your first name, Dr. Murphy?" He puts out his hand to her and she takes it and says, "Sherri Morrison."

"Well, I'm going to call you *Doctor* Morrison because you are the authority here, and I need to show you the utmost respect."

"I'm actually not a doctor. I'm a doctor's assistant."

"Well, as far as I'm concerned, you're the doctor, and I'm going to treat you like royalty. First of all, Dr. Murphy, let me say that I'm a little slow. You need to turn your chair around so that it's facing Pete because you and

Pete will carry on a discussion that has meaning. I'll just waffle around. All I'm good for is asking questions, not for understanding answers. That's what Pete's for." I ask her the various questions my mother has written on a blue slip of paper.

Without being invited to do so, Ms. Morrison reaches down and starts unbuttoning my father's pants and says she will remove the stitches now. I feel a bit ashamed that I find this to be slightly erotic, watching her pull my father's pants down with no shame whatsoever in a bold and mildly curious way a sensitive hooker might behave toward a shy boy who's about to lose his virginity.

Finally she tells him he will need to stand up, and he does. His pants fall all the way to the floor, and he is wearing a senior diaper. His legs are sticks. She leans down and pulls his pants off the floor and holds them up for him as she probes his stitches. Then she cuts the stitches out with scissors while holding up Blaine's pants for him with her free hand. I am wondering if this is the type of thing that very old, very rich men pay young women to do for them as a quasi-sexual expression of their last remaining power.

Blaine is totally fixated upon his navel, whose general area will become the focal point of the next thirty minutes, in fact of the entire day.

"Dr. Morrison," my father interrupts, placing his bony blue fingers gently on her wrist while she is in mid-sentence. She stops talking. "Here's the only thing

I really care to know. Am I permitted now to take one of those things…what are they called, Pete?"

"Q-Tips." Blaine and I have already discussed this.

"Right. Can I take a Q-Tip and put it in my navel after a shower and twirl it around? Because when they let me out of the hospital, they told me not to do that. But you said I could now. Is that right?" Ms. Morrison looks at me and winks. She takes his arm tenderly again and says, "Yes, Mr. Gorham, you can do that or not do that. Either one is fine."

"Well I like to do it every time after I take a shower because I don't want a lot of water slogging around in my belly button." She reaches over to the supply cabinet and removes a "two by two," which is a two-inch-square piece of gauze, and shows Blaine where to put it in the crease in his belly in order to absorb moisture. Blaine stops her and takes her other arm and stares at her deeply. She stares back just as deeply, not as a challenge but as an acceptance of my father's intimacy. They are now holding each other's arms like dancers. "I have one more question," Blaine says. He stares at her with his invincible salesman stare. "Are you ready?"

"I'm ready." She looks at me and winks again.

"Okay, here it is. Are you ready?"

"I'm ready."

"How am I doing, Dr. Morrison? Do you know anything that I don't? Is there anything you need to tell me but are afraid I can't take it? Because if that's what you think, you're right. But tell me anyway."

"You're doing fine, Mr. Gorham."

"Am I?" he asks again, suspiciously.

"Yes, you are. You don't have to come back unless you feel you need to. Like I told your son, you will need to see Dr. Strauch about those other things, but you're free to go."

We do finally all leave together and emerge triumphantly into the hallway before noticing that Blaine's pants are still mostly not on. Dr. Morrison reaches down and pulls them up and tightens his belt. He shakes her hand and holds on to it and pulls her into him and puts his other arm through her arm and says, "Thank you, Dr. Morrison, for patiently spending your precious time with an old geezer like me."

Instead of simply letting Blaine off at the front door of Seminary Estates and coming back later or tomorrow to explain it all to my mother, I elect to do it now, sensing that uncertainty would not be good to leave her with at this time.

It's Friday, and I feel good. My only obligation today is to pick up Blaine's walker and take it to be repaired. A day to myself. Finally.

I walk in the front door of Seminary Estates at 12:10 p.m. There's Blaine walking ever so slowly in front of the dining room. He sees me and stops. He looks terrible. He has what is developing into a permanent grimace on his face from pain. His skin is whitish-yellow. When he speaks, I can barely understand what he's saying because his words are so garbled. The right side of his mouth is distorted, too. Two days ago I'd noticed this on a brief visit to Seminary Estates, and I'd pointed it out to my mother. She'd said she hadn't noticed it herself, so I had dismissed it. But now it's clear to me that something is wrong. He seems to have had a stroke.

I mention that I am here to get his walker. He doesn't remember. Suddenly he becomes confused. I offer to get him a tray of food and take it back to their apartment, and he can go on back now, and I'll meet him there.

Roberta is sitting alone at their usual table, and I tell her the plan. She grabs me by the arm. "Pete, sit down a minute." She leans over and whispers in my ear, "Lots of other people out here have noticed what you noticed the other day about Blaine. In fact, they discussed it in a meeting this morning." I tell her I noticed it again, and it seems to me that he's had a stroke. "Should he go to the hospital, Pete?" I tell her I think so. Tears come into her eyes, and she says, "Connie who works in the kitchen said to me, 'Maybe he's just tired of all this, and he's getting ready to pass now, Roberta.'" My mother breaks down for a moment and sobs and then gains her composure.

I leave her table to catch up with Blaine who by now should be well on his way to room 142. But just five feet outside of the dining room, he is sitting in a chair, slumped over in pain.

"Are you okay, Dad?"

"Just hurting, Pete."

"I know you are. Dad, I think you should go to the hospital. What do you think?"

"Is the hospital a place where I can lie down and not get up?"

"Yes."

"Then I want to go."

"Can you get up now and walk back to your room?"

He struggles with great effort to stand. His knees are wobbly, and his feet point out asymmetrically like a clown. He is hunched over in pain. His walker meanders from side to side as he pushes it elliptically with effort from only one hand at a time and with all of the might of his slight remaining strength. I am tempted to carry him, but I'm afraid it would crush more of his bones. He is walking so slowly that only with great concentration can I keep pace with him and not move out ahead. Every few steps he stops. Finally we make it to the Oasis, but he doesn't sit down at first. "Pete, you know what time it is, don't you?" He stands as I sit as if he's a lecturer and sternly pronounces, "I *have* to tell you something. I've known that this moment was coming, and here it is. Things are changing. It's the time of the Walrus. 'The time has come, the Walrus said, to talk of many things. Of cabbages...and kings...and whether pigs have wings.'" He sits down.

My father looks very serious and also as if he's going to cry. "I *have* to tell you and your mother some things that are very important to me, and I don't want you to get pissed off. These are things I've never told you." I can't imagine there's anything he hasn't told us at least once, but I am having a slight novel fear that he is needing to say something critical of us—totally out of character—that he has been holding inside his whole life, and now at the end he must say before he dies. Something like, "I was only kidding all those times I told you I loved you."

I suggest we continue walking. Then I see my mother come around the corner and walk toward us. She arrives on her walker, and he repeats it all again. Roberta, ever practical, insists he not talk about walruses now but that he prepare himself to go to the hospital.

She keeps walking toward their apartment. I sit with him another minute and then tell him I'm going to walk with her, and then I'll come back and help him.

My mother is very alarmed. I tell her I'll call Dr. Strauch's office and say we want Blaine admitted to the hospital. Then Blaine arrives. "I have a proclamation that must be spoken before anyone can do anything else." My mother and I become quiet, ready to listen.

"There are changes that must come now. 'The time has come, the Walrus said, to talk of many things'."

"Oh, Blaine!" my mother sighs.

"I know! But I need to talk, too. There are things I have to say now, and I don't want to be interrupted by either of you, or I don't want either of you to get pissed off!"

My father is as serious-sounding as I've ever heard him be. My mother senses it, too, and we both fall silent.

Blaine repeats the walrus theme and then with great effort and chagrin starts talking about not being able to help Roberta with the dishes anymore. She tells him that's okay, and she understands. But he continues to berate himself in a lengthy diatribe. After several minutes of self-flagellation about not being able to do the dishes anymore, Blaine stops and looks at us and says, "There, I said it!"

"That's *it*?" I say to myself, astonished. Only later does Judy help me understand that he was saying that he cannot go on living the way they've been living and that he needs to go to a nursing home, or maybe that he's going to die, and we need to get ready for that.

"Your father can't say things directly, you know that. He probably can't even tell himself directly, especially now after he's had a stroke."

I call Dr. Strauch's office and ask them to admit Blaine to the hospital. They can't, they tell me. He'll have to go the emergency room and have them examine him and find something wrong and then call Dr. Strauch and ask if he will give his permission to admit the patient.

What combination of doctors, lawyers, and insurance moguls came up with *that* procedure, I wonder? And then I remember the last emergency room visit weeks ago. It was the same thing only then they *wouldn't* admit him. I tell the nurse this. She assures me he'll be admitted this time.

"This is how I see it going down," I tell her. "We'll wait hours in the waiting room while Blaine suffers horrible pain because he can't lie down. Then they'll take us to the examining room, and we'll wait more hours, and they'll x-ray him and manhandle him while they do, take blood, and perform other tests and have him fill out forms and disclaimers and promises not to sue them, and then hours after that they'll say they have to call Dr. Strauch, and by that time Dr. Strauch will be gone for the weekend."

"No," the nurse says, "They'll be able to reach Dr. Strauch at any time on his pager."

"Sure," I say cynically. "Do you mean there is *no* way that you can get a ninety-two-year-old man who has had a stroke and is in excruciating pain and who has been your loyal patient for nearly forty years admitted to the hospital without going through all of that?"

"No, there's no other way according to Medicare's rules."

I hang up and return to the living room and ask Blaine if he's ready to go to the hospital.

"I need to eat something first, Pete." So I heat up his lunch in the microwave and get him silverware and a glass of milk and a napkin.

"I'm leaving to go change my clothes and eat some leftovers at home. I'll be back in an hour."

When I return, Blaine is gone. "Where's Dad?"

"He's in his bedroom, changing clothes," my mother tells me. I walk back to his bedroom, and he's sitting almost naked on the side of his bed with his trousers down around his ankles, wearing only a diaper. "Dad, we have to go."

"Pete, I'm confused. I don't feel good. I think I want to take a nap."

"Dad, I'm afraid if we get to the hospital too late, that by the time they've taken you in and done their tests, we won't be able to get hold of Strauch, and he is the one who will have to admit you."

"He is? Well, I'll take a *short* nap."

My mother, by now attempting to take a nap herself, says from her bedroom, "Blaine, you need to go, or it'll be too late."

"I'm just going to take a short nap. Well, maybe she's right, maybe we should go. I need to get dressed, though."

"Dad, you lie down and take a short nap. I'm going to leave, and I'll be back in a half-hour."

"No, no, Pete, stay here in the room with me, will you? Sleep here, please." There is no place to sleep except on the floor or with him in his single bed.

"Dad, I'll tell you what. I'll go lie down on the couch, and you lie down here, and I'll come and get you in thirty minutes."

"All right, Pete. But wait, maybe she's right. I think we better go to the hospital. Can you help me get my clothes off first? I gotta take this thing off first." He points to his diaper. "Will you help me?"

I think of *Tuesdays with Morrie* where Morrie's friend eventually had to help Morrie wipe his butt. I'm almost sure I will never wipe my father's butt, but then I probably once was sure I'd never help him take off his diaper.

I take my father's diaper off and then help him on with his boxer shorts then his trousers, his T-shirt, and his body brace. Then I put on his gleaming-white sneakers and get down on the floor on my knees and lace them up for him. Now he needs a shirt. We walk into their only closet to find a shirt. He has a very specific shirt in mind. He finds it. It's a striped T-shirt. I point out to him that he already has a T-shirt on. He doesn't care. He wants *this* one, too.

Now begins the tedious process that my mother has complained of so many times—trying to get Blaine to actually *leave* the apartment. Many minutes later, we finally get out the back door into the terribly hot sun.

We are moving so slowly through the fire of midday that it feels as if we are two men, a father and his son, who bravely started out by foot to cross the Sahara Desert, and we've reached the middle of it and realize we've miscalculated, and that now in order to reach coolness and rest, we have ahead of us in *any* direction a distance equal to the distance we've already traveled. Our spirit of adventure is gone, and so are our energy and resources.

Finally we get to the car. We drive to the hospital and pull up at the emergency room. It's two in the afternoon. "Blaine, our goal here is to have you be regarded as someone in need of being admitted to the hospital. You know what I mean?"

"That shouldn't be a hard part to perform."

"Well it might be harder than you think. Remember last time?" He doesn't.

"Try to look dazed and crippled with pain."

"That's how I am, Pete. Who's going to do the talking here?"

"I am. You just go sit down as if you have no idea what's going on."

"I don't."

To my surprise and disappointment there are four other people ahead of us at the emergency room. I help Blaine to a chair and go to the check-in window.

For some reason, I have not been able to mention to my father that I think he's had a stroke. Broken hips first and then strokes signal the end of life, it seems. However, I whisper it to the nonchalant emergency woman behind the window, after telling her that my ninety-three-year-old father over there is in agonizing pain and that he appears to have had a stroke, too.

"When did you first notice it?" she asks.

I foolishly answer honestly that I noticed it two days ago, realizing at once that that will probably give them license to let my poor father suffer for an hour an a half, sitting upright on his fractured spine in a chair in the freezing cold waiting room before being called to the back.

We must wait twenty-five minutes before being called. Blaine is already feeling compelled to act and perform and tell jokes and make witty observations to various attendants even though he's delirious with pain. I'm worried that the staff will quickly decide that, "This old man does *not* need to stay in the hospital tonight." I want to communicate to my father that he needs to return quickly to the dazed and crazed cripple role, but I have no opportunity to do that.

Now the action starts. After first having my father sign a galaxy of forms delayed by Blaine's constant query about *how* he should sign them—Charles Blaine or C. Blaine or just Blaine—they hook him up to various test instruments and take his pulse and blood pressure and temperature. Then a nurse named Chris asks him, "On a scale of one to ten, how bad is your pain?"

"Is ten the worst?" Blaine asks.

"Yes."

"I'd say about five."

Five! Why did my father say that? Is he being falsely modest? Or brave? My God, they might release him right now! Blaine is casually conversing and joking with the two attendants and making them laugh right there in the ER. If I'm unable to stop him, he will give an award-winning performance acting the part of a man who has *not* just had a stroke and is *not* suffering torturous back pain. I need to change their perceptions radically and quickly. He has forgotten why we're here, and he is being blinded by the limelight.

I am freezing, and I am angry that the purpose of our visit—to get admitted—seems not to be coming together. While in the waiting mode, I tell Blaine I need to go for a walk. He is fine with that. As I walk away, he sings Benny Goodman's song, "There'll Be a Change in the Weather": "When you grow old, you don't last long. You're here today, and then tomorrow you're gone. There's a change in the weather, there's a change in the sea, so from now on, there'll be a change in me." The lyrics fade out as I walk farther away and go through the ambulance emergency room door and into the hot parking lot, which feels so good on my cold skin.

I ponder what's going on as I walk in the sun around the hospital parking lot. On my walk, I watch the people entering and exiting the hospital. Many of them are old, and most of the old ones are being followed or pushed or led or given aide in some way by others who seem to be their children.

Caregiving one's parents is a heroic thing. Like parenting, and like the Hippocratic Oath itself, it has to do with keeping the good of the patient as the highest priority. It requires that the caregiver attend to the needs of the patient while sacrificing his own needs— an act that seems to defy human nature. Caregiving one's parents often requires—just like parenting— having to recognize, in the course of giving care, that one's own self-image, built up layer by layer protectively, perhaps over decades of time, is faulty or illusory or self-deceptive or all three.

The person who gives physical care usually must also provide mental and spiritual care. To do so, he must honestly recognize and acknowledge who he is as it becomes revealed, however flawed or ugly, however contradictory or inconsistent. To give care to one's parents is to enroll in an intense years-long session of psychotherapy, which in the end will make the caregiver more aware of who he is and why he is who he is but might also leave him depressed to have found out that he is not who he had thought he was.

To care for my two parents day-by-day for years has made me see why I am contradictory and divided and how I can legitimately hold two or more opposing beliefs at once. It has given me an understanding of why I have two natures: one is detached and organized and opinionated and clear and believes in the scientific method; the other one believes in every sort of voodoo that has ever been uncovered or devised by man in his hour of fear and need. Part of me is angry with the stark and bitter reality I am forced to clinically perceive, but it is juxtaposed beside a belief that in some mysterious way, which most likely will never be understood, the world makes compassionate sense. So I am obliged at last to forgive everything and everyone and ultimately surrender the perception that life has as much or more evil as good, in favor of the higher belief that all people are essentially angels who have fallen.

In the hospital again, I ask Blaine how he's doing. He said they handled him pretty rough when they x-rayed him even though he told them over and over to be careful. Despite this, he is actually quite alert and in very good spirits, which get better and better as we talk. He says his pain is not bad.

After we are together awhile longer and he begins joking around and talking faster and faster, it occurs to me what has happened. They have given him a powerful pain suppressant, probably a hypo, and he feels great. His pain is gone or at least successfully set aside so that his effervescent personality can emerge to front stage again.

The doctor comes in and says immediately, "Wow, you sure look better!" He leaves again before I have a chance to ask him what painkiller they've used or to ask him for the third time if they're going to admit my father to the hospital. Blaine starts singing "Old Man River." "I gits weary and sick of tryin', I'm tired of livin' but scared of dyin', but ol' man river, he just keeps rollin' along."

"Blaine, you're looking and acting like a different person, and you know why?"

"No. Tell me."

"Because they gave you a painkiller. You've been living with excruciating pain all the time because you won't take painkillers because they constipate you. Dad, you're going to die from this pain. Or have a stroke. Or at the least you're going to end up soon in a nursing home because you can't handle day-to-day life because you are in such pain. Your priorities are wrong, Dad. Your first priority should be to get rid of this pain. And far down the list below that is taking a crap. Who cares about taking a crap when you're in such pain? If we have to, we'll get you an enema once a week, but you have to start taking pain medicine or else life is going to be over for you. And for Mom, too. You can no longer be obsessed with your bowel movements because if you continue to be, then the next stop is the nursing home. Do you understand what I'm saying, Dad?" I sound every bit as stern as he sounded earlier, and he can discern that.

"I hear what you're saying, Pete. You make sense, and I've been thinking about that myself, and I'm going to make some changes. I really am."

"I need to talk to you about something else. Don't joke around with this staff anymore. Our goal, as you'll remember, is to get you admitted here tonight, and you're presenting a picture to these people that you're just fine. They'll tell the person who ultimately makes the decision what they think, and if they say, 'Mr. Gorham said he was experiencing a pain level of only five,' like you told Chris, these people are going to conclude that you're just screwing around with them. And you'll never get in here, and we'll end up at Seminary Estates tonight, and tomorrow you'll feel like you did at noon today. You know what I mean, Dad?"

"Yes, I hear you, Pete. I'll tell Chris I should have said, 'Ten.'"

"Don't charm them or joke around with them or call them heroes or ask them their names and how many kids they've got and why their mother named them Sandy. Just sit here stoically like an old man in pain and don't talk. Let them talk. And don't interfere with what they're doing. Let them think that they have no other choice but to admit you. You know what I mean, Dad?"

"Yes, I know, and you're right. And you're right about the pain medicine, too. I'm going to change." He starts singing, "There'll Be a Change in the Weather" again.

"And don't sing for them, either."

"I'm singing for you, Pete. When they come in I'm going to close my eyes and moan."

We wait and wait. No other doctor or nurse or attendant comes back in. They are all gravely attending a train accident victim and also the other victims that have just rolled in on the next ambulance. We're way down on the emergency list now, and we'd better not push. But I do see the doctor who talked to us earlier standing at the counter of the central staff area. He looks extremely somber and unapproachable, but I go out to him anyway and ask him two questions: does it look like they're going to admit my father to the hospital, and did they give him a pain killer, and what was it?

"Yes," he says to the first question. "It looks like we'll admit him, but we have to get hold of Dr. Strauch first and get his permission, and we've been trying for an hour, and he doesn't answer his pager." To the second question he answers, "Yes, we gave him a hypo, and the medicine was Dilaudid."

Later, in reading about Dilaudid on the Internet, I find that it has two to eight times the painkilling effects of morphine and that its abuse potential comes from the fact that its euphoric intravenous rush is very similar to heroin's. This explains Blaine's euphoria and agreeability. I'm going to ask them for a fifty-gallon drum of it before he leaves.

I return to the room, and we wait and wait. It's almost eight o'clock. I'm tired, I'm hungry, and I'm almost convinced that they'll keep my father for the night. He is now extremely agitated in a good way and happy and is singing non-stop. "You're Irish to the core, just like your mother," he tells me when suddenly a plan occurs to me.

"Blaine, I think I should just leave, and then they'll *have* to take you even if they don't want to because you'll essentially be homeless. Tell them you fell asleep, and when you woke up I was gone. Call me if you need me to take you back home only if they are going to refuse to admit you. Or call and tell me if they have decided to admit you. But don't call after ten o'clock. I'll be asleep."

"That sounds like a great idea. Go ahead and go. I'm fine. I know the part I have to play, and I'm up for it. They'll take me. They'll have to take me. You have my blessing, son. Go ahead now. Run along. Go." He hands me his wallet and his keys to the apartment and the yellow envelope and tells me to take them with me so they don't get stolen. He shakes my hand again and tells me he loves me.

"I love you too, Dad."

I slip away like a thief in the night down the dark hallway to my freedom. I feel certain that there is *no* way any lightweight administrator the hospital might have on staff could *ever* keep my father from spending the night there after they've made the mistake of inviting him into the back room with the forklifts and the secretaries and the dockmen and the traveling salesmen and the truck driver who'll pilot the sixty-foot trailer full of carpet, being committed to the destination my father has set out for it: Blainie's Carpet Barn.

He'll bewilder them and charm them and captivate them and invade their souls until they beg him to stay for the night or for longer if he will. They'll be like his customers in the old days: if they walk through his door, or let him walk through theirs, they'll never leave without buying something.

From down the hallway, I can hear him start to sing again. "I gets weary and sick of trying, I'm tired of livin' and scared of dyin', but ol' man river, he just rolling along. I *love* that song."

At nine o'clock, I get a call at home. It's a nurse who says, "We have decided to admit your father to the hospital."

Dr. Strauch calls me at home. I'm not sure if it's best to tell people bad news directly or indirectly, but it's probably best to tell them in such a way that they understand it. I don't understand what he's saying.

"Is it bone cancer?"

"Well, yes, I think so. Things are pointing to that. With a younger person, we'd begin tests to find out where it metastasized from, but I don't know if that makes sense with your dad. When we find it, we would have to do surgery and treat it with chemotherapy, and I don't think Blaine could survive that. If he were my father, I'd simply try to manage his pain from here on out."

"Did you tell Blaine?"

"Yes, we discussed it. Blaine agrees that he doesn't want tons of tests done."

"How is he taking it?"

"Well, I think okay. He kept talking about how he's been waiting for Godot his whole life and now Godot's here. Do you know what that means?"

"Yeah, you know Blaine." Dr. Strauch laughs.

I debate whether to wait and tell my mother in person when I pick her up at four p.m. to take her to the hospital to visit Blaine. I decide that that would be too abrupt, and so I call her now.

She's shaken and almost loses control. She asks me to call my brothers and says she'll call her sister and that she'll meet me at four p.m.

On the way to the hospital, my mother sobs several times. At one point she says breathlessly, "I don't know what I'm going to do, Pete." I put my hand on her leg and squeeze it, and she grabs my arm and holds on like it's a ladder on a lifeboat.

Surely, I think, *she has to have considered this possibility.* But how does one properly consider life's extinction? I tell her Dr. Strauch said he's talked to Blaine about this but that when I talked to Blaine on the phone, he made no mention of it, so maybe we shouldn't either, yet.

She agrees and says, "He's probably forgotten it like he always forgets whatever Dr. Strauch said. And everything else now, too."

Blaine seems distant and detached when we visit him, and he has a hollow and slightly frightened look that takes him over these days more and more. He offers nothing, holding his cards close to his vest as usual. Finally my mother says, "So what did Dr. Strauch say to you this morning when he came in?"

"I don't remember. I can never remember what he says." He sounds convincing, and so my mother and I say nothing else and agree on the way back to Seminary Estates not to mention it yet or maybe ever.

The first thing Blaine asks upon seeing us at the hospital is, "When does everybody have to leave?"

"I don't know. We'll be here awhile."

"How long?"

"I don't know, Dad. Why?"

"I just don't want anyone saying, 'I gotta go now!' I just *hate* that. People keep *pouring* in here, and then they say, 'I gotta go!' and they leave. I can't keep up. I can't grasp the significance of anything I do. And anything I'm going to have to repeat to anyone, or say it for a third time to someone else, I'd better write it down because they'll be hovering right over me like Sherlock Holmes."

I stand up to move to a more comfortable chair.

"Are you leaving?"

"No."

"Well I need to know how long you're going to be here."

"Why?"

Blaine produces a small spiral notebook with notes scribbled all over the first page. "Because I have a galaxy of things here."

"Like what?"

"Like I need to know what I've done and haven't done and why not and what I have to do yet. And all these other things that have happened, I need to tell you about them."

"Like what?"

He reads the writing on the notebook—slowly. He stares at it and seems to be dumbfounded. "'Brush teeth.' I haven't brushed my teeth in five days, and I usually brush them several times a day. 'Have a bath.' I haven't had a bath today. I can't remember if they've even given me a bath since I've been here." My mother disagrees. "And Roberta, what about the stuff for my eyes? Where's that? And take a walk. They haven't taken me for a walk yet. I *have* to walk! And my stuff for athlete's foot. I put that on every day and have my whole life. Where is it? When are you all leaving?"

"Blaine, I don't know! We can't stay here all day, but we'll be here awhile. And I'll bring the stuff for your eyes and the athlete's foot ointment when I come next time. People have other lives, Blaine, they can't be here all the time."

"I know, but you shouldn't have anything else to do when you come to me except *me*. Like not having a telephone at your hip like a six-shooter! So I need to know when you're all leaving because I have a galaxy of things to talk about." He picks up his notebook and stares at it again, transfixed. "What about the stuff I'm supposed to snort every day?"

"Snort?"

"You mean the salmon?" my mother asks him.

"Salmon? Dad's snorting salmon?"

"Yes, it's for protein. I'll bring it next time I come."

Blaine stares at his list again.

"Let me see that thing, Dad." I take the notebook out of his hand. There are scribbles going in every direction, and some are crossed out, some underlined, some written in capitals or highlighted by exclamation points and question marks in quotations and different colored ink. I study it a long time and then discern a pattern—things Blaine needs to do on a regular basis but doesn't remember if he did them or not, and things that happened that he knows he'll be questioned about and that he'll forget happened. So he's written them all down.

"Blaine, I am going to print a list here of those things you need to do every day like brush your teeth, walk, have a bath, etc. The other things are things that happened that you've already talked about. This is too confusing here. No wonder you can't make sense of it."

"Thanks, Pete."

I make a small list of five or six things to do every day, which certainly constitutes a lesser galaxy than Blaine had imagined. Then I read the other scribbles out loud and ask his permission to throw away the page. We are left with a small list of daily items that are legibly printed, which I hand to Blaine. He stares at them peacefully.

"You're not leaving now, are you?"

I look at the clock on the wall in front of me. It's four minutes until two o'clock. "Not for four minutes."

"Oh no, stay longer than that, please. I *have* to discuss something with you both. Who will be here when you all leave?"

"*You!*"

"Oh no. Don't leave yet."

"I'll come back later, Dad. Tonight after dinner."

"Oh no, stay longer. Please."

"Then let's discuss what you have to discuss right now because I have to go."

"Don't say, 'I gotta go.' I just hate that phrase."

"Well I do. What did you want to discuss?"

"We don't have enough time now."

I get up and walk over to my father's bedside and take his hand. "Don't worry so much, Dad. We'll discuss it later. I'll be back later."

"I will have forgotten it by then."

"Alright, I'll stay until we're done discussing it now. Go ahead. What it is?"

Blaine stares straight ahead, motionless, as if not wanting to nudge out of line the delicate balance of things that must occur in his mind for recollection to happen. He almost has it, I can tell. But finally, it won't come. "Pete, I can't remember now. I'm sorry."

"Write it down when you remember it, and we'll talk about it when I come back, okay?"

"Yeah, if I can remember that I remembered." He smiles his playful matchless smile at me, which says, "I can still make the ship sail and keep the remaining mates from mutiny a while longer, but I have no control over which harbors it enters now. So be prepared."

"I am," I say to myself. I hope.

It's seven thirty p.m. when I return to Blaine's room. He is lying peacefully on his back, staring out the window while watching the natural light fade away. He greets me gently. We talk casually for awhile, and then he says to me, "How am I doing, Pete?"

"Well, you seem to have some problems, Dad."

"I do, don't I?"

"Yeah, a few. All you need's a new body."

"And a new mind. I ain't gonna get that though, I'm afraid."

"No, you're not. How are you feeling, Dad?"

"Not so good, Pete. Like they used to say about old cars back in Olds at the auto repair garage, 'It becomes harder and harder to just jack up the jalopy's radiator cap and run a new car under it.'"

"What's wrong?"

"I just can't keep track of things anymore."

I walk up to him and take his hand. He loves to be touched and to touch.

"Dad, you're a good man. You know? Everyone loves you, Dad, because you are good to everyone and take time with them and don't just give them the bum's rush. You're not here lonely at the end of your life with no visitors. There are constantly people coming in and out to visit you because you were good to them as perhaps no one had ever been before. In fact, to some of these people you might represent the first mercy they ever knew. You have touched a lot of lives while you've been here on earth, Dad. You've done more than your share to make this world slightly better. I don't know what comes next, Dad, and I'd be lying if I told you I did. But if there's justice in the universe, which I think there might be, you've got only good things ahead of you."

"Thanks, Pete, I needed to hear that."

"Are you ready?" my father would ask his customers. Then he'd look at them a long time without blinking, and he'd smile mischievously to prepare them for the Double Rabbi Low, the price which they had thereby tacitly accepted. They couldn't escape him, and they couldn't resist him, and they loved him. They came from miles away to be around him like moths sidling up to a flame. He was an entertainer and a clown and a mystic and a counselor and a con man and

an evangelist. It was vaudeville and stand-up comedy and a revival meeting and live TV all at once.

My father had no enemies. Everyone loved him and wanted to be around him because he made them laugh, and he made them feel good about themselves and feel worthy. He was a lighthouse on a black sea that was constantly lighted to aide every ship to see its way to shore that passed by our harbor. His beacon was always visible. He was a good and clever captain of a worthy pirate ship that sailed a treacherous but merry sea.

There is often a visitor or visitors in the room when I call on Blaine in the late afternoon or early evening. I have gotten in the habit of walking over to the hospital around eleven in the morning when I stop home for lunch. Blaine is usually all alone then. I prefer to see him alone because if he doesn't need to entertain people, which he prefers not to do now, he and I will just drift off into a freefall with our conversation. He likes to be with me because I don't care where his mind takes us or if he's accurate or consistent or even rational. I just like to be with this creative man, my father, since his last moment could occur at any time. I am able to coax him out of his obsessions and into tranquility for a moment now and then.

I walk back to the hospital at night after dinner. It's a perfect evening outside, and I cherish the walk even more as I realize that my father will never freely walk again wherever he wants, which he always did.

Blaine is alone in his darkening room, looking out the window up at some non-focal place. I whisper, "Hi, Blaine."

"Hi, Pete. How nice of you to come by."

We sit together quietly a long time in the last light, and then I say to him, "Dad, you're looking more and more like your father, you know?"

"Am I, Pete?"

"Yes you are. I think you're becoming inhabited by his spirit."

"How nice that would be. My father meant the world to me. He was a wonderful man."

I stand up and walk to him and say, "You mean the world to me, Dad. You're a wonderful man, too."

He leans up in bed and asks me to walk closer to him, and I do. He takes my hand in his. "I can't tell you how much it means to me that you said that and how much it will help me."

I squeeze his hand, and he squeezes back. "Pete, you still have a good handshake."

"You shake good too, Dad."

"*Shake* is right!" We both laugh.

Just as I'm about to leave, I remember a phrase he used the other day that I've heard him say a hundred times before. "Dad, what does it mean to 'buck against the goads'?"

"Isn't that a wonderful phrase, Pete? That's one of my favorite sayings from the Bible. It says so much, doesn't it?"

"What does it mean? What's a goad?"

"It means, Pete, don't fight what's inevitable. Don't bang your head against the wall. Don't buck like an oxen when the Master uses the goads to tell you which way to go."

"Don't fight authority, huh?"

"Yes, don't buck against the goads the Lord uses to keep us going in the right direction."

"Have you ever done that, Dad?"

"Buck against the goads? Pete, *always*. Even now as I lie here, I'm thinking of where there might be a break in the fence and wonder if I can walk that far or maybe crawl and slip under it while the Master isn't looking. It's funny, isn't it? *Buck against the goads*! At age ninety-three!"

Today is Blaine's birthday. He's ninety-three. So much has changed in three years. Then he was still walking without a walker and still driving even. He weighed one-hundred thirty-five pounds, and his sole mission in life was to look after my mother, who we all had decided would die first. Now he can't help but be concerned with himself first of all. It is hard for noble intentions to prevail over bad health.

My mother, not long ago the parent primarily in need of care, has had to reverse roles with him and be the stronger of the two in addition to having to witness his dramatic and probably irreversible decline. To think that three years ago my mother would end up a caregiver rather than the one in need of first care is hard to believe. It is a role she does not fondly embrace, considering that she herself has been declining for years and has little resources left beyond what's needed to look after herself.

My father charms the nurses. They all say to me, "Your dad is *such* a sweet man. He never forgets to call us by our name even if it's the wrong name. He treats us all so wonderfully. Some of these people here are so mean." Blaine tells them how wonderful they are as many times as he can in front of as many other people as possible.

In the wee hours of the darkness when the desperate wolf cries and fear and loneliness prevail and he wakes up, I know that Blaine enlists these nurses to sit with him and talk. And they do. At first they do because it is their duty, but later they find nourishment from him to deal with their own fears and loneliness—their problems at home and in their souls. Eventually some seek *him* out as so many people have always done. I heard a nurse whisper to him once, "You have helped me *so* much with my marriage." He knows that by healing others, the healer also becomes healed.

His memory is elusive yet sometimes quite clear but is usually a hodgepodge of loose ends and thoughts that have strayed from their bearings and which make sense only according to a chaotic logic. And with this come increasing pathetic obsessions designed to bring order to some compartment of his mind that is intent now upon protecting itself from primordial fears. The nurses give back to him by helping him to organize his thoughts without being critical.

The best way to stop his obsessing is to make him laugh. Then the preoccupations float off and wait for a while on nearby perches like buzzards frightened away only temporarily from their helpless victim.

My older brother Mike has been here for a week, and I have happily bowed out of the picture for that time, feeling that I needed a break. Mike has lived at Seminary Estates and has slept in Blaine's empty bed and attended to all of my parents' needs. He's helped move Blaine from the hospital to the Bounce Back wing of Seminary Manor Nursing Home, which is where he is now in room 607.

In a vague place in his apprehension, Blaine is aware that he will probably move yet again. He does not want to change again. He wants a constant spot where he can reliably live out his last days and where he can spend his time left interlacing with the same people.

Mike calls me in the afternoon. I can hear voices and laughter in the background. He tells me Blaine is exhausted. All day long people have been stopping by to wish him "Happy birthday," and they've been staying on and on. He doesn't know how to tell people to go away. He needs a nap. So they are calling off the birthday party until tomorrow morning. I tell my brother I'll stop by after dinner and just say "Happy birthday."

I enter Blaine's room just as brother Bill calls from Cleveland. Blaine talks to him for twenty minutes, joking and conversing in a very normal way. When he hangs up, he says to my brother and me with an intuition that we are about to leave, "I want to ask one of you guys to do me a favor before you go. I don't care which one, but one of you, please." Mike and I look at each other and know to wait before consenting to an open offer from our ever-calculating father. "All of the Barbarians are gone now as night has fallen and we've raised the drawbridge. And there is no more tumult. 'That's good,' most would say. But I'm feeling shaky because the party's over, and I'm going to be alone soon. Would one of you guys, I don't care which one, stay with me until I go to sleep?"

I think Blaine is worried about dying on his birthday. I look up at the clock on the wall, and it's ten after seven. I'm hungry and getting tired. I know that my brother would stay if I refused to, even if he didn't want to, but I can see that he's wary, too. He's been there for hours. Neither of us says a word. Therefore Blaine keeps talking. "I don't want to say this in front of the women, but I'm not brave anymore. I never was. But now I can say it. I want one of you to do like I did with you when you were kids—put me to bed and make sure I'm asleep before you leave." Mike makes an affirming sound to indicate he understands but signifies no commitment yet. He probably hopes I'll volunteer, and I hope he will. We both know that one of us will *have* to because it's our father's birthday, and he's ninety-three, and he's scared of being alone in yet another new place. "You see, boys, not only am I here alone tonight, but they haven't even gotten my phone working yet, so I can't even call you if I need to." Mike and I glance at each other expressionless but astonished. Blaine has forgotten the twenty minute phone conversation he *just* had with brother Bill.

"If one of you would just stay until I get ready for bed and fall asleep. I'll go to sleep anytime."

"You want to go to sleep right now?" I ask him in jest.

"Sure, Pete, come get in bed with me right now, and we'll sleep together."

All at once in come Roberta and her sister Phyllis for a last visit before bedtime. Suddenly there is commotion everywhere. Phyllis is already talking on her cell phone to her daughter who wants to talk to Blaine. Just then the regular phone rings. It's Mike's wife. Mike's cell phone rings seconds after that. It's Mike's daughter Nicole who wants to talk to Blaine. Phyllis puts her cell phone up to Blaine's ear, and he starts talking to Allison, and then Mike puts *his* cell phone up to Blaine's other ear for him to talk to Nicole. Mike talks to his wife Mary on the land phone. With a cell phone in each ear and their speakers on both sides of his mouth, Blaine sings "Jesus Is Calling" to the two callers at once.

Blaine cannot feel lonely anymore, and he cannot fall asleep for some time yet and probably will not be lonely later either, and so I feel justified that I will not have exploited my brother's good graces by leaving. I stand up and walk over to my father and put out my hand and say, "Good night, Dad. Happy birthday." He pulls away from all phone conversations and pulls my head down and kisses me on the forehead.

"I love you, son."

"I love you too, Dad."

The door is open only a foot, and I push on it quietly and slowly. Blaine and Roberta are sitting next to each other, talking like boyfriend and girlfriend—he in the recliner and she in the overstuffed chair just beside him. The therapist will not let him lie in bed all day anymore because she is afraid of pneumonia.

Before I announce myself, I hear my father say to my mother, "Because I'm afraid I'll pee on myself." They look and sound very serious. I'm afraid I've interrupted something between them, but as I walk closer and say hello, I can see that Blaine is holding the urinal in one hand and his penis in the other.

"Hello, Pete, I'm going to the toilet. Or I should say, the toilet is coming to me."

"Dad, every time I visit you now, you've got your penis in your hand. Maybe you ought to just let them insert a catheter, and then you could conduct life as usual."

"This *is* life as usual, Pete."

"Why are you always taking a piss?"

"I think I'm frightened, Pete."

"Of what?"

"Frightened someone will come in here, and I'll have to leave and won't be at a place where I can pee if I *have* to."

"Where do you go?"

"Everywhere. I'm busier now than when I owned the carpet business. Therapy, lunch, dinner, and all day long people come in here to talk to me. I can't just excuse myself and walk in and use the toilet while they're here because it takes a half hour to pee, and I'd have to be yelling through the closed bathroom door. And of course I have to try to remember what they said so I can tell Roberta when she comes over, which means that I have to be writing in my notepad here like a stenographer while they're talking to me."

"That probably puts pressure on him, too," my mother says nonchalantly.

"Yes, I'm constantly under pressure to perform and have answers to her questions as always, and it makes me so nervous I have to pee."

The phone rings. It's closer to me than anyone, so I pick it up. "I'm sure they're not calling for me," I say and hand it to my mother. She sighs. To her it's a form of dishonesty to avoid talking on the phone.

She's happy to hear from whoever it is. But her face suddenly becomes slightly frowned, and her voice gets a bit serious. I listen to her responses but can't tell who it is. Then she says, "Let me put him on. Hang on," and she tries to hand the phone to my father.

"Just put it up to my ear a second."

"*What!*" My mother is getting deaf again.

"Just put it up to my ear," he says, and she does.

"I can't talk to you because I've got one hand on the urinal and the other hand on my penis. Can you call back? I love you."

My mother takes the phone back. "Who was it?" I ask Blaine.

"I don't know," Blaine says.

At exactly five o'clock, Roberta rises from her chair and struggles onto her walker.

"The party's over," Blaine declares sadly.

My father reaches out and shakes my hand. "Thanks for coming, Pete. I'm sorry we didn't have a chance to talk about how *you're* doing, but we did talk about something important—and that's *me!*" He smiles.

"I love you, Roberta," he says to my mother as she walks toward the door. It is very tender the way he says it.

"And I love you, too," my mother says back in a way she has started to say good-bye to my father that is overflowing with warmth and affection and love. They miss each other badly, I can tell. Every night my father calls our house once or twice by mistake, thinking our phone number is theirs, a telephone number which they've had for forty years but which he's forgotten. They call each other like high school lovers.

I sense that my mother is changing. She has been alone now for nearly a month and a half, which is the longest ever in her life. Even in college she lived at home. Her natural personality has begun to assert itself, the one which she would have had apart from my father.

Being away from my mother is changing my father, too. Both of them have mentioned how odd it is to suddenly be separated after sixty-seven years together. It is likely that they will never live together again. Even the final assurance of aging—that one's mate will literally be there until death—can leave, too, and one can then enter into one of the most fundamental types of change right when it had appeared that, for the most part, change was over.

My visits to my parents are now bifurcated since they live in two buildings that are separated by several long hallways. I have stopped visiting my father late in the afternoon because that's when my mother visits him, and I don't want to invade their precious moments of intimacy. Nor do I want to be relied upon to prepare my father for dinner, which is the nurses' job and which they seem to prefer to do.

So tonight after dinner, I go first to Seminary Estates to see my mother. She gets lonely at night now. However, it's Halloween, and there are children in costumes everywhere. I can barely get in the door. The dining room is still full of residents getting ready to hand out candy to astute children who have sensed over the years, no doubt, that they can access a hundred candy-givers at once at Seminary Estates and then pass through the hallway to Seminary Manor and access another hundred of them. So I go back to Seminary Manor where the trick-or-treaters have not yet come. Some of the residents are lining up in wheelchairs, but my father is not among them. I go to his room. His door is almost closed. I open it slowly and see him sitting pensively in the recliner, having been covered with a white cotton blanket with the lights low. He is staring into some indefinable space of thought out in front of him. I can feel the depth of his acceptance. The TV is on in front of him, no doubt as a foil, for it is an almost inaudible black-and-white rerun of "The Addams Family." He doesn't notice me until I speak his name twice. Then he pulls away from his thoughts and turns toward me and puts out his hand.

Each time I see my father now, I feel more helplessly that the end of his life is near. He senses it, too. He still has a penetrating sense of humor and a profound gentleness. But he is slipping onto an astral plane of existence and starting to leave this earth behind.

I say good-bye again and turn to leave. Blaine grabs my hand. "I wouldn't trade having known you for sixty years, Pete, for a farm in Kansas. That's what my Dad used to say when he *really* liked something, and this was back in the days when we didn't have *anything* and could have really used a farm in Kansas."

I slip out a side door of Seminary Manor into the cool, starlit night and am starkly visible in the total darkness between buildings. I walk over to Seminary Estates to find my mother. The last Halloween children are leaving the dining room, and I am free to walk unencumbered. I pass the mythical desert oasis where my father will probably never sit in repose again in the shade of the illusionary, hot sun, resting on his sandy way to some destination.

My mother's door is open, and she is on the phone. "It's your father," she whispers to me, "calling to say you're coming over."

It is perhaps the last beautiful Saturday of autumn. The leaves are falling but still colorful, and the sun will be out all day in an azure sky—a golden day diluted somewhat by the melancholy brown corn stalks shorn and lying in the fields after the harvest. Judy and I will take Roberta for a long ride before dinner out to the lake and the woods and through the rural grain fields or wherever our inclinations lead us. And then back to town around the streets where she walked for nearly ninety years but walks no more. She needs a tour of her life, for it is changing quickly. We bring her back to Seminary Estates in time for early dinner.

I return to Seminary Manor at six fifteen to see my father for a few minutes. I assume he'll be done with dinner by then and facing the long, lonely night, and so I'll interrupt it slightly for the better. I have embraced both places now—Seminary Estates and Seminary Manor—as my parents' homes, and I feel comfortable in either one of them despite the fact that Seminary Manor residents are much less communicative and less cognizant and are further along the continuum of life's ending.

I push Blaine to his room, and we talk. His face is clear now, and his eyes sparkle with understanding and are free of confusion. "You understand the situation as no one else does. All I really needed was to talk." We discuss the restraint he has pinned to his gown again, and he believes they should leave it on him and that he should not get up by himself. "I realize I'm weak and that I cannot fall or the party's over." I wonder how long this contentment will last.

I tell him I have to go eat. I've been here over an hour now.

"Before you go, Pete, I need you to take me to the bathroom."

I wheel my father to the toilet, put on the wheelchair brakes, get him up very slowly, retract the foot pedals, help him slowly undress, turn him slowly around, lower him with painstaking slowness onto the toilet, and then go out and shut the door behind me.

"I'll call for you in five or ten minutes."

I go lie on his bed and stare up at the ceiling and at the huge "Happy Birthday: Ninety-Three" sign still hanging on the north wall that Judy hung. His bed is comfortable, but I am incapable of putting myself into the Seminary Manor picture yet. I think how awful it would be to be suddenly thrust into it without a gradual matriculation through the entire saga of aging.

After twenty minutes, Blaine calls for me. He tells me to bring a flashlight in with me. "Why?" I ask.

"Just bring the flashlight, will you?"

I go back into the bathroom while carrying the flashlight. I tell my father to try to stand up on his own because I want to see just how it would look if he were all alone there in the middle of the night. With agonizing effort, only partially successful before I assist him, my father rises up ever so slowly from the toilet. His legs are so tiny that it gives me fear.

Blaine asks me to shine the flashlight into the toilet bowl to see how much he pooped. I summon the courage to look down into the gray toilet water, and there at the bottom of it, standing all alone, is one little, dark-brown turd that is perhaps three cubic centimeters in size that has bravely elected to come out for us in order to justify the activities of the last half hour. I describe his success to him.

We attach my father's diaper, a mean task, then pull up and zip and button his trousers and tuck his dark-green turtleneck sweater into them and finally drape him again in his maroon sweater. Then we reposition the foam cushion on his wheelchair—with 60 percent of it on the seat and 40 percent of it on the back—and lower him down into it.

But it's not over yet. He needs to wash his hands, so I wheel him over to the sink, and he washes his hands and dries them very carefully again and again with paper towels. Then I push him back into his room and ask him where he wants to be.

I wheel my father over to the recliner and go through the ritual of disembarkment from the wheelchair into the recliner.

I can now see the light of freedom shining just perceptibly through the forest of responsibilities I innocently wandered into two hours ago. At that time, I had simply wanted to say hello to my father to help assuage his possible loneliness from being without my mother.

In ten more minutes, I will be out in the parking lot and walking to my truck beneath the pale yellow stars of a cool Galesburg Saturday night.

My wife will have made me dinner, regarding me as she does in these times with these responsibilities as a noble warrior in need of nourishment, who can occasionally find his way home from that place of battle he feels compelled to return to again and again.

Maybe we'll watch a movie and then walk upstairs under our own power and go to sleep in our own bed... and get up by ourselves, if we have to in the night, and go to the bathroom.

My father, always being bold in his lifestyle, got bolder and bolder in his business style, too. He became known as a lovable eccentric who was awesome at business. It was impossible for customers to get out of the carpet store without buying something. It was a contest for him. He was hurt if people left the store and hadn't bought anything. So he often sold things for less than he'd paid for them just to "keep the men busy." That kept people flowing into the store. His style had a Messianic zeal that was a combination of ultimate truth and utmost chicanery. The best summation of his position in this regard was a statement that he made to me once after he'd retired: "I always treasured the truth or else shading it in a way that didn't hurt anyone."

He was genuinely gracious and compassionate to those in need. He once sold carpet to an old man who stocked shelves at Walgreens. The man told him he could only pay two dollars a month. Every month Blaine went by the old man's house to collect his two dollars, and they'd sit on the man's porch and talk.

At night my father would come home from work and talk about the carpet business before, during, and after the meal. It was our family's constant nutriment. He talked about it on the weekends and at nights and always. It was the metaphor for our existence then and permeated everything, even our vacations and our recreation. We all worked at the carpet store or went there with him to pick something up or to pay a carpet supplier's bill or to meet someone who wanted carpet after hours. The simplest projects oftentimes turned into lengthy escapades of strangers becoming his friends, or traveling salesmen taken into our family to have dinner and spend the night with us on their solitary travels, or a lonely carpet layer knocking on our door at midnight to vent to Blaine the dark thoughts which late night alcohol had brought into his awareness, or one more stop somewhere to *see someone about carpet, or one more carpet-related phone call to someone that extended minutes into hours.*

My father is alone in Seminary Manor dining room, slumped over the table, apparently asleep or passed out—or dead. I walk up and put my hand on his shoulder, and he rises slowly, obviously in pain. "What's wrong, Dad?"

"My stomach. It hurts, Pete." The food on his breakfast plate is untouched in front of him. "I don't want to complain, Pete."

"It's okay to complain, Dad. It *hurts.*"

"But I always wanted to be like the Spartan with the fox, but that's hard, Pete."

"The *what?*"

"You know—the Spartan and the Fox. He stole the fox, and when the soldiers came up to him, instead of admitting it and being shamed, he let the fox eat a hole in his stomach."

"Where did you learn *that* story?"

"Oh, Pete, in school in Olds. They were constantly teaching us kids about bravery and courage. I always wanted to be brave and heroic like the Spartan and withstand the fox eating my heart out. But in order to be brave and heroic, you had to suffer and be in pain, and I didn't want any of that. It was a real dilemma for me."

He lays his head back down on the table. "Dad, you want to go lie down in bed?"

"I can't, Pete, because then I'll get pneumonia and die."

"Well, Dad, I came over here to let you know I wanted to wheel you over to Mom around ten thirty."

"Oh? Where is she?"

"In her apartment in Seminary Estates."

"Oh? Sure, that would be fine." He doesn't understand where she is or how she's connected to Seminary Manor, but he wants to go.

Judy goes first to Blaine's room to pick him up. When I get there, they're sitting, talking about the doves and rabbits that Blaine's father raised. "He loved the little animals," Blaine says, "like St. Francis of Assisi."

We push Blaine's wheelchair through the neutral bright-pink-and-white-tiled corridor that leads to Seminary Estates, and then we're walking down the hallway to room 142. Suddenly it comes back to him. "I've been here before, haven't I? I remember looking out that door at the end, and this…this is the…what's it called?"

"The oasis."

"That's right, the oasis!"

The door is open to apartment 142, and we push Blaine through it. My mother is on the couch. She gets up, and they both become teary and hug. She says, "Hi, Darling."

Blaine wants to sit on the couch where he used to sit next to her, so I delicately get him up to his feet and tiptoe with him across the six-foot expanse of carpet and lower him gently to the couch.

"Don't drop me, *please!*"

Finally he is down on the couch where he used to sit, and my mother is at the other end where she always sits. He sighs. He's home.

Winter 2007

The horror of horrors is about to occur to Blaine again...*change.* Brother Bill and Roberta and I attend a meeting of the staff of Seminary Manor to hear a status report about Blaine. Jane, his therapist, notifies us that he has progressed quite well but that he is not going to improve more than this, so Medicare will not let him stay on the Bounce Back wing much longer. He will have to be moved to another area, probably within three weeks. We knew this was coming, but Blaine didn't.

I have spent days trying to negotiate for the best possible circumstances. I have tried to secure a place for my father which my mother could still access from Seminary Estates. The staff has suggested moving him to another building entirely, which I looked at and thought was much nicer than Seminary Manor, but which my mother would not be able to visit except by car. No private room is available, which we want. So I plead with the therapist not to release him yet; I try to get a few more days until a single room will be vacated. They are all cooperative and love my father and want to help, but they can only stretch the Medicare guidelines so far.

Blaine's stomach is worse and worse. I ask them to remove him from any medications except what is absolutely necessary in order to keep his stomach as peaceful as possible. He keeps referring to the "grinding" sounds there. He is sick to his stomach often, and his back hurts constantly. He is a prisoner not just to his room but to the chair they put him in each morning—with its restraint—where he can do nothing but sit and stare in pain and wait for an aide or a nurse to come in and take him for a short painful walk or take him into the bathroom. It is sad, this man who a thousand times referred to himself as a "striped-assed zebra" to illustrate his constant fast movement through life. He walked thousands of miles and as an adult was never overweight. Now he is immobile, stopped dead in his tracks, and his self-worth and his purpose and his identity are all damaged by it.

I sit in a chair and wait for my father to wake up, which he does in a few minutes. "Hi, Pete."

"Hi, Dad. How are you?"

"Not good, Pete. I've been throwing up."

"Does your stomach hurt, Dad?"

"Yes."

"And your back, too?"

"Yes. Pete, I need to talk to you. Can you stay awhile?" I nod. "I can't talk to your mother about this. You're the one I can talk to because you listen, and you can take it." Then he gets right to the point. "I'm going to die, Pete.

Things are different. I don't know why I say this, but I feel it. I'm going to die."

He goes on and on, discussing his death. His tone and attitude and awareness have a disturbing ring of truth to them. He needs to talk. But then I wonder if he needs my approval or else my release or my assurance that I'll be okay.

"Dad, we've said everything we need to say to each other. I don't have anything left I have to say to you or you to me. We know what we feel about each other. There ain't no secrets, Dad."

"That's right. I'm glad you said it. It's true. I'm hurting, Pete. There's nothing left but sitting in this chair all day long, staring at the beautiful 'Happy Birthday: Ninety-Three' sign Judy put on the wall." He spits bile into the bucket on his lap, and his dry lips stick together as he tries to talk more but can't.

While he's struggling to part his lips, I say, "Dad, you have my permission to die, if that's what you need."

"Thank you, Pete. Yes, I want your permission. I'm *totally* dependent upon these people, nice as they are. I'm not used to being dependent."

"I know you're not, Dad."

"Don't tell anyone I'm telling you this, Pete."

"I won't, Dad."

"Don't tell anyone what I've said to you about dying, Pete, please. Here's why. If you tell everyone I'm going to die, people will start coming and sit at the foot of my bed, waiting for me to die. And then if I don't die, they'll be upset with me."

"In fact," I point out, "*they* might die first, hanging around here waiting for *you* to die!"

"Either that or *they'll* die waiting for me to get out of the bathroom, trying to have a bowel movement before I die." He starts giggling.

We're both laughing like two kids not afraid to make a joke of death.

"Oh, Pete, I'm so glad you came by here this morning just at this time. I'm feeling better."

I tell Blaine that Dr. Strauch is coming. He says we must get ready. To most people, this would mean tidying the room, but to Blaine it means preparing his case like a lawyer going before the Supreme Court…or more like a vaudevillian, practicing his high-court gig.

"Pete, can you take that stuff off the chair and then pull it around so it looks like we have a circle of elders? The thing you *must* do with doctors is to get them to sit down. Their goal is to get out as fast as possible."

I sit down in the circle. Blaine starts to say something and then stops. I wait and wait for him to finish, and then finally I say, "Did you want to say something else?"

"No, we're having a Quaker meeting before the good doctor gets here. You can speak if you feel the Spirit move you."

Dr. Strauch walks in. He's a cheery, middle-aged, handsome doctor with curly hair and a long, white beard. A young woman is with him. I offer my chair and say to them, "Sit down, sit down." They continue standing.

"Dr. Carl Strauch, my friend, my friend in ages past, my shelter from the stormy blast." Blaine grabs hold of Dr. Strauch's left hand and holds onto it. Strauch introduces his new assistant, Karen, from Peoria. She is formal and deferential. Blaine says to her, "Carl has kept me alive for ninety-three years." She nods with ardent compassion. Blaine tells the two of them to sit down. I give Karen my chair and sit on the bed. "How are you doing, Blaine? You look good."

"We were having a Quaker meeting before you came in. But, 'How am I doing?' Well, Doc, here's what I told Pete yesterday and was about to tell him again today, but now I can tell you too since you're my doctor and my friend and know everything about me." He turns to Karen. "I'm one of the reasons his beard's so white, Karen." Karen seems unsure and doesn't know quite how to respond. "Carl has kept me alive for ninety-three years, Karen, but now I'm going to die..." Her face portrays unspeakable pity. "...sometime."

"When?" Dr. Strauch asks.

"Well, Doc, you tell me."

"You promised me you'd never die until there was a Cubs-Orioles World Series. That's a few years off yet."

Blaine stares at that "Ninety-Three" on the wall and says, "What a blessing! To be allowed to live for ninety-three years. But now is the time of the Walrus, and now

I'm going to die…sometime. When am I going to die, Dr. Carl?"

"We don't know that, Blaine. You'll probably live to be a hundred."

Jenny comes out and asks us into her office, and we all sit at a tiny table right next to her door, leading to the reception room. Were it my office, the first thing I'd do upon receiving visitors would be to close the door. But she doesn't. I noticed that the other time, too.

I ask who should speak first. Finally Roberta does.

"We understand that you are going to move Blaine and were wondering just when it will be and where he'll go."

"Yes, his Medicare Bounce Back time will run out on December first, I believe, and we will move him to another area.

"Will he still have a private room?"

"That's what we're trying to arrange, yes."

I ask what area, and she doesn't know. I say we were told it would be on the same corridor, and she says no. Then I ask which corridor it will be. She's not sure yet but says it will be on "the floor" in probably hallway two, three, or four.

"So in other words, Blaine will be moving to an area that will have different nurses, different residents, and a different dining room, right?" She agrees. I sigh. "But you will move him somewhere where he will not have to move again, right?" She's not sure.

It seems silly for me to plead for understanding of the plight of the aged from the manager of a nursing home, but I do. I point out to her that Blaine's reality now is corridor six, and his friends are Nurse Amber, Nurse Jillian, Nurse Dominique, all of the other ones, and Roy and Paul and John and all the other residents he eats with three times a day and sees when he goes on walks and goes to therapy. (Which, she has pointed out, will end, too.) "He's a ninety-three-old man who no longer has a home and no longer lives with his wife and whose good health has almost run out. Corridor six is his taken-for-granted reality. He will be freaked out if we move him. There is *no* way to get him to understand that he will then have to move *again*. Why can't he just stay where he is until you need his room or until a private room becomes available? I can see that there are at least four other empty rooms on corridor six." I tell her I need to be assured, as does my father, that his next move will be the last.

I feel fairly certain that neither Blaine nor Roberta would consider leaving Seminary Village for another center, but if they would, I would accommodate them. It would mean a total disruption of all of our lives, and in the end it would probably be worse, but I *know* that if they wanted to do it, I'd comply. I hint that gently to Jenny.

"Can I say one more thing, Jenny? Yesterday I walked with my father from his room to go see the birds. He walked the *whole* way by himself, and after we'd sat and watched the birds awhile, he walked the whole way back to the dining room. What your therapy has done for him here is miraculous. I am grateful to Jane and to all of the other staff here who walk my father and take care of him. I truly am. Can't he now, though, since he is able to walk two hundred yards on his walker without any help, go by himself into the bathroom and use the toilet and come back without being shackled to an electronic restraint, having to call for a nurse to help him and wait for fifteen minutes when he's done for the nurse to come back and get him?"

"Let me see if I can find Jane."

Jane arrives instantly as if Jenny has pushed a button under her table.

The first thing I tell Jane is that what she has done for my father with her therapy is miraculous and that she appears to have seized him from the jaws of death and has restored his ability not only to walk strong but to walk with will and hope.

"Your father is a *very* determined man," Jane says.

"How well I know that, Jane."

Then I discuss the bathroom issue with her. Jane defends the procedure, saying that in the bathroom Blaine has to turn around and sit down and turn around again when he gets up. He is very vulnerable when he does that. Because I simply cannot imagine having to ask someone to undress me and to put me on the toilet and take me off and wipe my butt and re-dress me and then put me back in my chair, I say, "You know, it's *so* important to my father who has lost most of his freedoms now to at least be able to go to the bathroom by himself that I'm wondering if there is a way we can authorize him to go ahead on his own, and if he falls and breaks every bone in his body, then at least he will be able to say that he fell freely."

Jane seems barely able to disguise being appalled. She becomes strident in advising me that that's *not* what we should do. I intuitively know not to press it. I listen to her go on and on, defending this policy, and then I thank her for talking to us, and she leaves. We sit with Jenny with not much left to say except that we need to think about all of this. "I'm disappointed," my mother says. Jenny says she's sorry, and I think she is. She says, "There's nothing else we can do," which is the retort of all bureaucrats.

I walk my mother back to Seminary Estates— the slow shuffling meander of the old and tired and dispossessed and weary—through the last corridor before the double doors that go back through the neutral pink corridor that separates Freedom Denied from Freedom Curtailed.

Blaine knows vaguely that the move is coming, and he is re-embracing the life mode he finds to be most appropriate in such situations: obsession! When I walk into his room, he looks like Stephen Hawking hunched helplessly over his confinement chair with his glasses low on the bridge of his nose, writing *A Brief History of Time* furiously on hundreds of cranberry-colored Post-it notes.

"How are you doing, Dad?"

"Not good, Pete. I'm confused. I'm trying to organize all my notes before Roberta gets here and asks me, 'What happened today, Blaine?' I don't want to come across to her as the incompetent, old geezer I've become. I still want to impress her with what a command I have of everything."

As soon as Roberta arrives and sits down, Blaine takes over by saying, "Okay, folks, we're all together, and we've all been hiding from the truth, and sooner or later we have to confront it. We all know that tomorrow I'm going to move. We need to have a big discussion about that. Not now! But soon."

It becomes evident in a short time that Blaine's concern is double—the concern for tomorrow's move and the broader and graver concern for *tomorrow*, for his ultimate fate, and for where he is or is not ultimately headed.

"Dad, we're not hiding from anything or hiding anything from you. Let's discuss these things right now." I get up and close the door.

"Why can't I go home?"

The room suddenly has a denser gravity. It's not my place to speak next, and I don't, and finally Roberta does.

"Blaine, I can't take care of you. I can barely take care of myself. You need a lot of attention. I can't give you a bath or get you on and off the toilet or even get you out of bed or get your clothes on."

"Well, when *can* I go home?"

"I don't know, Blaine. When you can take care of yourself again, I suppose. Seminary Estates wouldn't let you live there if you couldn't take care of yourself."

"Are you saying I'll never go home? This is what we've all been hiding from, right here. Why can't we just hire a nurse to help with all these things? How much money have we got?"

"About a hundred fifty thousand dollars."

"Okay, that's plenty. Can we rent an apartment and have someone move in with us?"

"Dad, a hundred and fifty thousand is not enough to hire a full-time live-in nurse indefinitely plus pay for all your other costs."

My mother is at a crossroads. Blaine actually *could* move back to Seminary Estates. The people there would welcome him back—they miss him and ask me all the time when he's going to return—and would probably overlook some requirements. He might even improve for a while and hold his own.

In my opinion, my mother could allow it to happen and could even encourage it simply to give her husband of sixty-seven years one more breath of freedom and independence and a final sense of connubial wholeness. Maybe Blaine, if he could say it, would prefer to have his fate sealed in this way by finally exhausting all possibilities of living life the way he once did and eventually being carted off to the hospital or back to Seminary Manor or even to the grave. My mother could say, "Let's try it, Blaine. Let's just go for one last fling at life and know that in the end there was not one more drop of it left to savor."

But she doesn't. She is not this way at this time and maybe never was. She is not willing to dilute her own last remaining ounce of painful but tolerable freedom with his. She makes that clear, and he understands it and will not insist.

When the bell tolls five o'clock, my mother and I rise. She kisses my father so tenderly, and we walk together through the two sets of double doors that go back to Seminary Estates. We are quiet most of the way, walking ever more slowly, further burdened by this implicit option she's refused. Before I let her go, she turns to me and pleads, "I just couldn't do it, Pete. I couldn't take care of him."

"I agree, Mom. I don't think you could, either."

Each morning now when I awaken, I wonder if my father will have died in the night and I'll never see or hear him again. Each morning it seems closer. Often throughout the day I fantasize about being with him at his last moment on earth, holding his bony hand and comforting him. Once, long ago, in some abstract solemn moment of promise, I vowed to myself that before turning back, no matter how much I should tremble with fear, I would go with my parents as far as I could toward the edge of eternity. I have pictured myself many times here at this nexus of ultimate understanding, letting go of my father and watching his spirit shimmer away into what I wish to believe will be heaven. It is frightening, for each time in my fantasy it is I whom he is relying upon for assurance, and I wonder if I can genuinely give it to him or at least give it convincingly like the great salesman that he himself was.

I spend one afternoon with my mother, going over the bill she just got from Seminary Estates, which includes her apartment expenses plus all of Blaine's for two months. It is astronomical. She worries now that they will run out of money and tells me she wants to die first.

I push her over to see my father each day at four o'clock in Blaine's wheelchair. I must stop by his room first to get it. He is always prepared like a jackal to unload all of his most recent worries upon me.

Yesterday, I wheeled Roberta to him, and after being with him in his never-ending anguish, she said on the way back to her dining room, "I feel sick to my stomach from dealing with all that, Pete, I don't want to eat. Please just push me back to my room." These are only some of the trials that have taken place since Christmas.

Today I call Blaine and say that I'm coming out to visit him. I introduce what I want to say by first saying, "I don't want you to think I'm treating you like I'm your father, but…"

"Hold on! Hold on! I'm just fine with that. Let's just say right now at—let me look at my watch and call for a notary—that at 3:10 on Sunday that the transfer has been made! You are *now* my father, and I am your son. I hereby transfer *all* responsibilities to your shoulders. I'll get Kim to seal it with wax."

"Dad, Mom has one hour a day to see you at four o' clock. She does *not* want to come over here for that hour and listen to you rag on and on about all of your problems and your obsessions."

"Well, I need *someone* to help me with these myriad of things that I just can't grasp anymore."

"Dad, you have a myriad of people helping you. You don't need to plague Mom with it."

"Like who? Who do I have?"

"Well, you have me, you have Kim, you have Jane and Amber…"

"Amber's gone now. That's why I'm so glad we've christened you as my father because now I won't have to bother her or anyone else because I have you!"

"Dad, listen to me." Blaine is silent. "You're not listening. I can tell that all you're doing is preparing to talk again."

"I'm listening."

"I have a life, Dad. I can't devote all of my time to taking care of all of your problems. That's why you are here and we're paying these places sixty thousand dollars a year! They're supposed to provide the help you need that I can't provide. And they do. And you take advantage of it like you should. But, Dad, you have to chill out and enjoy life some and not just think all the time of the next catastrophe that might happen. You're driving yourself crazy with all of this. Watch television, read a book, listen to the CD player Mom gave you, but Dad, don't keep being the boss of Blainie's Carpet Barn and in control of everything and everyone. Have some faith in somebody. These are your last years. Enjoy them."

Blaine looks like he's going to cry. "Do you think Roberta and I should move back in together to save money? How much money have we got left? Is it enough?"

"She can't take care of you, Dad. And Seminary Estates doesn't provide care the way this place does. Nobody's going to come around and do the things these people do here."

"You're right, Pete."

"Do you miss her, Dad?"

I'm not sure what his answer means. It clearly has a *yes* component. And, of course, it has a component of obligation and a vivid sense of not bringing about a situation that would do harm to my mother. I ask him if he's happy at Seminary Manor. Of course he would never—could never—answer without in his own subconscious mind either feeling he's betrayed someone or some side or else caused the world to become deceptively clearer than he sees it as being. There is even a hint of loneliness about his answer, which now is turning into a convoluted justification of the status quo. I'm not listening anymore.

I rise and prepare the wheelchair for its mission and announce I must go get Roberta. My father, as always, by the simple effort of having had an interaction with me, seems less anxious. There is some great empowerment I can give him, not necessarily because of who I am but because of who I am to him, that lets him re-enter the domain where his world is once again somewhat more radically free with possibility.

"I'm going to get Mom, Dad."

"Okay, Pete. I won't bother her with these things."

I return to Blaine's room where he's still sitting, waiting to be taken to dinner. I try to calm him down, but he says, "What am I going to tell Bill when he calls and asks me if I've listened to the Bible yet?"

"Tell him you've only listened to the Old Testament so far."

"I can't lie, Pete. Not about the Bible." We laugh.

"The only time I'm not fearful now," my father tells me, "is when you or Roberta or Judy is here." I mention all the people who love him and visit him, and he says, "Pete, they're all just interruptions." I explain to him again why Mom can't take care of him and all of his needs. He seems to understand.

Sunday morning, I feel sad and drive out to see him. He is very much at peace, sitting calmly in his chair with his legs up and the afghan covering them, going through the piles of notes he's written.

"Going through your notes, eh?"

"Pete, I made a decision. I'm going to throw out these notes, all except the ones I *have* to keep—which I'm deciding now—and I'm not going to write anymore. I am facing up to something finally. I'm losing my memory. I can't hide it from others anymore or hide it from myself. I can't keep trying to remember these little girls' names or who came in here or what they talked about. From now on, all I'm going to do is talk about what I *do* remember, if anything. When your mother says she heard that Dr. Strauch came by to see me and asks me what he said, I'm going to say, 'I don't know!' And then when she rolls her eyes up and says, 'Blaine, how can you forget what the doctor who was just here said?' I'm going to say, 'Because I'm ninety-three, and my memory is shot.' If I hurt these girls' feelings because I can't remember their names even though they come in here and help me all day long, that's just the way it has to be. I can't keep trying to be Roberta's star pupil, either."

"Dad, I think that's a great decision. It's too much work trying to pull the wool over everyone's eyes. It's easier just to let the truth be known."

"Pete, that's so true. I've always had trouble with that."

I hear lots of noise coming from my father's room as I approach it again. Upon entering, I see a clutch of people holding hands and singing, "It's a Wonderful World," accompanied by Blaine's Kermit the Frog doll that is sitting on his dresser that he got for Christmas. If you wind it up, it sings in Louis Armstrong's voice. The people with Blaine are staff members—a janitor and a couple of attendants I've never seen before and someone else. They're all smiling and happy and dancing. Blaine is at the center, holding two people's hands and laughing with them. He sees me and introduces me to them all. Finally they all slowly disperse and go their own ways, and then Kermit winds down to silence. Blaine and I are standing in the middle of the room. The party's over. He looks at me and laughs and struggles over to his chair and sits down and sighs.

"Hilarity in the morning," he says, looking up at the sky. "This is how it was every morning, Pete, at the store. I'd get up at five thirty so I could get down to the store by six thirty and have thirty minutes alone before the celebration started. Then Dobbie would show up, and then Francis, and then the installers would come in all at once, each hoping to get there first so they could get the easiest job for the day. And they'd be gruff and hung over and angry and unshaven and demanding. The salesmen from the carpet mills arrived about that time, too, because they knew they could find me then before I scattered to the wind and disappeared. Then maybe a sixty-foot trailer full of carpet from a mill in the South would show up and have to block traffic in the street while it unloaded. The cops would show up to see what the neighbors were complaining about. It was chaos, Pete, just like this morning. But then all at once, just like this morning, everyone left, and I was all alone again until the next wave of chaos. I loved it, Pete."

"You love chaos, don't you, Dad?"

"Oh, Pete, you're *so* right. I loved it!"

"Why did you marry a woman who loves organization and order?"

"I suppose because I'd never had any of that. 'I try,' Pete, just like Earl (Blaine's employee who hired himself) used to say."

He laughs, remembering the mentally challenged dwarf who came into his store one day and said, "Mr. Gorham, they've closed the rug-cleaning store (where Earl worked for twenty years), so I'm going to work here now." And he did for twenty-five years.

"You look happy, Dad. Maybe you need this hilarity in the morning like you're back at work."

"You're right. I think I *do* need it—just at first in the morning, a flurry of chaos with people running everywhere in utter confusion trying to put together a destiny for the day. And somehow I'm the center of it. And then it all goes out like the tide, and I'm left alone on the beach to contemplate it all and to write my ads in silence."

My mother is in the hospital with pneumonia. Judy called me after visiting her and said she seemed terrible. It doesn't look good; her pulse rate is 132 beats per minute, and her blood pressure is off the chart. If she was an ordinary woman and not my mother, I'd say she's not going to make it.

In the midst of all of this, I have to take Judy to the airport an hour away to catch a flight to Florida. I stop by the hospital first, though, and find that Roberta's no better. I tell her I'm going to take Judy to the airport and that I'll be back later. She can hardly hear anything anymore, but I finally get it across to her. The last visit to the ear doctor revealed no ear wax. Her deafness has made her irascible and unpleasant to be around. She yells at everyone, thinking they're not speaking loudly enough for her to hear. Even though the ear doctor's office is just across the street from Roberta's hospital room, I can't imagine when she'll be energetic enough to make the trip to see him, and he'll not walk over to the hospital to remove her ear wax.

I check in with Blaine one last time before going to the airport. I assure him over and over again that Roberta's doing okay, which she's not. Nonetheless, he will worry as he's done most of his life but slightly less now. He is comforted mainly by the fact that he didn't *give* her the pneumonia since they haven't seen each other for weeks.

On the way to the airport, Judy tells me I must not take upon myself such graven responsibility for my parents and that I must give myself periodic relief from it and not worry about the consequences. Driving back from the airport, I decide she's right and decide not to go see my mother again until around four thirty in the afternoon.

Immediately upon entering my mother's hospital room at four thirty, she says to me "Where have *you* been?"

"I took Judy to the airport. I told you I was going to do that."

"I *know* that. When did her flight leave?"

"At one o'clock."

"Where have you been since then?"

I'm blown away. "That's two and a half hours from the time I got back to Galesburg. Am I not allowed some time on my own? I have a life, you know."

My mother and I get into a mild verbal fight as she's lying on her death bed. She begins to breathe heavily and turns her head away, sulking the Irish sulk, the same one I have. I now feel not only anger but double guilt— first for not returning immediately to her bedside and second for potentially killing her with anger and resentment once I do.

Blaine calls me at seven in the morning and says in a gravel-like whisper, "Pete, can you come out here and see me? I need to talk to you about some things."

"What's wrong, Dad?"

"Pete, can you come out here and talk to me?"

"I've got a lot of things to do this morning, Dad, and I have to get Judy at the airport at noon. I could come out later this afternoon."

"Can you come right now before you go?"

"Can you just talk to me about it here on the phone?" I'm not going to win this struggle, I know, and

I'm possibly eventually going to kill *both* of my parents with anger and resentment. How horrible that would be—to kill both of one's ninety-year-old parents with anger and maybe even have to go to prison for it. What jury would find in my favor no matter how justified I was? "Yeah, I'll be there in a half hour."

"Thanks, Pete."

When I open Blaine's door, which he keeps shut all the time now, he is scurrying around like a rodent. He has improved so much that his walking is almost normal in every way like it was ten years ago, except that now his posture is severely hunchbacked from years of favoring his back. He has a deeply worried look on his face. He sits down and looks up and says, "Pete, I've got a problem. You know the flashlight you got me? Where you screw the head off to get the light to come on?" He is referring to a very cool, pen-size, twenty-dollar replacement flashlight I got him last week, which works by slightly screwing the head counterclockwise until the light comes on and then slightly screwing it clockwise to turn it off. I knew immediately upon giving it to him and seeing his befuddled amazement at how it could produce light that way, that I'd made a mistake.

"Well, I was looking in the toilet to see if I'd had any luck with my bowel movement, the way I check every time, and I screwed it too far, and the whole top of it fell into the toilet. I want you to get me another one—the old kind with the button you move up and down."

"It went down the toilet?"

"No, no, not that. Forget that one! I want you to get me another one."

"Where's the old one?"

"Pete, I don't *want* the old one. I want a new one like I used to have."

Suddenly I see the flashlight on his table by the bed, and I go over and pick it up.

"Pete, don't touch that. It fell in the dirty toilet. That's why I want another one. That one's filthy now, and we need to throw it out."

I turn it on, and the light comes on. "It's fine, Dad."

He rolls his eyes up and sighs and says again firmly, "I don't *want* that flashlight. Just throw it out. I'll pay you for it. Buy me another one, please!"

Recently I have noticed that even though my father still insists upon paying for everything, he never actually does pay for anything. This is because he's not had even one dollar on his person for months and months. He intends to pay me later or at least tell Roberta to pay me, but he forgets. I've started to say, "Don't worry about it. Just leave me a big inheritance."

"I'll keep the flashlight for myself and get you another one."

"Pete, get me one like that other one I had. Remember, with the little lever on the side that you just push up or down? Where is that old flashlight?"

"We threw it out, Dad. I know what you mean. I'll get it for you."

"You will? Thanks. I'll pay you back. You know which one I mean, don't you? The one with the little lever on the side that you push up and down?"

"Yeah, I know Dad, I'll get it."

"Thanks, Pete, I just have to have a little flashlight for when I get up in the night, and I liked that one there a lot, but I screwed it too far, and it fell in the toilet. You know which kind I mean, don't you? With the lever on the side?"

Finally, my father gets around to asking about his wife. "Pete, how's Roberta?"

"She's got pneumonia, Dad."

"I know, Pete, and that makes me so sad."

"She's had it before, Dad, lots of times, and she got over it. I think she'll get over it this time, too."

"Do you, Pete?" he asks wistfully like a boy might ask his father whom he trusts.

"Yes, I do. She's getting better, and besides, she's indestructible." He laughs. "So are you, Dad."

I drive by the Dollar General store on my way home. I ask them if they have flashlights. A woman leads me all the way to the back of the store to a rack of flashlights. They are all too big except for a package of four that has two big flashlights and two pen-size ones like Blaine likes. Eight batteries are included—four for the two little ones and four for the two big ones. The price is five dollars!

I buy them all and take them back to Blaine. He is ecstatic. This tool—the flashlight—somehow symbolically represents and actually is for him a type of freedom—one of his few left. We put the batteries in and try them all. "How much were they? I want to pay you." I tell him the price. He can't believe it. I show him the receipt. "Dad, these are so cheap that you can just throw them in the toilet if you want to after you check for poop."

He laughs. "Pete, how's Roberta doing?"

"She's much better, Dad."

"Oh, I'm so glad to hear that, Pete. I worry about her so much."

I've been to the hospital to visit Roberta. She's getting a little better, but she goes up and down. Her pulse is closer to being normal; however, the doctor is worried that her heartbeat is irregular. She's put on a pound or two but hates the food there. She's extremely tired and weak.

Being with her is awkward because she is so deaf. I wonder if other patients in the hospital think I'm verbally abusing my mother since I seem to be—and am!—yelling at her all the time. I pleaded with a nurse two days ago to clean out her ears, which she promised she'd do but hasn't. I'm tired when I get home and start to make dinner.

Judy comes home. She's stopped by to see Blaine and is upset and needs to talk about it. She said when she'd got to his room he was lying in the dim light with his eyes closed. She'd sat down in a chair to the right of his bed out of his vision. Eerily he'd whispered, "Is that you, Judy?" They had whispered back and forth, and then he'd told her he was dying.

Before she could respond, a nurse came running into the room and shouted, "Blaine! Blaine! What's this about you dying?" She came over to the bed and pulled his sheet down to his knees and looked at his skin. "You're not dying, Blaine. I've seen lots of people who are dying, and you're not dying."

Another nurse had popped in and sat down on his bed and held his hand. "Blaine, why are you telling everyone you're dying? You're not dying! You're going to live to be a hundred!" He held one nurse's hand while smiling beneficently at the other.

Nurse Amber came in the room and up to the bedside. There were tears in her eyes, and she was wiping her cheeks with the heels of her hands. "How is he?" she said to the second nurse.

"He looks okay. I don't think he's dying." She smiled at my father. "You're not dying, are you, Blaine?"

"Not if you say so, honey. But that's not what the nurse told me this morning."

"Who told you what this morning?"

"I don't know. I'm confused now."

Amber came up to him and said in a mock scolding voice, still crying, "You shouldn't say that, Blaine. There are a lot of people here who love you. We don't want you to die."

While still holding onto the second nurse's hand, Blaine reached out and took Amber's hand and started singing, "I Can't Stop Loving You." Gradually nurse one and nurse two slipped back out into the hallway. Then Amber said she had to go, too. Blaine sang "If Ever I Should Leave You" to her as she left, and then he and Judy were alone again.

Soon Judy had gone into the hallway to find out what was going on, and Amber had said, "I went into Blaine's room, and he told me he was going to die tonight. He thanked me for all the help I'd given him and promised we'd see each other again in heaven. I couldn't help it. I just started crying and ran and got someone to look at him."

"What was that all about?" I wonder to Judy.

"I stayed and talked to your dad a long time. I was there an hour and a half. He was having hallucinations that seemed to be telling him that he was going to die tonight. He was totally convinced of it. He felt better when I left."

"Should I go see him after dinner?"

"It might not be a bad idea. He was scared, but he was funny, too."

Blaine is still lying on his back in bed when I get to Seminary Manor. His eyes are closed. The light is dim. I stand in front of him, and he opens his eyes and greets me and puts his hand out to shake mine. I clear three or four sweaters from a chair and sit across from him.

"How are you doing, Dad?"

"Not good, Pete. Did you talk to Judy?"

"Yeah, I just did."

"Did she tell you everything?"

"She said you thought you were going to die." He smiles. "Why did you think that, Dad?"

He looks furtively at the partially open door and asks me to close it and points to his head and says, "I'm no good anymore, Pete, this doesn't work right."

"What happened, Dad?"

He struggles a long time to get it straight in his head and then finally just gives in. "A nurse today came up to me and said, 'Blaine, I've got some bad news. I'll come back later and tell you.' All day long I was scared because I knew she was going to come back and tell me I was going to die. But she never came back. I looked for her all day, but she never came back."

"Do you know who she was?"

"No."

"Maybe she went home at four and forgot to tell you, Dad. First of all, they're not going to send a nurse to tell you you're going to die. If they have to tell you that, I'm sure it's going to be your doctor who tells you. She was going to tell you something else. Probably something mundane, like a time change."

He points to his head. "Pete, I think she was up here. She wasn't out there. I'm no good anymore, Pete."

"Dad, you are good. These nurses don't gather around and cry at the bedside of someone who's not good. They love you, Dad. You know what?"

"What, Pete?"

"You're not crazy, Dad. Your memory's not as good. But it's good! You just don't feel in as much control of your thoughts as before. But that's okay."

Peace is returning to my father's face as I ramble on. I keep talking the way a father might talk to his baby son who's just awakened in the night from a nightmare. When I leave, Blaine is ready to go to sleep even though he is still absolutely convinced that a spirit spoke to him and told him that his time on earth was almost over.

That night I awaken from my sleep every hour or so and lie there, wondering if the angel has come back yet to take my father home.

I had planned on a rare day to myself with no visits to Seminary Manor or the hospital, but the phone rings at eight thirty. It's Dr. Strauch who tells me he'll visit my father around ten and invites me to join them. I assume Blaine is still alive, but I don't know.

When I enter my father's room, he is standing up and invites me to sit down. Just then, Nurse Tina knocks on the door and comes in. She sees me and says, "Oh, I'm sorry, Blaine, you probably don't have time for me now."

Blaine struggles over to her and puts his arms around her neck and his cheek on hers and says, "I always have time for you, honey. You are as valuable to me as gold interlaced with diamonds!" She smiles broadly.

"What's new, Blaine?" Dr. Strauch asks.

"Spring training?"

Images of baseball have cemented these two men's friendship from the start.

"What's new with you?"

"Well, Carl. The other day I thought I was going to die. Before, when I told you I thought I was going to die, that was just playing games. This is the main show."

Dr. Strauch ignores this and starts asking real questions about Blaine's health. The sad but happy truth is that Blaine is not able in any way to demonstrate to the good doctor that he is dying. In fact, it appears that he is living more forcefully. He is walking almost normally and is oftentimes not even using his walker. His heart is perfect, his lungs are perfect, and all of the rest of his internal organs seem to be perfect. Blaine mentions his stomach, which he says continues to "grind." Strauch goes through the litany of tests and operations he or others have conducted to try to discover what's wrong with Blaine's stomach, but it always appears to be fine. He mentions that Blaine has gained twelve pounds in the last four months.

Strauch finally brings up the subject that is on all of our minds—what to do next with Roberta. She will have to leave the hospital in a couple of days because Medicare won't cover her after two weeks. She herself believes that she is too weak to return right now to her apartment alone. Strauch suggests that Blaine is almost well enough to go back to the apartment at Seminary Estates and live with her. Dr. Strauch and I have a lengthy discussion in front of Blaine about the possible evolution of my parents' lives together or apart for the immediate future based upon their current and projected states of health. There is even the suggestion that they could eventually move together to the other facility in Seminary Village, Hawthorne Inn, which provides a greater level of care to its residents but is not a nursing home.

It has been bewildering to both me and Judy over the last few months what has happened to the sixty-seven-year relationship between my mother and father who were once inseparable. We have speculated about every reason why they have not made much effort to get back together or even to see each other. We have tried to get them to agree to a daily visit of Roberta to Blaine by wheelchair. I proposed once that we hire someone to see that a daily visit happens even if Judy or I can't be there. They didn't go for that. We have offered that they move back in together. That conversation goes nowhere.

Finally, I have had to conclude that my parents' sixty-seven-year marriage has resulted in an amicable separation. By being obliged to be apart, they have discovered that they like being apart. They still love and get lonely for each other, but generally, life without the burdensome patterns that they unconsciously impose upon each other is simply easier to manage. At ninety-one and ninety-three, people seem generally to opt for the easiest solutions to things rather than the noble or the principled or even the right solution.

Blaine is confused by all of this talk of reunion. He continues to maintain that by being together in any fashion, he risks making Roberta sick, which has become his weak but intractable argument for why they must remain apart. I can't penetrate his irrationality or his will with logic. I'm not sure that I know, or if they do either, what are the true reasons for his or her desire for separation. In fact, I'm not sure there are reasons. I think at this point there are only feelings and complexes and deep-seated fears that are driving both of them along with a sense of relief at not having to interact with each other as before when they were more capable of sorting things out.

Strauch tells us he has recommended to Roberta that she come here for a while to Seminary Manor— to Bounce Back—to receive therapy with the goal of eventually going back to her apartment.

Blaine is aghast! "You mean here? Right here with *me?*" To Strauch, who is not in touch with my parents in as holistic a way as I am, this appears to be perfectly reasonable. But I know that for a galaxy of tangled reasons, my mother and my father cannot be together now and maybe never can be again.

Strauch compares Roberta's and Blaine's health using actuarial logic, which, of course, Blaine doesn't listen to. But I do. I find it interesting. His conclusion seems to be that even though Roberta is two years younger than Blaine, due to her inferior health she might not live as long as he. That's all that Blaine hears—that Roberta won't live as long as he will.

All at once he stops the discussion, assumes a stance of mock anger, and announces boldly, like a knight preparing sternly for a battle, "I have made a decision, and the two of you must listen to it and abide by it and take the appropriate actions, whatever they should be. Let there be no moaning at the bar!" he says cryptically. "I will not allow my wife of sixty years to die first. I will not drag her down to her death by having us live together so that I can selfishly get what I want. Someone needs to volunteer to go first! Someone needs to be courageous and stalwart and true—to be a he-man. And that's me. I'm the man! I need to be the one to step up to the plate and die!"

I would never have believed it possible, nor would I have believed that I could be an accomplice to it. But today an ambulance has taken my mother to Seminary Manor's Bounce Back wing, not to be with my father in his room there but to be in her own room just across the hall from his. However, she is not alone. She has a roommate—a woman, a *deaf* woman. My mother has elected to live with a total stranger who is totally deaf rather than live in the room just across the hall with my father to whom she has been married for sixty-seven years.

I am now the child of a broken home.

Spring 2008

Jenny calls me. "Pete," she says, "I just wanted to let you know that a single room has finally become available, and we are going to move your father into it."

"You are? When?"

"Tomorrow!"

"You're kidding me!"

At the end of the conversation that ensues, Jenny says, "Thank you for understanding, Pete."

"Wait a minute. I do not understand this at all— why you have to move my father to the other side of the building away from my mother? And do it tomorrow! It will blow his mind!"

"I'm sorry."

"You know, Jenny, these old people just get pushed around like chess pieces. They have no power anymore, and they are like prisoners who are only technically free."

"I'm sorry."

"Please don't tell Blaine tonight. Just move him tomorrow. And would you please inform Roberta that I'll be out to see her after dinner."

My mother is sitting in a chair in her room, reading the paper, and is still dressed elegantly from dinner. It is possible to believe that she is sitting in their living room of their house in the country, waiting for Blaine to come home from some adventure he's had, with dinner in the oven.

She sees me and smiles and says, "I figured you'd be out tonight."

"Has Jenny talked to you?"

She nods yes. She is amazingly even-tempered and accepting of this new development, which comforts me, since I am one-half her and one-half my father, who will come unglued, and at this time I need to be reminded of my rational and receptive and stoic side.

We talk back and forth like two old friends, deciding that it's best for both of us to stay out of the way tomorrow and just let them move Blaine. Otherwise, we both agree, we'll get caught up in the flurry of manipulations in which my father's superhuman ability to get at least his portion of his own way will no doubt prevail. Some sort of complicated gerrymandering will take place which no one but Blaine will completely understand until the dust clears and it's too late to reconfigure the boundaries.

I walk by room 401 on my way out—the room Jenny has told me will be Blaine's. It's half the size of his present room. It doesn't seem like a place in which I want my father to spend his last days on earth.

On my way home, I once again contemplate bringing both of my parents to my house to live out their last days. Again, it doesn't compute. Again, I can sense the regret I'll possibly feel after they die, knowing that in the old days (with which I have always been emotionally identified) the parents would have gone to live out the rest of their lives with their children.

This is how I see it happening. My mother will love it; my father will be afraid of another change and be confused. He will resist; she will embrace. Probably in the end she will be living in an entirely different building, Hawthorne Inn, and he'll still be in room 401, which is becoming more and more a dark little pocket of solitude and withdrawal for him.

The details of arranging the trip to the adjacent building, Hawthorne Inn, just fifty yards away, are proving to be typically burdensome.

Blaine's door is closed all the way, and the room is dark. He's asleep with a towel over his face. I sit down across from him, and soon he wakes up. There would never be a good time to tell him that on Thursday we're going to visit Hawthorne Manor, but just when he wakes up would be the worst. So instead, I talk to him slowly and gradually for twenty minutes before bringing it up.

"What's Hawthorne Inn?"

I tell him as benignly as possible.

"You mean to another building entirely?"

"It's right next door. It's part of this place."

"Why would I move right next door?"

When I tell him that Mom would go, too, that's all he needs to hear. "You mean we'd live together again?" No matter how many times and how many ways I have explained to him why Roberta lives someplace besides with him, he cannot understand how it could be. He accepts it by believing that he's being quarantined to keep her healthy, which is an explanation he himself has conjured up.

I suggest we go visit her.

"Right now?"

"Yes, right now."

"Oh, Pete, I can't do that. I don't want to give her anything."

"What are you going to give her, Dad? You don't have anything."

After various reasonable assurances from me, he agrees that we should visit my mother, his wife.

They see each other and smile broad smiles like two initiates to love. My mother puts out her hand, but Blaine says he can't touch her because he might give her something. She pretends to understand.

Quickly my mother brings up Hawthorne Inn. Obviously, she has talked to others about it and is excited and can't wait to visit Thursday. He is excited like a little boy that he might be invited to live with my mother again, and that's all he needs to know. The rest of the details are unimportant.

So it's not really surprising after all, when I think of it, that my father loves Hawthorne Inn and is prepared to move to it as soon as possible. What is surprising is that my mother hates it.

"It's too quiet here. There's nothing going on. I can't imagine living here."

My father has no strong opinions about anything that are not always subject to change. My mother has strong opinions about most things, and they are often intractable. The subject is closed. We eat a nice lunch in the guest dining room. It is very quiet—rather, *shockingly* quiet.

Before we leave Hawthorne Inn, my mother makes a mind-blowing statement. She says, "I think your father and I will just share a room in Seminary Manor. Pete, maybe you could ask Jenny if one's available."

That night I say to Judy, "The next time we talk to Mom, she'll want to go back to her apartment at Seminary Estates."

My mother has been living back at Seminary Estates on her own for three weeks now. My father is still in little room 401. We all go for a ride this Sunday to see the spring emerging around town, then join Judy back at the Seminary Estates dining room to have Sunday brunch. It is somewhat like old times. Many residents come up to Blaine and hug him and ask when he is coming back and say they miss him. "Your dad's the nicest, sweetest man," a woman whispers to me. "We all miss him." At the end of the meal, Judy has to leave, and the three of us sit while Blaine finishes picking at his food.

"Are you done?" my mother finally asks him, being anxious to leave.

"I am, but I want to go back to your apartment with you for just a minute."

"Why?"

"I want to look around and see where you live."

Blaine is enraptured with my mother's lovely, bright, and spacious apartment. "This is fascinating!" he says. "Roberta, did I ever live here?"

My mother is deaf again, so everything my father says to her in his soft voice needs to be repeated several times before she understands. It's easier for me to answer for her. "No, Dad, you never lived here. You lived down the hall with Mom."

"That's what I thought. Why did I leave?"

"You had to go to the hospital, and then…"

"I went to the hospital?"

"Yes, and then you had to leave the hospital, but you weren't well enough to come back here, so you went to Bounce Back." I can see that he's confused, and so I stop explaining it because he doesn't care to understand, anyway.

Then he stares at my mother and says, "Roberta, tell me, what is my future with you?"

She doesn't understand his words. He repeats it. She still doesn't understand. Or does she? I repeat what he said to her, and she gives a heartless, generic explanation, offering no solution or hope. I can tell by his uncharacteristic acceptance of what she's said that he knows her feelings won't change. When she picks up the Sunday paper and says, "Let me see what the headlines are today," I stop her, saying, "Mom, I think Dad needs to discuss this with us, okay?" She puts the paper down and pretends to suddenly understand that he's not—or *I'm* not—through discussing his future with my mother.

She says, "Well, Blaine, you don't think you are well enough to take care of yourself without help from the nurses."

"I don't?"

The discussion that ensues is sad. He clearly wants to be back with her in this happy spot of normalcy, but she doesn't want him to be for reasons I will never fully understand, and I don't think they will, either. To me, my parents should want to be together until death do them part, in sickness and in health, for better or for worse, no matter how old they are. But Blaine has already accepted her disinterest by the time he suggests I walk him back to his room, rather in the way a homely schoolboy quickly accepts and intuitively understands that the best-looking girl in the school is only willing to talk to him cursorily for a second or two before moving on to higher fields.

Before we leave, my father tells my mother how beautiful she is.

Upon opening the adjoining door to the Seminary Manor nursing home, the scene changes radically.

Wheelchairs are the common mode of transportation, buzzers sound constantly, the faces of many of the residents are blank and hopeless, and nurses scurry everywhere to attend to constant demands.

My father's asleep in his dark little room when I arrive, as he is so often now. His face while asleep looks like his father's but is upsettingly feeble and old and helpless. I sit in the recliner right next to the bed. "Hi, Pete," he says.

"Dad, go ahead and sleep."

"Okay." So Blaine sleeps in bed, and I sit beside him in the chair in the small, dark room that I'm sure now is where my father will die. There is constant noise in the hallway—the nurses talking to one another at the nurses' station just outside his door; the wails from a man my father calls "Mohammed" that never stop, like a ship lost in a foggy night, beseeching the world to notice it; the TV from the nearby lounge where various unconscious and semi-aware residents sit all day in wheelchairs, pretending to watch what's on, and buzzers going off without end. It is actually comforting to me to hear all this background noise, and I think, "If I was here, I wouldn't want to be at the end of the hall where no one comes."

Eventually I fall asleep, and I have a dream. It's a lovely dream, and I feel sure and peaceful when I wake up. It's dark. Blaine is asleep. I wake him up slowly by speaking his name just once. "Blaine?"

"Oh, hi, Pete."

"You have to go to dinner in thirty minutes."

He sighs then reaches for some notes he's written that are lying on the table close to him. He puts his glasses on first, asks me to turn on the light then studiously reads several pages over and over. It's totally silent for at least five minutes. "Ah, here it is," he finally says. He puts the notes down on his stomach and takes his glasses off. He looks extremely serious. I am sitting parallel to his bed, so we don't really engage each other the way speakers usually do, which is rather nice. He waits through silence for his thoughts to organize themselves and suggest a direction, and then he says, "When's dinner?" I tell him five thirty. He looks at the clock. "What time is it now?"

"Five o'clock."

He sighs again. "It's mayhem down there, Pete."

"It is? Why?"

By 5:25, I think I know why. I don't know if its fear or disappointment or frustration or disgust or all of them that Blaine is experiencing at mealtime, but whatever mixture of emotions it is, I am beginning to see that that's where his stomach problems might originate.

Howard, the obsequious quiet man who's eaten with Blaine for months, is now gone. No one knows why. In his place is an unpleasant man whose wife lives at Seminary Estates and dines with Roberta. Blaine can't remember his name. The man is stone-deaf and has had a heart attack. His wife sometimes comes at the beginning of the meal to be with him, but she leaves soon. Blaine is left alone then with this unpleasant deaf man. The man needs help but rejects it and is sour.

Blaine pulls the notes out and reads two quotes from the man at last night's dinner, over and over. "Keep your mouth shut!" in reference to Blaine and, "She's crazy!" in reference to his wife. My father is upset and needs to talk to me about this man. The man apparently threw up on the table one night, too, which is part of the "general mayhem" Blaine referred to.

"You can't reach some people, Dad. You've got to accept that."

"Pete, you are so right."

Blaine asks if I'll walk him to his table. He seems to want me to see this man. He probably believes that by seeing the man, I'll change the dynamics somehow.

We get to the table, and there are two men sitting there. Blaine introduces me to Reggie, who shakes my hand and says very softly, "Nice to meet you."

Then he introduces me to the other man. I reach for his hand, and he puts his out to shake mine weakly, and he mouths the words, "Nice to meet you," without really saying them. He has an angular face, thin and resolute, strong, stubborn, and has a detached body language that suggests to me bitterness. I help Blaine sit down, and I push him up to the table and then put one hand on his shoulder and shake his hand with the other and say good-bye.

On my way out, I pat Reggie on the shoulder, and then I pat the other man on the shoulder and squeeze his deltoid slightly, hoping that he'll feel a transmission of kinship with me and through that a new and protective affinity with my father. Either that or he'll realize I'm my father's principal keeper, and that I contain all of the dutiful and possibly even fearsome qualities that attend that fiduciary relationship of one man standing in respectfully and honorably for another.

Before sunrise, on the morning after our late night return from Florida on our first visit to our first grandchild, the phone rings. It's Cottage Hospital. My mother has told the nurse to call and tell me that she has just been brought to the hospital by ambulance. She's had chronic diarrhea for over a week and is exhausted. I walk to the hospital.

I meet with my mother's pulmonologist, Dr. Soyangko, a chipper, optimistic Asian fellow who, after reading her extensive file, guesses that she has MAC again (mycobacterium avium complex), but he calls it MAI (mycobacterium avium-intracellulare), which is apparently the same thing. "It can cause chronic diarrhea," he says.

He performs a battery of tests, including a stethoscope exam and an immediate chest x-ray, which reveal rattling sounds and dark spots. He orders a bronchoscopy for two days later, a procedure in which a tube is inserted through the nose, down the air channel, and eventually into the lungs to look for tumors and other problems. This *procedure* has all of the elements of an operation, meaning for me that I will spend almost an entire day in pre-op, waiting, and post-op.

When I meet with the doctor after surgery, he says, "The good news is that your mother doesn't have lung cancer or MAI. The bad news is that she has another similar virus that is just about as bad." Then he hands me a card with four small photos of my mother's airways.

For some reason, doctors think that I am more than a layman and expect that I can discern subtle abnormalities in x-rays and such. It is tempting to act shocked at what I see, but I have to tell him I don't understand any of it. I point to a repulsive-looking mass of yellow tissue and say, "What's that?"

He tells me it's pus from the infection clogging Roberta's bronchial tubes. "It's a wonder she can breathe at all. She's one sick woman!"

Roberta is in the hospital for two and a half weeks on high doses of antibiotics and steroids. Meanwhile, they find that she also has what they call a "Super Bug," which is a euphemism meaning she's caught a contagious hospital disease; in other words, the hospital made her sicker. She has to be isolated. Her visitors quickly back away when they learn that they are required to wear a mask in her room.

It surprises me how vigorous and happy my mother seems to be during this period. Then I realize why— the steroids. Steroids give you boundless energy and optimism in addition to ecstatically voracious hunger. Watching my mother willingly and happily endure her two-week quarantined hospital stay because of happiness-boosting steroids, makes me wonder why such drugs aren't handed out in nursing homes and mental hospitals every morning with breakfast. No doubt it's possible to create too much joy and optimism, which could lead to an unruly awareness.

During this period of my mother's hospitalization, I keep my father informed in as gentle a way as possible of her condition. He asks me how she is doing when I first go to his room, and we discuss her for a few minutes. He often lies back in bed and looks up at the ceiling, and I sit in the recliner next to him. Sometimes he falls asleep. Sometimes I do, too. Or he tells stories, and I listen.

Blaine takes my hand and says, "Pete, I need to ask you something. How's Roberta doing?" After I assure him again that she's doing fine and is happy and vigorous, he says, "I'm so glad. Your mother means everything in the world to me, Pete."

"I know she does, Dad."

He takes my wrist again and says, having completely forgotten he just asked me, "Pete, tell me how your mother is doing." I say she's doing fine, picturing her smiling high on steroids. He decides that we should call Roberta while I'm there. He seems to understand most clearly where my mother is when she is in the hospital, but he's never sure how to reach her there by phone. So I dial the hospital number, give him the phone, and tell him to ask for room 311.

Blaine holds the receptionist with conversation and confusion and charm for fifteen minutes, having her call Roberta again and again without an answer until finally the woman has to take another call.

My father immediately says to me, "Pete, could you dial the hospital again, please?"

"Dad, give it a few minutes."

Blaine stares at the ceiling for thirty seconds and then asks me to dial again.

I have finally now, after sixty years, come to appreciate my father's bizarre subconscious championing of humanity. For over six decades, often in horror, I've watched him patiently but with dogged determination use the most outlandish methods to successfully resist the inevitable onslaught of technology grinding us all down into automatons. His tiny triumphs of the interpersonal over the impersonal probably have delayed for a few microseconds, by some negligible calculus, the eventual irretrievable total loss of human freedom. And now, despite the never-ending frustration of dealing with my father, I consider him my hero in this effort, a man who can, within the blink of an eye, bring the most hardened, humorless person back snickering into the center of his own hidden heart.

Twenty minutes later, after having made five more calls to the receptionist, Blaine finally reaches his wife who says after thirty seconds of talking to him, "I've got to go now, Blaine. The doctor just came in!"

My father sighs deeply and hangs up. "Why would anyone choose to leave an important conversation for any reason, especially simply to talk to a doctor who has just come in and who is probably late himself? Even a doctor could be made to wait for at least five more minutes before threatening to leave and then another five minutes before he actually does."

It's Father's Day. Judy will be visiting her father for the weekend. I've decided to make dinner at our house for my parents. I've planned for it for a week. The logistics of this won't be easy. There are six steps to climb at my house to get to the main floor. I'll have to practically carry my parents up them one parent at a time. But they haven't visited our house for so long, and they love it. The weather is supposed to be lovely, temperate, and sunny. It will give them at least a fleeting sense of renewal by being in the presence of the late spring.

Before Judy leaves, she makes quiche for them, which my mother adores. We purchase fresh fruit and poppy seed bread at the farmers' market on Saturday. Judy makes a cake and sends my father a bouquet of flowers and balloons. I go to the store and get Blue Bunny ice cream, which is my father's favorite. I call Seminary Manor and arrange to have someone get Blaine ready and to get him to the front door by 3:45. And I tell my mother to meet us at her front door at four p.m., and we'll all go for a ride in the sunny countryside before we eat. My energy is high for this.

I wait until mid-Sunday morning to call my mother and confirm our party. It takes both her and my father a long time in the first of the morning just to wake up and to move beyond debilitating aches and pains and whatever new infirmities might accompany each new day for them. To expect anything even remotely close to optimism before ten a.m. is foolish.

"Hi, Mom, how are you feeling today?"

"I don't feel very good, Pete. I still have chronic diarrhea, and I don't feel like eating. I won't be able to make it to your house today. I'm going to go to the doctor tomorrow. The diarrhea won't go away, and I'm worried it's something else. I dread another colonoscopy, but I know that's what they'll want. I'm sorry, Pete, I just don't think I can do it today."

"What if I bring food to your place? I'm already planning to pick up Blaine at 3:45, and I could just bring him over there, instead. I've got a quiche and some cake. Any interest in that?"

"Well, maybe we could do that then. I love quiche."

"I know you do, Mom. I'm going to call Dad and remind him to meet me at 3:45. I'm not going to tell him we've changed plans. I'm just going to bring him over there, and we'll all eat together at your place. It's no problem. It's already made."

She sounds relatively pleased about that.

Blaine answers after six rings. "Blaine, it's Pete, your son. Happy Father's Day."

"Thanks, Pete. And I'm a lucky father to have you as a son."

"You're going to meet me at your front door at 3:45, right?"

"Just a minute, Pete." I can hear papers shuffling near the phone, and my father sighing. He's looking for the notes he took yesterday when I told him to write down that I'd be there to get him at 3:45, as if finding them will somehow certify the appointment. He comes back in two minutes. "Pete, can you talk?"

"Sure, Dad, it's Father's Day. What kind of guy can't talk to his father on Father's Day?"

He laughs weakly. "Pete, I don't feel good. My stomach's bothering me. But I don't know if it just bothers me all the time now as an excuse or what. It may be an obsession about not giving your mother anything. As you know, Pete, I have a terrible fear of giving your mother something. What if I had visited her the day before she went into the hospital the last time and she had died? I just can't stand for that to happen, Pete. That has become a huge fetish for me. I want more than anything to be in the presence of your mother all the time, but I'm afraid I'm going to give her something. I'm sorry, Pete, I just don't want to go and take a chance on that."

I'm beginning to think it's more than that. I think they're tired of each other. I think they've come to regard each other as yokes around their necks after having found uncommon relative peace in being unwittingly separated. Neither of them could or even should now admit that to themselves, but it's true, I think. In a way, realizing this makes it easier for me because then I won't have to strive so hard to get them together. I have to accept this cruel truth—that what was once regarded by many people as an ideal marriage between my father and my mother is not that any longer. It actually may never have been ideal but instead the mechanical workings of the respective and mutual needs of two basically good people, their determination, and their loyalty to old-fashioned family values and religion, all held together in a snare of symbiosis. But more likely it's simply been transformed by the exigencies of aging and ill health, and they are now in the final uncharted stage of their relationship. Who knows?

At any rate, the party's off. I offer to take my mother a piece of quiche and a piece of cake for dinner. And I tell my father I'll stop by his room later to say, "Happy Father's Day," in person.

A few minutes later, the sun goes away, and the sky turns nighttime black. I turn on the TV, and there are warning messages flashing across the screen on almost every channel, telling me to run for the basement. Suddenly the sky shakes, and lightning flashes to the ground, and heaven erupts in a downpour of wind-driven rain.

At four p.m., I take a big piece of quiche and two pieces of poppy seed bread and a piece of cake to my mother. She's asleep in her chair, and when she wakes up, she looks depressed. She talks about her health worries, as usual. Then she asks me in an uncharacteristic moment of weakness, "What do *you* think I should do, Pete?" This has the alarming feel to me of a general asking one of her troops which direction they should go, and realities taken for granted suddenly disappear in yet a new upsetting way that implies my weary leadership.

My instinct, as always, is to tell her to stop taking *all* of the medicines the doctors have loaded her down with in the last twenty years, but she is such a dedicated loyal patient that my suggestion would be tantamount to asking her to join a mutiny. And then I'd have to be the new captain. We do decide, however, that she should stop taking the antibiotic they gave her at the hospital for the Super Bug that they've never discontinued. She's buoyed by this—given hope, a life raft—at least for a few hours.

I heat up her piece of quiche in the microwave and serve it to her. She likes it. She's a great cook and loves good food even when she has diarrhea and is sick to her stomach. She's happier by the time I leave at ten minutes to five, telling her I should walk over and see Dad before he goes to dinner and wish him Happy Father's Day.

My father, as is often the case now, is lying asleep but has his eyes slightly open, somehow allowing him to quickly regain partial consciousness if need be. He looks like a cadaver. He says, "Hi, Pete," in his gravely

Marlon Brando-like distant sleeping voice. I wish him Happy Father's Day. While still staring at the ceiling, he puts his left hand out to shake mine. It moves away from his body toward me like an independent lever on an otherwise unmoving robot. He voices a return greeting to me while staring up, sounding as if his mouth is full of stones.

In time, my father's sleep voice disappears, and he tells me he wants more than anything to be in the presence of my mother at all times. He sounds genuinely disturbed that this can't be because of his obsession with "giving her something." I know that like all obsessions, his can't be reasoned away. My father does not disrespect logic and reason; he simply is not amenable to them, and to blame him for being illogical and unreasonable is like blaming someone who understands only French for not understanding English directives. But I can see that he needs clarification of why my mother and he are not living together now, and so for Father's Day I do my best to explain it as I see it.

I mount a monologue that I must say is somewhat inspirational in its ability to cast light upon important areas. I am able successfully to find common grounds, which all three principals share—he, my mother, and me. I am able to point out why my mother, even though she still loves my father, cannot live with him now, and why my father, even though he loves my mother just as much, cannot live with her now. And while still being honest, I am able to leave open the possibility that they will one day live together again but not in one of their present circumstances. It will be when she has reached the stage of aging that he is in, I suggest, when she will also have to surrender her last freedom that now she is clinging on to tenaciously, which to her he represents the loss of. He happily agrees with me as if he's been thinking about all of these same things, too, and had arrived independently at these same conclusions.

We talk for an hour in the deepest intimacy—a son to his father and a father to his son—on Father's Day. Finally I tell him for the fifth time that he must go to dinner since he is already twenty minutes late. How much I—who am aware of and can call out by name each separate individual minute that passes by me each hour—finally now envy my father who has always had the rare freedom of having *no* sense of time whatsoever. One either possesses this freedom at birth, or one does not. I am one who doesn't.

We walk together to the dining room, and all along the way people greet my father. He stops and talks to each nurse and attendant we pass, and he introduces them to me, but he forgets all of their names. They play a game with him and give him hints until finally he guesses correctly. They love him. He never forgets them, just their names.

A short distance past the final turn that opens into the cheery dining room whose light comes abundant from the lofty, airy ceiling, my father stops and turns to me. The beautiful, yellow birds in the big cage on the other side of the lounge are singing merrily and seem to be staring instinctively at the sky-lit cathedral ceiling above them as if it constitutes their theoretical, elusive freedom. To be in this spot in this facility gives one hope and seems uncharacteristic of the reality that lies beyond it.

My father takes my hand in both of his, and he leans against me with his forehead like a runner about to cry because he's won the race and it's over, and he whispers in my ear, "I love you, son. Happy Father's Day." Then he trundles off to join his comrades at their dinner table.

I head the other way and feel the gasp of sweet, cool air as soon as I close the front door to Seminary Manor behind me and step alone into the reverie sunlight of the late Sunday afternoon Father's Day springtime.

"Jenny, since talking to you last about my father's fate, I've had several discussions about it with him and several with my mother, and we have reached a decision. You told me he could stay where he is as long as he wants, right?"

"Yes, I did."

"And I told him that. And I told him about the room in the Bounce Back wing that will soon become available. He rejected that outright because it wouldn't be permanent. He hates change. I think he wants to stay where he is, but he's very worried, Jenny."

"He is? About what?"

"He's worried that, to quote him, 'They'll sweep down on me again in the middle of the night and carry me off to a room where I've never been, and I'll have to live there until they sweep down again in the middle of the night and cart me off again. And I hate change.'"

"Ohhhh," she says, sounding genuinely touched by my father's fear. "It wasn't in the middle of the night, Pete."

"I know, Jenny. As I remember, it was after lunch. My father's pretty dramatic."

She laughs. "I know he is. Everybody loves him."

"But he can stay where he is forever, right?"

"Right. Or, Pete, he can decide later if he wants to go to Hawthorne Inn. Or if another single room like he's got now comes up in a different wing—one where the people function at a higher level—he could go there."

"Jenny, that sounds great. Thank you. I'm going to tell him now, okay?"

"Yes, Pete, that's fine. Go ahead and tell him."

I call Blaine at eleven in the morning. His voice is almost inaudible, as if he's had a stroke, the way it is now whenever he wakes up. I tell him I'll call back, but he wants to talk. We talk a few minutes until his voice and his head start to clear up, and then I tell him I just talked to Jenny.

"Who's Jenny?"

"The head of the place where you live. I just told her you want to stay in the room where you are."

"What do you mean, Pete?"

"Do you remember Sunday you and I and Mom went for a ride?"

"Yes, that was very nice."

"And we discussed you moving?"

"Yes, I remember that."

"And you decided you want to just stay where you are?"

"Oh, Pete, you mean I can do that?"

"Yes, Jenny said you could stay there as long as you want or until *you* decide to change."

"In other words, I have all the options."

"Right. And they have none."

"Oh, that's how I like it, Pete. You are so smart to get that in cement. Tell me once more what she said." I tell him. "Oh, Pete, that's just wonderful. To be in the catbird's seat. That's where I always wanted to be in the carpet business, too, but I never was. Now and then they'd let me sit there for a few minutes and dream about how it could be, but then they made me get down right away and go back to having no options. Tell me once more what she said, will you, Pete?" I tell him. "Do you think we should get it in writing?"

"I thought about that."

"Wait a minute. Maybe we shouldn't. It might piss them off, and then they'd come in the middle of the night again while I'm sleeping and sweep me away and tell me it's my only option besides death."

"I don't think they'd do that, Dad."

"Well, let's not ask for it in writing. You never know. Let's just trust that they won't come back and handcuff me and read me my options." He laughs. I laugh, too. "Pete, you are the one who watches over me and protects me from harm, which I'm helpless to do for myself now," he says, although it certainly does still seem to me that he's just as masterful as ever about getting what he wants.

"Okay, Dad, I gotta go. I'll talk to you this afternoon." He thanks me again and again, and then he says, "Pete, before you go, would you just tell me one more time what she said?"

I tell him.

My mother kept all of the records, did the payroll, wrote checks, and balanced the checkbook for our family and for my father's business until he retired and then later for just the two of them. I learned to my shock just a few years ago that my father did not know how to balance a checkbook and that he never recorded checks he wrote. My mother and his employees eventually forbade him from doing it.

At the carpet barn, Blaine was allowed to have only twenty dollars a week to spend and was not permitted to enter anything in the checkbook or the ledger, or rather *fail* to enter anything. He was easily the number-one salesman. But after clinching the sale, he was required by his employees to turn the customers over to Francis who took their deposits and entered their sales into the ledger and made an appointment for them to pay the balance when they picked up the carpet or when the draperies were installed. My father was an astute buyer of carpet, a genius at it, but here, too, after making the buys, he turned over the details to someone else. Otherwise there was never any closure, only chaos, which my father relished. He was able to run an immensely successful small carpet business because he could delegate authority. In was more like "joyously surrendering" or "happily relinquishing" authority to anyone. He only wanted to buy and sell and talk and be totally free, which he almost was.

It is the morning after my birthday, and I am on my way to Chicago with Judy to spend the night and return late the next day. We have no plans—just to rest and experience some sweet inaccessibility.

One hour out of Galesburg, my cell phone rings. It's Tina at Bounce Back. Roberta is having trouble breathing, and a test has revealed that her oxygen level is low. Tina's called Dr. Strauch. He's out of town, so another doctor has ordered a chest x-ray, which will require that Roberta be taken to the hospital. This, of course—without me there—will require an ambulance, and Seminary Manor seems to think they need my permission to call one. I tell them I'm not a doctor, and if Roberta's doctor has ordered a chest x-ray that requires hospital admittance, then so be it; it should be done. Tina tells me she'll keep me informed. Thirty minutes later, she calls me again and says they've decided simply to "watch" Roberta's oxygen level until Monday and then take her (or probably have me take her) to the hospital for an x-ray. I say "Fine." Tina says she'll keep me posted. An hour later, Tina calls me again. Roberta's oxygen level has dropped to a dangerous level, and they've re-called the doctor, who has ordered an ambulance.

The first time Tina called, I had said, "We're on our way to Chicago." The second time I had said, "We're almost to Chicago." The third time I had said, "We're actually in Chicago now!" I keep apprising her of our progress to illustrate to her my helplessness. That way I can also convince myself that turning around, cancelling our single-day vacation of inaccessibility, and returning to the scene of the fury, would be pointless.

I would like Tina to say, "Don't even think of coming back. We've got it under control, and if you did come back, it would be pointless, and you so badly need to have a day of being inaccessible," but alas, she doesn't. The Hippocratic Oath does not provide for doctors to keep the good of the caregiver as a high priority—only the patient's. It is the caregiver's decision whether or not to turn off his cell phone.

Chicago is beautiful, perfect weather—sunny and blue. I lie in bed and look out over the Chicago River and Marina City and Joe Kennedy's Merchandise Mart where Blaine used to go to buy carpet. I remember once a salesman there saying to me, "Your father's style would never work in a place like Chicago." Then Blaine talked him into lowering the price again.

After two hours, I forget about my mother. I go for a long walk. After I've walked two blocks, my cell phone rings. It's Tina. She says Roberta's breathing is not good and that she has pneumonia in her left lung and that they are going to admit her to the hospital. "Is that okay with you?" I tell her again that I'm not a doctor, so she should do whatever the doctor orders.

I'm on the phone many more times before leaving Sunday afternoon early in order to get back to Galesburg to visit my mother in the hospital. I talk to my brothers, my aunt, Seminary Manor, the hospital, and I even have a call from my father. He says, "Pete, tell me something. How's Roberta doing?"

"She's in the hospital, Dad."

"Pete, I know. I was there. I went down to visit her just as the medics arrived with a gurney and loaded her onto it and wheeled her down the hall to the ambulance. I thought she was dead."

"Well, Dad, you probably know more than I do then. I'm in Chicago."

"You *are*? Well, tell me something. How's Roberta doing?"

"She'll be okay, Dad. She just needs a rest. She'll be okay. I'll be back soon, and I'll go visit her."

"You'll be back from *where*?"

"We're in Chicago, Dad, just for the night, we'll be back tomorrow."

"You *are?* Are you having a good time?"

"A great time, Dad."

"Pete, relax and have a nice time in Chicago, and I'll see you tomorrow. You think Roberta's going to be okay?"

"Yeah, she'll be fine, Dad. She just needs a little rest. Don't worry, Dad. She's in good hands."

"Okay, Pete. I love you."

"I love you too, Dad. Bye now."

•

Summer 2008

I visit my mother at seven p.m. and have to wear a mask. I ask a nurse why, and she says, "Because of her recent history of MRSA, we require everyone to wear a mask around her." I'm sure the nurse later regretted saying that, since "MRSA" is the complication my mother picked up in the hospital itself the last time she was there and which the hospital staff referred to euphemistically then as a "Superbug." As a matter of fact, MRSA and Clostridium Difficile infection—C. Dif.—are notorious for being spread in hospitals themselves, purportedly by employees who don't wash properly between seeing patients. Actually, I think this excuse is offered to the public instead of saying the brutal truth: going to a hospital in modern America practically insures that the sick will become sicker, especially those with compromised immune systems, such as older people who are taking antibiotics that wipe out bacteria that fight these "bugs," whose habitat is hospitals.

Roberta is discouraged. I try to cheer her up, but she's a realist and won't buy that pie-in-the-sky stuff like my father will. The next day they move her to the third floor, which is usually a good sign because it's the therapy wing. But she thinks they're simply appeasing her.

I go to the hospital again Tuesday night after my dinner. Dusk is beginning to fall earlier. The sun is heading boldly back toward the next solstice, dreamily unaware that it will eventually be hijacked by the cold winter. My mother is sitting with the light off, staring ahead of her at a blank spot of contemplation I don't remember seeing her look at ever before. I greet her.

She greets me weakly. She is fairly lucid and to me looks better. I tell her so. I think it pleases her even if she doesn't believe it. I sit with her a long time, and then a nurse comes in and tells my mother she needs to do her breathing procedure. The nurse puts a mask on herself and then hooks Roberta to an open tube into which she must breathe. Her breathing spews dry-ice-like smoke from the opposite end of the tube, and the sharply outlined, cold, white fumes look eerie, being silhouetted against the falling dusk in her lamp-less room. The nurse stands beside me and watches Roberta breathe like a fiery dragon—in and out dutifully.

I ask the nurse if she has to work late tonight. She works twelve hour shifts, she says, and even more of them now since Burlington, Iowa—where she lives with her daughter—is flooded. The bridge over the Mississippi River that goes from Iowa to Illinois is washed out, and she has to go south to find another crossing. This results in her having to drive two hours to work and two hours home instead of the usual one hour each way. "During the week," she says, "I just sleep here at the hospital. But I get the weekends off. I can't wait for Friday nights because then I get to see my daughter again."

Finally Roberta finishes, and the nurse unhooks her and leaves. I ask my mother if she wants to walk. She does. She hasn't walked for days. She is so feeble on her walker that I am afraid she'll fall, so I walk a step behind her with my arms ready to catch her as if she's a toddler. She stops every few steps to catch her breath. We walk across the hallway and back, and then I ease her back into her chair. She's pleased to have completed the marathon and is in a slightly better mood when I announce I am going to leave. She looks vulnerable, like a little girl, which is a rare appearance for my strong mother. I stand over her and take both of her hands in mine and, wearing my yellow mask, say, "Mom, you're going to get better. Really. Believe me. Remember when you had your heart operation? I didn't see how you could possibly come back after that, and you did. This isn't as bad as that." She smiles weakly. I lean my head down as if to kiss her on the forehead, and she ducks down a bit like a decent sensitive leper in a colony of outcasts, as if shielding me from her contaminated breath that contains MRSA and pneumonia and Clostridium Difficile. So I kiss her on her curly, white hair. She is compliant and surrenders to my affection.

"You've uplifted me, Pete. I feel better."

✳ ✳ ✳ ✳ ✳

Judy arranges two vases of flowers from our backyard and takes two homemade peach muffins—one for each of my parents. We visit Blaine first. "I'm not well," he says. "I've been trying to call Roberta all day, but I keep getting a recorded message from you, Pete. What's going on?" I cannot get him to understand that when Roberta was in Bounce Back—a concept which he also doesn't understand. "Bounce back from what?"—I loaned her my cell phone with *my* voice message on it. I pull the cell phone out of my pocket and show it to him.

"But where is Roberta now?"

"She's in the hospital," I tell him.

"Why does Roberta live so many places, none of which is with *me?*" He is so happy we've come, however, because we can help him call Roberta. "Where is she now, right this minute?"

"She's in the hospital, Dad."

"What is that number?"

"Dad, I'm sure you've got that number here somewhere. Let me look." I shuffle through piles of notes on his bed table, which he's paper clipped and bound tidily in rubber bands and has put into stacks of ordered chaos to be forgotten. Within ten seconds, I come up with four notes that have the hospital number written large on them—labeled "Roberta, Cottage Hospital"—all of which I've given him in person or over the phone, each time waiting more or less patiently for him to slowly write the number down. Several other notes have my cell number written on them and are labeled as Roberta's number. I throw those notes in the wastebasket, hoping to take away some of his confusion.

I guide Blaine through the steps of calling the hospital and asking for Roberta Gorham, which he does admirably. My mother answers, and he says, "Roberta, this is Blaine. How are you?"

By his facial reaction, I assume she has said, "Not well."

His face melts into worry, and he says, "Tell me everything about what's wrong with you," and I can hear her say, "I don't want to talk about it." He says, incredulous, "You don't want to talk about it?" and she says, "No, and my dinner is coming soon, so I have to go."

"Can't we just talk until your dinner gets there?" She says she has to go and hangs up. My father lies there, staring up at the ceiling with the phone on his chest.

"Pete, what is wrong with your mother?"

"She's sick, Dad. Don't take it personally. She's like that with us, too. She's sick, and she's worried, and she hurts. She's going to get better, though, Dad. Really, she is."

"You think so, Pete?"

"Yeah, I think so, Dad."

"Why won't she talk to me, Pete?"

"Dad, let me make a suggestion. When you call her next time, don't ask her right away how she's doing. Just talk about other things besides her health—anything.

Eventually she'll tell you how she's doing. You're too abrupt when you ask her right away what's wrong with her. It scares her off, and she runs like a rabbit back into her hole." He likes my suggestion; it rings a bell for him. He perks up and asks me more questions about how to talk to Roberta, which I answer wisely.

It occurs to me as I am giving my father advice about how to "reach" my mother, that I am now not just my father's son but am also his father and maybe even his grandfather and his best friend and his doctor and his counselor and his hope. I am also Marty McFly in *Back to the Future* who's traveled backward to 1945 in a DeLorean Time Machine to coach his father about how to court his mother in order to win her, so that his father and mother will fall in love and get married and then Marty can be born.

Every Day, Every Year

There are many heroic and worthy stories that play out silently among the aged that go unnoticed and unheralded. The world in general does not want to pay attention to the end of life. The time for flamboyance and pretension is finished with the aged in nursing homes. Headlines do not focus, for the most part, upon old declining lives that once long ago were relevant and newsworthy, but upon the young and the new, which are rising in brilliance. No one wants to be reminded that the sun also sets and that their own life will end, too, finally—most likely shockingly sooner than they ever could have imagined.

Every day when I visit Seminary Manor, an eighty-five-year-old man and his wife are sitting in chairs pulled together just outside of the front door, resting in the shade of the canopy, holding hands. Sometimes the man is asleep but still holding his wife's hand. She has Alzheimer's disease. She never speaks and rarely changes expressions, but they cuddle closely together as if they just met for the first time two weeks ago and are in the thrill of new love. He comes every day and spends the whole day sitting with her, holding her hand tenderly. He speaks in a monologue to her throughout the day. I greet them both every time I enter or leave the building and pat them on their shoulders as I walk by. She says nothing, but he is always cheerful. Every time I see him, I think with awe, "This man is a nobleman—a lord and a hero."

When I walk my father to dinner, the man and his wife are sitting at the same small table they sit at three times every day, waiting to eat together, holding hands. His whole life is given to her. Even though her expression doesn't change, the expression she keeps is a pleasant one and is lovely and contented. Once I said to the man, "You spend a lot of time here, don't you?" He said, "Well, yeah, but, you know, that's what I'm supposed to do now."

The woman named Eileen, who was my mother's star pupil in 1938 at Frog Pond one-room country school, now drives forty-five miles almost every day to Galesburg to visit my mother. Eileen is now in her late eighties. There is an unbelievable bond that has re-developed between her and my mother. It is heart-warming. Roberta influenced this woman in a transcendent way—when she was just a teenaged country girl—by injecting her with a life force that inspired and sustained the girl throughout her amazingly successful life and career. Her re-connection with my mother some seventy years later—two years ago—has apparently distilled her life and shown her its essence by placing my mother back at the center of it in such a way that Eileen cannot bear the thought that my mother will die. She senses it is happening, though, and so must be with my mother every day that she can.

These and other heroic stories happen invisibly each day amidst dire sadness and tragedy, and they can easily slip away unnoticed. They give me inspiration. They also give me fear, for some reason. They give me tears of profound emotion that I am not capable of labeling—bittersweet tears of tragic ecstasy for something that I am in awe of and terrified of at once, but which I have somehow, for this brief moment of my life at least, made peace with and have been transformed by.

There is good news. My mother has dodged another fatal bullet; she does not have lung cancer. She only has C. Dif and MRSA and, of course, chronic pneumonia, which is what has caused the infection in her lungs that has caused the extreme swelling. However, she's totally exhausted and still can't walk and is uninspired. A test of her blood reveals she's extremely low in immunoglobulins—the blood proteins involved in directing appropriate immune responses. The common word for them is "antibodies." Dr. Soyangco has recruited a new doctor, a cancer doctor, whose mother lives at Seminary Estates, too, to administer three-hour infusions of immunoglobulin several times a month into Roberta's veins. He starts the first one tomorrow.

I visit my mother at Bounce Back late Saturday afternoon, and she says before I can even greet her, "Oh, Pete, I'm *so* glad you've come. I'm so lonely. They've put me in isolation. I can't leave the room. I can't even go to meals. I have to wear a mask." She still has traces of MRSA.

My mother is humiliated and ashamed. I talk to her awhile, and then she asks if I'll take her for a ride in her wheelchair just down to the end of the hallway. I load her into it, and we don our masks and traverse the hallways like two pariahs. I eventually wheel her to the front door so that she can look out on the sunny day and see its pleasant wind gently bending the trees' smaller branches. "You want to go outside, Mom?" She loves the idea. We go through the two sets of double doors and roll by the old man holding hands with his wife and greet them. We wheel down to the parking lot. My mother is suddenly happy. "Real air! How wonderful!"

I meander on the sidewalk past Seminary Estates and into their parking lot where my new truck is parked. I show it to her and take her all around it, opening the doors and demonstrating the amenities. We end up walking perhaps a quarter of a mile, masked in the wind. She is temporarily healed of her malaise and even finally suggests we go back inside to the captivity of her room, which she's ready to re-occupy. I sit down with her and promise I'll get her a phone by Monday morning and offer to give her mine now. She refuses, saying she'll infect me.

My poor mother, a woman whose navigational system could always find true north in a storm and who could always give the sailors upon her deck a solid sense that in the end they'd safely find their way back home, is becoming confused by all of these moves and their attending sicknesses and partial recoveries. She is having trouble finding her legs at constant sea and is losing the kinesthetic feeling of her own life center. So, in a way, am I.

I don't sleep well anymore. The double helix code I inherited from my mother—"The very same Irish blood runs through your and your mother's veins," my father says—somehow seems compromised in me the same as it is in her and has made us both be out of focus, fractured, and misspelled—first in her because of her fading health and then in me because I have her same twenty-four pairs of chromosomes, and I'm heavily entrusted, as her replica, to carry on our genome.

So now, too often, I awaken in the middle of the night into cold awareness characterized by dread and helplessness, hearing the allegorical bay of a wolf close by me where I lie, which symbolizes a vulturous end to all of this.

Throughout each day, I'm driven by an urgency and a single focus to do whatever I can do, like a fireman in a raging storm of flames, to come up in the end with something meaningful from the fire worth saving rather than a heap of ashes soon to be borne away and scattered like dust upon the approaching winds.

My doctor opens the door to her examining room where I am sitting, waiting. She is clutching my folder underneath her left arm, and her right hand is resting on it, too. I can tell by her expression, which is even more serious than usual, that she is prepared to tell me something unpleasant that she's just learned from the EKG report.

It is an art to be a purveyor of bad news. She is a doctor and a woman who tells it like it is, however, and does not have time, she apparently believes, to attempt to be a news delivery artist, as well.

"You have a problem, Peter," she says even before sitting down. "You have what's called a 'right branch bundle block.' It could be serious and life-threatening. If it were up to me, I'd put you in the hospital and begin tests immediately."

The verdict is in! My mother is now innocent of all communicable life-threatening diseases and is free to leave her room without wearing a mask and will be invited to dine again with her fellow Seminary

Manorites in the dining room, rather than eating isolated in her tedious room.

I am walking down the Bounce Back hallway to visit my mother with my dear high school friend Johnny Humes who is here for our forty-fifth-year high school reunion.

Then we walk to my father's room. Johnny follows me into the semi-darkness where Blaine is lying in bed on his back. He seems to be asleep, but he quickly says, "Hi, Pete."

Johnny walks up beside me, and I say, "You know who this guy is, Dad?" Blaine rises up a bit and notices Johnny's white hair and says, "Well, I know one thing. He's old!"

Johnny puts his hand forward for my father to shake and says, "Mr. Gorham, it's John Humes." My father pulls himself up in bed and leans forward and puts his arms around Johnny's neck and pulls my friend to him, and they hug. When they finally release each other, Blaine grabs hold of both of Johnny's hands and says, "Mr. Gorham died many years ago. Call me Blaine."

But Johnny says, "I could never call you anything but 'Mr. Gorham,' Mr. Gorham." Johnny sits down in the chair beside the bed, my father still holding both of his hands. I go sit in the other chair at the end of the bed, and they talk to each other for forty-five minutes, in which time they never let go of each other's hands. Johnny speaks clearly and concisely in telling his amazing life story, and my father interrupts now and then with an exclamation of astonishment or to repeat for emphasis something Johnny's said. Approximately every five minutes, my father says either, "I love you, Johnny," or else "Give me a kiss!" and pulls Johnny's head down and kisses him on the top of it or on his forehead.

One of the many things that I loved about Johnny Humes, which is still in evidence, was that he was a rare teenage kid who could allow his hands to be held by my father for forty-five minutes or to have my father kiss him every five minutes and say, "I love you," and not be uncomfortable with it, in fact, never bringing it up again to anyone, except warmly, as if truly he didn't regard it as bizarre. During a time of my life when it was vital to me to appear to be from a place as normal as any other kid, Johnny Humes allowed it to be.

After forty-five minutes, we leave. As we walk out to the parking lot, I say to Johnny, "Thanks a lot, man, for visiting my parents. It made their day."

"It made my day, too," he says.

Fall 2008

At the heart clinic, I am lying half-naked on my back, waiting for the cardiologist. I am plugged up via numerous slimy electrodes to a huge, sophisticated sonic x-ray machine with an enormous high definition screen three feet from my head, showing every conceivable view of my heart beating currently from every angle, as it has done dutifully—gulp!—more than *two billion times* already in my life—without fail. Through a speaker somewhere, I can hear awesome but rather comforting sounds of my own heart's life force sloshing and glugging around rhythmically like seawater. An angelic woman nurse, who turns out to be the very person who originally set up the cardiology lab here some thirty-five years ago, talks gently to me for much of the time and makes me feel taken care of. The room has a whole wall of windows with sunny light pouring into it in front of a blue sky. It feels happy and bright and cheery. It seems generally to be a place of competence and healing. For just a moment, I can see how one might eventually surrender to this.

Finally the cardiologist arrives—two and a half hours late. He is a cheery Asian man whom everyone seems to love. He looks at the screen and says without hesitation, "Oh, that's a nice picture!" and then he and the nurse exchange opinions about various functions of my heart, which they both seem to be impressed with. They then inject me with the chemical that causes my heart to race up to 167 beats per minute, which allows them to determine its viability. It is odd to have my heart racing at terror speed but not to feel tired or even anxious in the least. I feel like a yogi who has attained enlightenment.

The stress test is over remarkably soon. All of the staff seem satisfied that nothing is wrong with my heart, and that in fact it is quite healthy and strong. I ask them questions about the debilitating pains up and down the back of my legs, about my left forearm that seems to be going to sleep off and on, about whether I might have a blood clot or an arterial blockage somewhere, if my heart valves are all opening and shutting as they should, if what had been diagnosed as a problem in my lungs is the result of a malfunctioning in my heart—all fears that had been instilled, perhaps, by my overactive imagination. They assure me that all of my concerns, which I've inculcated into my own powerful package of dreads, are groundless, stopping short of saying, "You imagined them all!" Those worries had come upon me like a tornado, graphically illustrating to me how fragile life is and also how the mind and the body are tied together into a strange symbiosis of warning and denial.

I leave the heart lab. It's dinnertime, and there is still sun. I am so happy that one of my major organs has been found to be intact that for days and days I bask in the glow of being healthier than I had thought I was. For weeks, I decide not to spend every day worrying about my parents. They feel neglected, of course, but seem to understand remotely.

My mother is living independently back at Seminary Estates again now, making one last attempt to hold on to her freedom. It is my father who seems to be unraveling. Without knowing where Roberta lives or why she lives there, Blaine has persuaded an administrator at Seminary Manor to walk him over to her apartment every day at four thirty and to return thirty minutes later to get him. At exactly five o'clock, even if it's in the middle of a sentence he's speaking, Roberta announces to my father, "Blaine, I've got to go to dinner now!" and saddles herself up to her walker and starts for the door, leaving my father there alone in her living room to wait for his carriage.

My mother has stopped inviting my father to eat with her because he never accepts her invitation. He's told me he's afraid people who know him will ask him a lot of questions, and he won't be able to answer them. So he eventually goes back to his own dining room at five thirty, where he's comfortable around people functioning at a lower level with lower or no expectations.

I stopped by a little after four thirty to see my mother a couple of days ago, and they were both asleep, one on the couch and one in the chair beside it. They told me they had been having a disagreement about something, and my mother suggested that they stop disagreeing and take a nap instead, whereupon they had both immediately plopped down and had fallen asleep instantly.

"How long can you stay?"

"I just got here, Dad. You want me to leave already?"

"I don't *ever* want you to leave, Pete. When you're here, I feel at peace. Otherwise, Pete, I'm afraid."

"What are you afraid of, Dad?"

"I'm afraid of fear itself, like Roosevelt said."

"I don't know what that means, Dad.

"I don't think I'm afraid of dying. I think I'm afraid of living. I'm afraid of tomorrow and talking on the telephone. If you can be right there to answer the phone and explain to them that I can't talk. Pete, I can't cope anymore."

Memory, which is able to coordinate fluidly an infinite array of ever-changing situations from the past and present and to project them into the future, is at the center of coping. Once the flow of memory becomes damaged, one's confidence in coping goes away and leaves one powerless and vulnerable. When this happens, those who've needed to be in control of every aspect of their lives, like Blaine, are faced with the unthinkable; they must surrender control to the object of their trust, if they have it. This is a test of faith in its rawest, most fundamental form.

✳ ✳ ✳ ✳ ✳

"I don't want to talk to anyone, especially on the phone. I don't want them to hand the phone around from one member of their family to the next and have them all talk to Grandpa. Grandpa's not all here anymore. And I don't want people coming up to me wishing me happy birthday and asking me a lot of questions about when I'm coming back and every other thing that I can't remember. I can't even remember their names! Yes, I'm worried about tomorrow—a lot. And every other day, too.

"Pete, I hardly ever do this, but I need you to help me with something tonight." I look at him with grave suspicion, feeling that I should tell him no even before he has a chance to ask the favor. "Would either you or Judy, one of you at all times, stay here with me right through until tomorrow? Is tomorrow my birthday?"

From my deeply imprinted childhood memory bank of mandatory church upbringing and my father's insistent daily reading and rendering of the Bible, these memorable words of Scripture come forth to my lips. "Do not be worried about the morrow, Dad, for the morrow shall take care of itself."

My father's face becomes instantly peaceful, and his eyes become clear. "Isn't that true, Pete? I can't tell you how many times in my life I've said those words to people, some right here, and now I can't even take the advice I give."

I walk over to the table beside Blaine's bed and pick up the big, beautiful, dark-red, leather-bound King James Bible that he inherited from his father. There are countless dog-eared place keepers and notes that mark passages throughout the book. I pick one out; "Let not your heart be troubled," John 14:1, and combine it with mine into, "Let not your heart be troubled. Do not be worried about the morrow, Dad, for the morrow shall take care of itself." The passages seem to belong together.

"That's beautiful. Where does that come from, Pete?"

When I was fourteen years old, our family was chosen by the church to read and analyze a passage from Matthew in front of an audience at a famous pre-Civil War church in Galesburg known as Beecher Chapel. Beecher Chapel was named after the Reverend Edward Beecher, the brother of Harriet Beecher Stowe, author of *Uncle Tom's Cabin*. Beecher Chapel was a significant part of the Illinois Underground Railroad. It was torn down in the early 1960s.

Our family sat on a couch and overstuffed chairs on a raised stage set up in the middle of a second-floor sanctuary. We were supposed to represent a typical late 1950s church family, casually sitting around the living room, discussing the meaning of scripture. We practiced for days, right there in Beecher Chapel, and then at the appointed date we performed in front of an audience of believers from various churches in the city. Our goal was to make it seem as if insights were pouring like fine serendipity wine from our collective religious family heads all at once.

I was confounded by much of the passage we were to analyze. But these words especially confused me: "Lay not up for yourselves treasures on earth, where moth and rust doth corrupt and where thieves break through and steal. But lay up for yourselves treasures in heaven." The phrases "lay not up" and "moth and rust doth corrupt" were beyond me. They were like parts of a math problem that I couldn't fathom because I lacked a fully developed gene. And yet that passage was given to me by my father as the one I should elucidate publicly. After much discussion, I was able to appear to understand and articulate its meaning without truly understanding it. But I was scared because I knew that it would take only a single unanticipated question from someone to defrock me as a fraud. And not only that, I also knew that it was the worst of wrongs to perpetrate fraud not just in the house of the Lord but also by using His own words. So for days before the performance, I couldn't sleep. I read the passage over and over but ultimately couldn't quite get it. However, I ended up going over the entire reading—Matthew 6:19-34—so many times that I discovered these beautiful treasures that my whole life I've remembered at various appropriate times; "Take no thought for your life, what ye shall eat or what ye shall drink, nor yet for your body, what ye shall put on."…"Behold the fowls of the air: for they sow not, neither do they reap, nor gather into barns; yet your heavenly Father feedeth them."…"Consider the lillies of the field, how they grow; they toil not, neither do they spin: And yet I say unto you, that even Solomon in all his glory was not arrayed like one of these. Shall He not much more clothe you, O ye of little faith?"…"Take therefore no thought for the morrow: for the morrow shall take thought for the things of itself."

I read the entire passage to Blaine. He is comforted. I cut a paper towel into a long strip and I write in red magic marker, "Let not your heart be troubled. Take no thought for the morrow, for the morrow will take care of itself" and I place the strip into the book of Matthew, marking it, "Chapter 6:19-34," and I say to Blaine, "Whenever you start to worry or get afraid about tomorrow, I want you to open the Bible and read what I've written on this slip." I read it aloud again. I set the Bible beside my father's bed and turn it toward him and ask him to practice reading it. He does. I tell him again whenever he feels uncertain or starts to worry, to look at the marker and read what's on it. He agrees to do that.

"I've got to leave soon, Dad, but Judy said she'll come out and see you later."

Before leaving the building, I find Carol and tell her the pills are all now safely in Blaine's stomach.

Judy returns home late for dinner and is worn out after spending two hours with my father. In addition to giving him solace, as she always does, she perceptively convinced him to walk over to see Roberta after dinner and to watch Lawrence Welk with her at seven o'clock.

Judy has also gone shopping for various items and foodstuffs for Blaine's party tomorrow morning at Roberta's apartment. Among other things, she's bought him a big "Four" to replace the "Three" in "Ninety-Three," hanging on his wall, which she wraps as his present. She's a bit concerned that she didn't buy him a typical present.

"That's all right," I tell her. "The only thing he really wants for his birthday is to not have to talk to anyone on the telephone. I've tried to make Mom understand that, but she doesn't. To her, it's a sin of the gravest sort not to talk to someone who calls on the telephone. She keeps saying, 'He'll be just fine once he gets over here.' But he won't. He's putting his trust and faith in the two of us to protect him. I don't know what to do. Just pray nobody calls, I guess."

That night, Blaine doesn't call me to come over or to detail to me his fears as I'd expected him to do. His visit to Roberta, which Judy sagely orchestrated, has apparently calmed him down enough that he is able to sleep untroubled.

I call Seminary Manor, and Carol answers. I ask her if she'll remind Blaine to be ready to go to Roberta's at 10:30. But when I get to Blaine's room at 10:45, he's sound asleep. I wake him up, and he is stunned when I tell him we have to go to Roberta's for his birthday party. I wish I could just let him go back to sleep and sleep through the whole day as he wants to do. He sighs and moans and slowly rolls up to an upright position and lets his partial memory slip back gradually into his clouded awareness.

"Happy Birthday, Dad."

"Is today my birthday?"

We arrive at my mother's apartment at eleven, which is fine since Judy is baking her egg casserole in Roberta's oven. The sun is out and shines through the many east-facing windows of my mother's lovely, cheerful nest. While we're waiting, we sing Blaine happy birthday. Everyone seems happy.

"My sister's going to call at eleven thirty to wish you happy birthday, Blaine. They all want to talk to you."

"I don't want to talk to *anyone*."

"Blaine, listen. It's your birthday. These are your relatives. They love you and want to talk to you on your birthday. You need to talk to them."

"I don't want to talk to *anyone*. I can't cope."

"Don't be silly, Blaine. When they call, I want you to talk to them."

Blaine sighs deeply. I look at Judy. She smiles.

The egg casserole is ready to eat at 11:40. With it, Judy serves homemade bread, fresh orange juice, and fresh fruit. For some reason, the phone hasn't rung. My mother's sister is always punctual just like my mother.

"I wonder why Phyllis hasn't called yet," Roberta says.

"Well, let's eat," Judy says. "If she calls while we're eating, we'll just talk to her and eat at the same time."

"That's not like Phyllis. She always calls when she says she will."

Before we eat, Blaine insists upon saying a prayer, which starts out, as usual, "Dear Heavenly Father..." He thanks his Heavenly Father for everything he can think of.

The meal is wonderful. The room is bright. Everyone seems happy. Judy has arranged to have the events of the celebration flow smoothly in a timely manner from breakfast to card opening to present opening to singing happy birthday again to the final act of eating cheesecake with fresh strawberries. Somehow she's able to keep Blaine from spending inordinate amounts of time on a single activity. Our discussions are lively and cogent, and my father has rallied once again and has assumed his rightful place at the center of the festivities, laughing and talking and adding a general overtone and assumption of glad predestination to our little get-together, sure that God Himself had wanted this birthday to happen just the way it's happening.

"I can't understand why no one has called," my mother injects from time to time.

"I don't want to talk to anyone who calls," my father adds each time.

We spend three and a half hours together, and then the natural time comes to end the party, for my parents need to take a nap. I am simply dumbfounded that the phone hasn't rung.

We pack the plates and the remaining food and the presents and get ready to depart. Just before we leave, my mother excuses herself and goes to the bathroom.

Blaine gets on his walker and goes into the bedroom to get his sweater. Judy has a big Cadillac smile on her face as she turns square to me and bounces on the balls of her feet and raises both of her thumbs up in a sign of victory. Then she turns and picks up the phone, and I notice that it's disconnected from the cord that goes into the wall.

"I've got to plug the phone back in now while they're both out of the room."

She laughs and reconnects the wire to the back of the phone with a tiny click. She sets it down and says, "I wonder why nobody called," and laughs again.

"Wow! That's brilliant, Judy! Just brilliant! So simple. So effortless. You gave Blaine the only present he really wanted for his birthday." I stand up and give her a hug and hurriedly gather together my things as Blaine walks back into the room. Judy says, "Let's get out of here before somebody calls."

"Amen," Blaine says. "Isn't that something? Nobody called the whole time. What a nice birthday you planned for me, Judy. I love you. And the phone never rang. Hallelujah!"

Winter 2008

The phone rings at four thirty in the morning. Judy answers it as I pretend to be asleep. I hear the conversation. It's my mother. She's at St. Mary's hospital. She's explaining things to Judy that I happily can't interpolate, but I'm glad she's there and not breathless in her apartment. Judy gets off the phone, and I continue to pretend to be asleep, hoping she'll just go back to sleep herself, knowing my mother is safely admitted to the hospital. But she gently shakes my arm, and I pretend to wake up suddenly.

"That was your mother. She's at St. Mary's and needs a ride home."

"She *what*?"

"Your mother is at the hospital and needs a ride home."

"*Now?* They won't admit her?"

"No. They said there was nothing they could do, that it's the congestive heart failure."

I sigh and begin to move slowly towards getting up, hoping that my mother can wait until I've had a cup of tea at least.

"You mean she wants a ride right now?"

"Well, she says she's not quite ready yet, so wait a few minutes."

I sigh again.

"What's it worth to you if I go get her?"

I can't believe it! My sweet wife is proposing that she herself suffer, instead of me, in the cold and the darkness and with stern pre-sunrise hospital administrators and with my likely grumpy mother. She's asking me only half-jokingly how much it's worth to me. Knowing her, I could probably get her to do it for nothing.

"What is it worth to me?" I ask myself. A thousand dollars? No, a hundred thousand dollars. A million dollars. I'd give my wife a year of my remaining lifetime if she would go out into the cold, dark, five o'clock morning and take my mother back home and let me sleep another hour. "Fifty dollars!" I say.

"Hmmm," she considers, trying to sound only half-interested. But I know better. Despite her considerable success, this is a vast sum of money to her—a girl from a small farm who helped her mother clean houses for extra money—an almost usurious amount of money for what amounts to, basically, a cab fare for a mile ride.

"A hundred dollars!"

"Hmmm. It's sounding better. Will you make me tea, too?"

"You bet I will."

"And bring it to me in bed?"

"Right now!"

I scramble out of bed, go downstairs, and make two cups of Earl Gray tea and put them on a tray. I put two fifty-dollar bills under her cup and carry it up to her.

She picks up her tea and sees the money and snatches it up and starts laughing hilariously and rolling on the bed.

"This is just *crazy*," she says. She can't stop laughing.

Nor can I. Laughing with joy and with thanksgiving.

Another Christmas. A simple one. Dinner with Judy and my parents in Seminary Estates' dining room at eleven thirty. No gifts. My mother says correctly, "At ninety-two, I don't need anything else. Except maybe… well, you know."

Judy goes to my mother's apartment at 10:20, and I walk over to pick up Blaine. Roberta reminded him last night and again just this morning that I'd be there to get him between ten and ten thirty.

Along the way, the nurses are dressed in various festive Christmas garbs and are happy. There is food everywhere, brought by relatives. There is even a huge potluck family reunion in one of the lounges.

Carol is working today…on Christmas. I walk by her at the computer and ask her if she's playing poker. She laughs gently. She's probably never played poker in her life. The computer screen is filled with pictures of various Eli Lilly pills, which she's been studying. I wish her Merry Christmas.

Blaine's door is ajar—a good sign that he's awake. I ignore the "Do Not Disturb" sign that has been permanently affixed to his door—like everyone else does—and walk right in. My father is foraging, which is one of his two most prominent modes of existence now, the other being sleeping. In the foraging mode, he's always on a mission—either to find what he's suddenly remembered having started to look for before he forgets again what it was or somehow to fortuitously remember what it was he started to look for in the first place. Find or remember what to find. There is a constant shifting back and forth in his mind now between these two interrelated but different objectives—like a changing of magnetic polarities. He's still remarkably adaptive.

"Are you ready to go, Dad?"

He looks at me quizzically before even saying hello, as if my question has brought about another awareness of something else he was to do but has forgotten. "Go where, Pete?"

"We're going to Mom's for Christmas dinner."

"We are? Where's that? This is Christmas?"

"In the dining room of the place where she lives. Yeah, it's Christmas."

"You mean we're going to eat with a lot of other people?"

"Yes, but they all know you and love you."

"Okay. You mean one of those dining rooms off to the side?"

"I think so, yeah."

"Good."

"So are you ready to go, Dad?" He starts foraging again, taking tiny, shuffling, but seemingly decisive steps away from his walker (which he never uses anymore in his room). "I'm trying to find something, Pete, if I can just remember what it was. When do we have to leave? Where are we going?" My father is a consummate delayer. He goes into the bathroom.

I notice that all of his flashlights are laid out on his bed table. So at some point, I think, he must have been cognizant that I was coming and got prepared for it. Before he asks me, I volunteer to check the flashlights' remaining battery power while he gets ready. "Oh, good!" I then notice that he's found the flashlight he'd lost, which I'd replaced recently. So now there are two little flashlights, two medium ones, and a big one, which are all necessary tools he uses every night to traverse the six-foot wilderness between his bed and the toilet. To have a low battery in even one of the flashlights is abhorrent and terrifying to him. "Pete, without these flashlights, I'm lost. More lost, that is." Several of them are low. I replace the batteries and throw the dying ones in the waste basket. I make a note to buy more batteries for him. When he emerges from the toilet with his pants still down to his knees, I shine them all in his face, and he smiles a big smile, knowing that tonight will be a worry-free night of peace and light.

"It's ten of eleven, Dad. Mom will be mad if we're late. Doesn't that scare you?"

"Pete, it always scared me, but I was always late, anyway."

"Well, we're not going to be late for Christmas dinner. Come on." I start to pull his pants up, and he helps me and asks me to fasten his belt so his pants won't fall down. His zipper is all the way down, though, which is the way he always leaves it now. He just covers his open fly with a sweater or a shirt. After fastening his belt, he reaches for another belt that is hanging on a hook on the bathroom door and puts it on top of his first one. "Two belts," I say, "One decorative and one practical. Just like you, Dad."

After the second belt is fastened, he looks up at me shyly. "Where are we going now, Pete?"

"To Mom's dining room for Christmas dinner."

"Do I need a coat?"

"No, we're not going outside, just over to her building." I can see in his face that he doesn't quite get it yet. He sits down on the bed and lies back on his pillow.

"Dad, we gotta go. Mom's starting to hyperventilate about now."

"Oh, I know. So is Blaine. We always gotta go. Everybody's gotta go. But I need to talk to you a minute about something. Sit down."

"I'll stand here while you talk, Dad. It's my responsibility to get you to Christmas dinner on time, and I'm not going to fail at it even if I have to drag you."

311

He laughs a big, absurd laugh. "The young, strong man dragging his one hundred-pound, century-old father down the hallway," he says and then laughs again. "You're just like your mother. She was the general, and I was just a general soldier."

My father leans up to a sitting position and looks at me timidly again. "Pete, I don't remember this."

"What?"

"Any of it. I didn't remember it was Christmas, and I don't remember your mother calling. My memory's gone. Pete, don't tell Roberta, okay?"

"I won't tell her. You don't need to remember anything, Dad. That's why you have me and all these nurses and attendants. What you have, which will never leave you, Dad, is the personal power to get others to remember what you need and to see that you get it and employ it properly and timely. And you also have faith that they'll do it, that is, after you've reminded them a hundred times each time you remember again."

"You won't tell Roberta that I forgot, will you?"

"Never, Dad, even if she breaks both my knees." He laughs.

"Let's go, Dad." I put my hand out, and he takes it, and I pull him up from the bed to his walker. I finally have a sense that we're going to make it on time. But first Blaine must go through his room-departure ritual. He checks the shopping bags I've permanently fastened to his walker, making sure his donut pillow is there along with a full box of Kleenexes—not a partial box. He arranges some things on his bedside table, picks up a ballpoint pen, and pockets it. He shuffles over to the mirror and picks up his brush and combs the front of his hair. He always leaves the back tousled, which is probably because he can't see it. He wipes his face with a towel. He wonders aloud if he washed his hands after peeing last and does it again. He dries them meticulously then announces he's ready. But first he must select a sweater from his closet. He has fifteen of them. I help him on with his selection, and then he turns to me and asks how he looks. "Like a prince!" I say. He laughs.

We've made it! He's moving forward through the door to the hallway, out into the world, with a destination. No doubt he'll be distracted again and again on our way, but I know now it's just a matter of time until we get to Roberta's doorstep. I only hope it's before eleven thirty. I feel like a cowpoke herding the last straggling doggy on the last mile home before the sun sets. Immediately outside of his door in the hallway, he greets a bewildered-looking fellow resident passing by, being pushed in her wheelchair. "Hi, honey. Merry Christmas." He waves, and she waves back and smiles a big smile and then disappears right away back into her bewilderment.

Carol's still sitting at the desk. Blaine makes a special move toward her and puts his hand on her shoulder gently and says, "Do you know this sweet girl, Pete?" Before I can say I do, he starts to tell me her name but forgets and then nudges it out of her. Blaine has started to rally amidst the public, to be unafraid to display his vulnerability—his fading memory. His double-belt holds up his falling pants with the zipper unzipped. He puts his arm all the way around Carol's shoulders now and turns to me as if posing for a picture and says, "She helpsa' me, Pete." Carol is busy but takes time to pose with him like a mother with her child.

"I know Carol, Dad. She's sweet, you're right. I think she's your favorite nurse here, isn't she?"

I shouldn't have said this. Words like "favorite" throw Blaine for a loop because they require him to make judgments that imply that some are good and some are not as good, which he would never do or even think. He would never think this first of all because he doesn't believe it but also because, as he told me many times, "No bridges should ever be burned because one never knows if he will need to retreat. Bridges must flourish everywhere in every direction."

Blaine answers in such a way that neither Carol nor I is sure if he has agreed that yes, she is his favorite nurse. But he might have, although not with enough transparency that possibly one could brag about it later and hurt the feelings of all of the other nurses who are also his favorites.

We move on finally into the lounge where throngs of family members are eating with their nursing home relatives. A fifteen-foot-long food table contains turkey dishes and stuffing and candied sweet potatoes and mashed potatoes and gravy and every manner of specially prepared holiday food. Blaine's eyes dart back and forth in the crowd, and he waves and smiles and speaks to them. He suddenly veers off our course into their midst to take their hands and greet them. I can see some of them are confused why this errant nonagenarian is joining their reunion. After some minutes of this, we get back on our trajectory.

There's only one major hurdle left in Seminary Manor—the main desk of the Bounce Back wing, which we must pass by before entering the final hallway that connects his building with hers. This desk is Command Central. Many nurses are sitting, talking, and laughing in permissibly gay, Christmas fun. Blaine knows them all, and they all know him. He introduces me to them one at a time (all of whom I know and have met through Blaine dozens of times before), not remembering a single name of persons he appears to be as close to as schoolmates. They love him and immediately correct his mistaken identifications of them. He tells stories about them all—which are uncannily accurate and some completely new to me—despite forgetting their names. They laugh, and they love him; one combs his hair with her fingers before putting a Santa hat on him. They pin a Christmas decal on his shirt and give him a drink of eggnog.

Finally, some minutes later, I see by the clock above the nurses' station that it is now 11:15. My mother will simply go to the dining room on her own rather than be late. I don't want resentment here, not on Christmas day. I say, "Ladies, we have to leave you because we're eating at Seminary Estates today, and dinner starts pretty soon. Will you excuse us?" Of course they will. They know Blaine. They know everything.

Blaine hasn't a care now; he is totally into and trusting the world that only fifteen minutes ago he was scared to enter. He's got all of the nurses laughing or crying or both. Finally, Linda, dressed like Santa, takes his arm and moves him toward the final hallway, and I move with her and him. Then she lets go of his arm, and he and I are off again on our final leg of the journey toward yuletide reunion. I feel supremely confident that we'll make it to my mother's room in time to sit a moment and talk before launching ourselves toward our destination. There is one more place that we'll be stopped—right after we enter Roberta's building where diners always wait well ahead of mealtime and sit and talk.

Sure enough, Betty sees him and pushes herself up from her chair to get to him before we turn right and down the hallway to Roberta's room. She waddles over and puts her arms around my father and hugs him and says, as always, "I just love this little man," and she tells the story, as always, of how his pants fell down while he was talking to her, and she had to pull them back up for him. We all laugh, as always. I inch him away, as always, and he's glad that I do, as always, for he senses that he's getting near to his wife to whom he'll have been married sixty-eight years tomorrow on December 26.

The clock on the wall says 11:25. We are right on the borderline between acceptance and resentment. As I open the door, I see my mother sitting across the room in the recliner. I call her name in a tone of holiday happiness, hoping her natural sense of duty and punctuality will allow her enough latitude on this day of forgiveness to accept her husband's near-transgression. We're late by the most rigid standard—hers—and certainly late according to our promise—that we'd be there by eleven—which of course my father has no recollection of ever having made. But today, we shall hope, we have sinned only a pardonable sin.

Instantly upon recognizing me and seeing Blaine walking into the room behind me, my mother smiles a huge and happy, uncontrollable smile and says, "Well, here are the boys of Christmas! Right on time!"

This morning I have canceled my work schedule with Jack in order to see Blaine and try to allay what I'm sure will be his growing panic. But I see to my amazement that today he is totally calm and eerily so. As I approach the table, his expression does not change, nor does he even speak until I sit down. Then he shakes my hand. I had expected him to assault me about the state of his deteriorating teeth as he did last night.

"Dad, I decided not to wait until this afternoon to see you. So I canceled my work with Jack in order to come out here this morning."

"Oh? Were you going to come out this afternoon?"

"Yeah. We talked last night. Remember?"

He doesn't remember and doesn't even try to deceive me that he does. "My head doesn't work right anymore, Pete." He reaches over calmly and picks up a piece of paper he's written upon and says, "Let me read you something." He carefully unfolds the paper, stares at it a long time, and then starts singing the words he's written. "I am weak, but thou art strong. Jesus, keep me from all wrong." He sings in a wailing falsetto voice. "Through this world of toil and snares, if I falter, Lord, who cares?" He starts to sing it over again, but I stop him and say, "Dad, how's your tooth?"

"It's okay, Pete," he says nonchalantly with confidence then picks up the paper again and sings, "When my feeble life is o'er, time will be for me no more."

I feel as if I've been pardoned from serving jail time. I had expected that what lay ahead for me this grim day would be to tediously arrange and prepare for the first of at least two dentist visits, which would each take hours and hours and would involve bewildering shenanigans from my father. But for some divine reason, the urgency of Blaine's tooth falling out last night has gone away.

"That's where we are now, Pete, 'Time will be for me no more.' We've come to that time. The Lord prepareth a table."

We rise from the table and move toward his room. At the nurses' desk, my father goes behind the counter and up to nurse Cindi—the woman I talked to several times last night.

He introduces her to me and says, "She helpsa me, Pete. And she's very sharp." I've known Cindi over a year. As he walks away, she whispers to me, "How's he doing with his tooth?"

"He hasn't even brought it up."

"I know," she says, "Let's leave it that way."

By the time I get to Blaine's room, only a few seconds behind him, he's already in bed and covered up. His eyes are closed. I turn out the light above his bed and push his walker back into place and cover his left leg with the afghan he's pulled up sloppily around himself. "Okay, Dad. I'm leaving now. You go to sleep."

"Good-bye, Pete."

I walk toward the door and put my hand on it. I pull the door open and start walking out.

"I love you, Pete."

Spring 2009

I visit my father, expecting he's had time to think about his tooth for two days and wants now to go to the dentist after all—maybe even today. I'm better prepared to deal with it. When I walk in his room, Leanne is there. She is the Seminary Manor administrator who for months has graciously volunteered to walk my father over to see my mother any day he chooses and then to pick him up an hour and a half later. She has just put eye drops into my father's eyes and is saying, "Okay, Blaine, I'll be back in fifteen minutes," as I walk into Blaine's room.

"Hi, Pete," he says to me soberly. "I have a dilemma." He looks at Leanne for help, but she's blank. "This is Leanne. Have you met her?" I tell him I've known her five years. "Leanne was going to take me to see Roberta." He sighs and then spits into a jar he's holding. "But now that you're here, what should we do?" He looks troubled.

"I'll stay here and talk to you for fifteen minutes, and then Leanne can take you to see Mom."

"I'm sure you've called the front desk and talked to them like you always do before you come out to see me, and so you know what's going on."

"I never call the front desk first. I just come out."

"Well you know, don't you, what happened yesterday?"

"No, I don't."

"You haven't talked to the front desk to check up on my condition like you usually do before you come out?"

"No, I never do."

He sighs an ostentatious sigh and then looks at Leanne. "Honey, can you tell him what happened yesterday and last night?"

Leanne looks at me sheepishly and says, "In the morning your dad had an upset stomach, and he didn't go to breakfast. In fact, he didn't eat all day. And then late in the afternoon he thought he wasn't going to make it, and he was very upset all night."

"You mean you thought you were going to die?" I ask Blaine. Leanne nods.

"Last night was mayhem, wasn't it, honey?"

"He didn't get much sleep. He was very anxious."

"Tell him the rest, honey, will you?"

Leanne looks to me as if to say, "I don't know how to say this," so I turn back to my father and say, "Dad, just tell me in your own words what happened."

"Okay, I will. I cried and cried like a baby for hours in front of them all. I couldn't stop crying."

Leanne takes my father's hand and retells the story so that it's gentle and acceptable and then says, "Blaine, I have to go, but I'll be back to get you in fifteen minutes." Blaine won't let go of her hand.

"Before you go, tell me what to do about going to see Roberta. Who's going to take me? Should we all go? Should I stay here? Will it upset Roberta so much when I tell her I cried like a baby in front of everyone that she'll get sick again?"

Leanne wisely suggests that my father should not go see Roberta today at all. I agree with her. She finally is allowed to leave, promising she'll come back to check on him.

I am there with my father who regurgitates the entire spectrum of possibilities with regard to informing Roberta. What becomes clear is that Blaine's main worry now is that someone will tell Roberta what happened before we do, and that she'll be embarrassed, upset, shocked, or maybe even will have lost respect for my father for crying like a baby in front of the staff.

I volunteer to see my mother and talk to her about my father's experiences before anyone else does. "I'll let you know when I've told her."

He grabs my hand. "Pete, I am so grateful for this."

Two hours later, I open my mother's door. It's dark inside. She's not sitting in the recliner as she usually does at that time of day just before dinner. I walk in quietly. The door to her bedroom is almost closed. The light is on. It is rather dark, and I glance at her bed and see the covers slightly raised and crumpled the way they would be if she had gotten up and gone into the bathroom. I stand and listen. There are no sounds coming from the lighted bathroom. I look more closely at her bed and finally realize that the slightly raised covers contain my mother's scarce body, which is now so tiny that it is hardly discernible with the blinds closed. I close the door to her room and start to leave. Then I return and open it again and look at her. Is she alive? I stand and stare at her, wondering, and then I hear a tiny volume-less exhalation of air, which is just enough to scrape the sound waves. I could probably count the number of carbon dioxide molecules departing from her defective lungs and into the stale bedroom air as she breathes.

I close her door and find a blank piece of paper and write her a note, saying I was there. Then I leave, relieved that I don't have to tell her about my father thinking he was dying and then crying in front of everyone.

It's almost spring. The light is lengthy. I go for a long ride in my truck, out past the hospital and north along the curving, two-lane road to the small farm town of Henderson, Illinois, and beyond that into the country, past historical farm homes and barns and animals grazing in the amber late winter fields flanked by rolling woods and creeks. I am lost in the benign wilderness of Midwestern agricultural beauty that has no parallel in America. I am thinking about my past and who I am and why and how I am the result of a line of descent that stretches all the way back to this land one hundred fifty years ago—a line I'll never know how to follow for sure. The self-understandings that I have gained recently, in fact, are more and more confusing.

I take out my cell phone and call my mother. She has just awakened. Her voice sounds as if she's suddenly reentered the world from the world beyond. She can't believe how long she's slept, which is almost through dinner. I tell her I was there and left her a note. "Yes, I just found it. I so wish you had woken me up. I wanted to see you." I tell her I was with Blaine for nearly two hours. "He had a very bad night last night. He thought he was going to die." She is understanding and asks me no particulars. I wouldn't know them, anyway. "He cried and cried for hours. He was most concerned that someone would tell you first—that he cried for hours in front of everyone. He thought you'd be ashamed of him. He'll call you after dinner tonight. I'm sure you'll comfort him about that."

I call my father back and tell him I talked to Mom, and she knows now about last night. "No one else had told her," I add. "She'll call you later."

"She will? So I should just wait to hear from her and not call her?"

"Yeah, just wait, Dad. She'll call you. She won't forget."

"Oh, Pete, thank you. I'm so relieved," he says.

My mother calls later, but I'm gone. She leaves this message. "Blaine called me and explained everything. I told him it was all right to cry. 'But I cried in front of everyone,' he said. 'That's okay,' I told him. 'If you feel like crying sometime, you can come over here, and we'll cry together.'"

Blaine calls at six a.m. He's very upset. "I waited the whole weekend for you to come out, Pete, because I wanted to talk to you, and when you came out, I fell asleep. How could I do that?" I tell him he must have been tired. "No, I waited the whole weekend for you to come out, and then when you did, I fell asleep. I don't know why. I think I was afraid to talk about it, and so I went to sleep." I manage to calm him down and tell him I'll be out there around four. He calls back at seven a.m. and repeats the same conversation. I try to get him to discuss what he wanted to discuss with me, but he keeps avoiding it, telling me he has to talk to me in person. Finally, he tells me he's scared. "Something's going on." He indicates, but only slightly, that he suspects a conspiracy.

I go out to see Blaine at four. Eventually he tells me that Bobbi, his favorite nurse at night, has gone to another area and is not with him any longer. In her place are two new nurses. He is not comfortable with them and doesn't trust them. He keeps hinting about drugs and being drugged. I ask him to give me the nurses' names, but he won't. He repeats that he's scared. Twice he says that it may just be in his head. I talk to him a long time and get him to remember the similar nurse change that happened when he was at Bounce Back and his similar reaction to it. He seems to remember. I tell him it's just change itself that he doesn't like, and that I understand that. He agrees but continues to express fear and says, "I *know* that something's going on," implying that his suspicious nature can detect such things better than others, and there is a design afoot to undermine him in some way. I keep asking him to show me the two nurses, and he says they won't be back until tonight. He asks me to come back. I leave around five, promising him I'll return after dinner, and he can point out the nurses to me then.

I return at seven p.m. Just inside of the front door, I see Blaine walking alone back to his room from the dining room. I join him. He seems fine and is pleasantly surprised that I've just dropped by. Foolishly, I remind him why I'm there—to identify the two new nurses—and he gets anxious. He had forgotten about it, or at least its urgency had receded. The pace of his walking picks up, and what was a gentle ramble back to his room quickly turns into a purposeful after-dinner mission. He's excited by it. I ask him if he can identify the two new nurses, but his purpose is somehow different than mine, as always. He wants to find Bobbi. So we walk the Bounce Back corridor. He sees her go into the room at the end of the hallway. We start after her together. Then he stops me. "Maybe you should go back to my room and wait for us, and I'll accost her alone so she won't feel overpowered." I agree to that, not sure exactly what it means. I go back to his room and sit for fifteen minutes. Then bored, I walk back to the lounge outside of the Bounce Back corridor and wait for him to bring Bobbi.

I can hear them talking out of sight but walking toward me, my father asking her to have a meeting with us in his room. She comes into my view, walking swiftly ahead of him, calling back to him that she'll meet us when she finishes her duties. She disappears into the nurses' room. Blaine comes up to me, frustrated, and repeats that she'll meet with us in his room for a discussion. I'm not sure what we're to discuss. I had thought we were to identify the two new nurses, but my father believes that Bobbi is the key to understanding all of this. He and I head back to his room, but then halfway there, he stops. "Wait a minute! Maybe we need to stay here where we can keep an eye on Bobbi and can keep the pressure on." I dissuade him from that and tell him she said to meet us in his room and that we should do as she wants. He agrees. He starts back and then stops again and says, "Okay, but it could be an hour or two until she gets there." I assure him that I cannot wait for her for even an hour. I fear a circumstance that I've been involved in with my father countless other times—where I am required to wait and wait for some projected set of conditions to arise, which finally never arise.

Now Blaine gets nervous because his plan is not being instituted as he sees fit by any of the parties to it. He doesn't know what to do, and so for five minutes we waver back and forth, literally walking one way and then the other in the middle of the hallway in front of the nurses' station until finally I insist we go back to his room as Bobbi suggested and wait for her. He follows me reluctantly and plops down in bed.

"I'm scared," he says. "I know something is happening. I'm lonely, Pete, and feel isolated. I miss your mother. I yearn to live with Roberta. Something's happening. They're realigning things." Eventually he realizes that Bobbi has not yet come after quite a long time and probably won't return before I decide to leave. "Go to the desk down the hall and bring back the male attendant who is sitting there and have him take my blood pressure, will you?" I resist. "Please, Pete," he says with panic nearing anger, "I can tell my blood pressure is spiked up."

I go to the desk and ask the young man sitting there if he will take my father's blood pressure. The way he quickly consents tells me Blaine has made this request before. Upon entering the room, Blaine introduces me in a way that requires the young man to fill in his name, which is Jerry. He's a sweet guy, tall and slim, and seems athletic and capable and reassuring. He quickly takes Blaine's blood pressure. It's normal. Blaine seems disappointed. "Would you take it again, old friend? I don't think that's right." Jerry assures him that it is, and Blaine instantly returns to his rally mode, asking Jerry to go get Bobbi then, telling him she was supposed to meet us in the room. Jerry naively scurries away to find Bobbi and returns in a minute and says—as Bobbi herself had said—"She's putting people to bed right now but will come after that if she can."

Blaine amends his plan. "How about Jennifer?"

"Jennifer's putting people to bed, too, Blaine. *Everyone* is. In fact, Blaine, you need to get ready for bed."

Everyone at Seminary Manor knows that a discussion with Blaine is never casual or of short duration and must be avoided when their plates are full. Now Blaine becomes upset like a trapped animal. He starts to get up from the bed, announcing to us that he needs to find Bobbi.

Jerry gently stops him and wisely suggests an Ativan, which is the benzodiazepine drug used for treating anxiety that I consented to several months ago that allowed Seminary Manor to administer as needed. Once every few weeks I get an acknowledgment form in the mail from Seminary Manor, telling me they've administered one or two pills of Ativan since the last report.

"I don't know if I want an Ativan. I need to talk to Bobbi." Jerry gently convinces Blaine that his anxiety level is far too elevated to sleep. "What do you think, Pete?" Blaine asks me.

"I agree with Jerry," I say. Blaine takes one half of a pill of Ativan.

Finally an attendant named Missy comes in like an angel. She is calming. As she stands close beside my father and holds his hand, I can see the drug begin to take its effect, and little by little Blaine's anxiety releases. "Will you put me to bed, honey?" Missy nods compassionately that she will.

"I'm going home, Blaine," I say.

"Don't go yet, Pete." I start to resist—I want to go home, I'm tired of this—but he pleads. I often suspect that my father's primary motivation in situations like this is to win. But it's impossible to unravel the truth. His motives are selfish and generous at once. They often concentrate a laser focus and a mule's determination upon gaining ownership of the tiniest spot of turf while at the same instant profligately deeding away the rest of the whole universe.

I wait a while longer, standing behind Missy, who has taken over the primary caretaker role. She comforts my father and holds his hand. He is improving. Sleep will come now, I can see.

"I'm going, Dad."

"Don't leave yet, Pete. Come here, please. Hold my hand." Missy, a nurse with some strength of her own character, is standing submissively beside him, susceptible, allowing herself to be drugged by my father's uncanny love. I walk over beside Missy. My father takes her hand. He takes my hand. He starts to sing.

"There's a place for us, somewhere a place for us, hold my hand and we're halfway there, hold my hand and I'll take you there." Missy smiles. My father starts to cry. I put my arm around Missy's shoulder and whisper in her ear. "Thanks for taking care of my father."

"Good night, Dad."

"Good night, Pete. I love you."

"I love you too, Dad."

Summer 2009

Judy is worried about Blaine. He's not in his room when she stops by in the afternoon to see him, but arrives momentarily. He's been visiting Roberta. "He is very confused," Judy tells me at dinner. She suggests we go out again and visit him tonight.

We arrive at his room at around seven forty-five. He greets us without cheer then excuses himself and goes into the bathroom and stays for fifteen minutes. I have come to realize that my father's incessant disappearances into the bathroom when I arrive involves more than simply pooping or peeing, although that is always part of his plan. He seems to be able to gather his otherwise elusive thoughts while sitting alone on the toilet.

Blaine feels comforted whenever both Judy and I are there. He opens up more directly in her presence, though I seem to be needed there, too, as a catalyst.

My father lies in bed and stares up at the ceiling. His profile is entirely different than it was just a year ago. It's now hawk-like but also handsome with a wise introspective intensity not there earlier in his life.

The only light on is the table lamp between Blaine's bed and Judy who is sitting in the recliner. I'm in a chair at the end of his bed as an audience in the darkness. The lambent glow from the table between them helps inspire with its dusty peacefulness a monologue from my father, which is really quite coherent and precise, especially considering how unglued his mentality often is now.

"Most nights just before bed, a nurse comes in and gives me a shower. I have now begun to fall asleep during the shower, taken over as I am by a feeling of euphoria, which is so wonderful that I lose consciousness. I also have this same feeling when I go to sleep. In fact, knowing that by going to sleep I will experience this feeling of ecstasy, I am finding myself wanting to sleep all of the time like when you were with me the other day, Pete. That's the thing I mainly want to do now other than take a shower—go to sleep. When I sleep, I go to a place so far away and so still and so benign that it is disappointing to return. I see a lot of my relatives there, not dreams of them or hallucinations, but *them*. They are real. I'm not dreaming. Often after I do return, I discover that I have peed the bed, which is mortifying to me. I feel like a virgin on the verge." He laughs. So do we.

I can't imagine any attendant or nurse there giving him mind-altering substances without my or Dr. Strauch's approval. No doubt such transgressions have taken place in similar institutions. In fact, the prevailing and disturbing sense one has in a nursing home is that most everyone there is in a drug stupor. However, Blaine has no recollection of having received any but his regular pills, the last of which are given at four p.m. The Ativan is only given occasionally, and it is closely regulated.

Blaine then gives us a textbook description of the allure of ecstasy, of the craving of the experience of well-being, which can rarely if ever be had with such a high quality feeling of well-being in any other ordinary worldly endeavor but maybe as a religious experience or a death experience. "It's this that has me most frightened," he says, "this war between my will to be independent and disciplined and in control and my true desire now as an old man to let go and to float off into perpetual bliss."

He says that the struggle he's having with whatever this bliss represents is between respecting himself, which he admits is now "just a senseless snare" and being truly happy. "When we are young," he says, "we know that bliss won't be perpetual because someone's eventually got to pay the fiddler. But when you're almost ninety-five, the fiddler is willing to fiddle for nothing for the short period of time you've got left just to keep everyone happy."

He finishes his descriptions and says, "Has what I've said made any sense at all to the two of you?"

Almost simultaneously, Judy and I speak a resounding, "Absolutely."

"Dad," I say, "it's okay to feel euphoria no matter what's causing it. You're at a point in your life where you deserve to feel as good as you can as often as you can. That's all right. Don't feel guilty about it."

"Thank you, Pete. Pete and Judy, I need to tell you something else. I am having more and more dreams about heaven and the end of life and the pleasant feeling of being asked by angels in chariots to climb aboard and ride away with them and leave this world behind."

By the time Judy and I leave at nine fifteen, Blaine is calm and ready to go to sleep. Aside from telling us he loves us, he says only one more thing.

"What I long for is Roberta."

Roberta is asleep in her recliner. She looks peaceful. She is smiling fondly, lovingly. She looks radiantly elsewhere. I sit down on the couch next to her and say in a voice slightly less intense than usual, "Hi, Mom." It is usually enough to wake her, but she doesn't move. A pleasant thought occurs to me that she has died and gone to heaven and has left behind upon her lips an expression of the last clearly wonderful thought that she had on earth before shuffling off her mortal coil.

I sit a moment longer then repeat my greeting. Still she doesn't move. Then she opens her eyes, and I speak her name again. She turns and looks at me and smiles and reaches over to get her hearing aids. Having them in her ears, she then permits herself to apologize to me.

"I have quit the Zoloft again," she tells me. This time—I know my mother—it's final. She gives me the formula for her decision. "My stomach was constantly upset, and I had diarrhea."

The medicine's true rewards, of course, are in the future, as it takes at least two weeks for the anti-depressant to begin to work. I might try to persuade her to give it a little longer and at least experience the desired effect of feeling happy before deciding to give up. But I know her. The decision has been made. There will be no going back again—ever.

"I don't really think I was depressed anyway."

She *was* and is depressed. She has been depressed a long time. Her sister has pointed it out for several years now as Roberta's life has wound down. Her sons- and daughters-in-law have noticed it, and her husband, too, in his oblique way, and others. Finally, I had talked her into taking the anti-depressant. She had taken one pill to appease me, and then she had quit. In a needy moment, I'd talked her into trying Zoloft one more time. She's done it for a few days this time. But now it's over. Her attitude is like someone's who has gone to Vegas with the goal of gambling only until they've lost a predetermined amount of money.

Actually, I'm not sure anymore that my mother is even constituted to feel as good as the Zoloft might eventually have made her feel. She has said, "I don't want to lose control." It seems that being happy for my mother has become tantamount to being out of control. After all, happiness is ecstatic, and what is ecstasy if not "standing outside of oneself in a state of being beyond reason and self-control." And she'll have none of that, thank you. To her, loss of control, however it's defined, is not worth putting up with for *any* price. Were she to get out of control in the wrong way, she might even invite Blaine back to live with her.

Happiness is fleeting. Self-control is forever.

Fall 2009

It is Blaine's ninety-fifth birthday!

All of the relatives are here from around the country. We have carefully planned a simple event in the "Green Room," which is a pleasant lounge just down the hall from Blaine's room.

My mother is in Bounce Back again after having spent nearly a month in the hospital with pneumonia, MRSA, and the "Super Bug." Her doctor solemnly informed us of these various, continuing maladies just after performing another bronchoscopy, gravely pronouncing her, as he did a year ago, "one sick woman." He "vacuumed" her lungs again, pulling out gobs of mucus and other infectants, which is enough to allow her to breathe on her own for a while without using oxygen twenty-four hours a day. She is one sick, angry, depressed, and lifeless woman. Kathy, her newest paid helper, was her only interest. Kathy was willing to serve her for an inestimable (and almost inhuman) number of hours each day, answering her ringing bell and serving her every whim. This was even while she was in the hospital where the hospital itself provided around-the-clock care.

When my mother was to be released from the hospital, I advocated strongly—against my own better judgment but at her insistence—for her to return to her apartment. Kathy stayed with her twenty-four hours a day for two days. And then Roberta had to go into Bounce Back when Kathy had to leave for a few days. My mother was afraid to be alone through the sleeping hours of the night. It seemed clear to me that her days of independence were over.

Blaine was thrilled that his wife was in Bounce Back just down the hall from him in the very same room of Bounce Back that he had been in. I tried to explain this concept to him over and over again, trying not to sound too positive about her being near him permanently.

He developed a pattern of seeing her. He would wander by her door sheepishly during the day and look in to catch a glimpse of his wife of sixty-eight years, hoping she'd see him and beckon him to come in. She did, occasionally. But she was one sick, angry, tired, depressed woman, and he got the hint quickly. After his supper, he often visited her again. His eccentric ways quickly annoyed her, however. Her only goal was to return to her apartment at Seminary Estates. Having surrendered to old age and dependence nearly two years before, Blaine couldn't understand why she wanted to be independent in her condition. "Why does she want to go back there?" he'd ask me.

It is with this backdrop that we feel the need to emphasize simplicity in regard to Blaine's ninety-fifth birthday. And, of course, we also feel the need to "keep it simple" because Blaine himself cannot seem to remember, first of all, that there is going to be a party and secondly what the significance of the party is. At least ten times he has said to me, "Now, what is this big event coming up?" He says it not with cheer but with trepidation. He dreads even the slightest deviation from his highly structured routines. And more than anything, he does not want anymore to be the center of anyone's attention except Roberta's.

It is not hard for me to understand, therefore, when the twenty or so guests arrive in the Green Room on Monday, October 19, at six thirty p.m. to celebrate with Blaine his ninety-fifth birthday by honoring him and opening presents they've brought for him and having birthday cake and even a few speeches, that Blaine is not there!

"Where is Blaine?" everyone wonders. He's not in his room, he's not in Roberta's room, he's not wandering the hallways, and he's not in the bathroom. He has not shown up by seven p.m.

I decide alone to walk to his dining room, which is empty except for him. He is sitting in the corner, having just been served his supper. This would mean, ordinarily, that he would be in the dining room for at least another hour.

"Dad," I say. "The party's started."

"Oh? What party?"

Twenty minutes later, a battalion of helpers, each carrying a couple of the many dishes that he orders at each meal and studiously picks at for an hour and a half before abandoning, arrives with Blaine in tow at the Green Room. We sit him down at a table in the center of the group where he will converse with anyone and everyone until after eight, when we must insist upon serving the simple fare we'd planned of birthday cake, even while Blaine continues to eat his cold, imported supper one molecule at a time.

After dinner, various people stand up to salute Blaine with touching speeches on his behalf, and he makes a few speeches of his own. One of them is a long and rambling soliloquy about his ninety-year-old friend and former employee Dobbie, his right-hand man at Blainie's Carpet Barn. The two men stand holding hands, both of them nearly in tears, heaping accolade after accolade upon each other, reminiscing incomprehensibly about the good old days in the carpet business. Dobbie was his boatswain on the pirate ship.

By nine, the halls of Seminary Manor are empty of residents, who've all gone to sleep. Only nurses remain who occasionally stop by the Green Room to offer their best wishes to Blaine and to implicitly urge us on. Soon after that, people start leaving the party. Finally there are just a few of us. Blaine hasn't yet opened even a single present, and there is a pile of them three feet tall. My father is tired. I suggest he say good night and go to his room, which he's happy to do, and that we'll open the presents tomorrow.

Winter 2009

I have insisted that my mother's sister and my brother attend the Seminary Village staff meeting with me to evaluate my mother's status. It is my belief that they are going to tell us that Roberta cannot go back to Seminary Estates because by their definition (or almost anyone else's) she cannot live independently. I want the others with me to hear it themselves and to comment upon it, if they wish.

That's what the staff tells us; she cannot go back. I ask them four different times to repeat it, so that I know unequivocally that that's their will. They all agree. They tell us to tell the front office.

I call Seminary Manor's front office the next day, and they assure me that at least two if not three of them have informed Roberta.

"That's not true," my mother states. "Only one of them told me, and that person said I'd have to go to Hawthorne Inn. I'd rather die than go there. I'm not happy about this. And I want Seminary Estates to tell me the verdict themselves, or else I'll demand to have an ombudsman. In fact, I just may get an ombudsman anyway." They arrange a meeting.

The word comes down through the grapevine to my brother that there will be a representative from Seminary Estates, one from Seminary Manor, and one from Hawthorne Inn present at the meeting. They will all tell her unanimously that she can no longer stay at Seminary Estates.

We arrive at my mother's room at the designated morning hour. The staff has failed to tell my mother there is to be a meeting! When we tell her, she is appalled to have been slighted, and rightly so. When they arrive, the first thing my brother points out to them is that they failed to tell my mother. They apologize profusely. Jenny sits next to my mother and bravely takes her hand and weakly begins to tell her the verdict. Verdicts should never be handed down weakly, especially to someone like Roberta, and especially while holding her hand. My mother begins arguing her case by pointing out that, "There are others at Seminary Estates who also have helpers, some at night even. In fact, there is one woman whose husband never goes to dinner and is hardly ever seen. The wife brings him his meals. Another woman, who sits at my table (and I'm sure you know who I'm talking about) is the mother of a prominent local doctor. She has fallen six times and is still there." Roberta says they are picking on her and mentions the word that terrifies institutions—discrimination. She also mentions that she has heard good things about the new care center out on Linwood Road and that she will go there and take Blaine with her rather than come here to Seminary Manor. My brother and I sit silently in the shadows and listen, amazed at our ninety-three-year-old mother's still-adept mind, performing youthful feats of reason and memory even though she's practically deaf. The staff begins to melt, not with warmness but with uncertainty in their own confidence. The only addition my brother and I make is to point out to the staff members that they have an obligation, first of all, to lay out precisely what the rules are and show where they are clearly set forth in a document that would be available to anyone. And secondly, they must enforce them evenly.

By the end of the meeting, the staff has waffled. They give her a possible "second chance" but insist that unless she can prove her ability to be independent by heartily embracing physical therapy (which she hates) in order to improve her locomotion, they will return to the position they had earlier and insist that she not go back to Seminary Estates.

We do not try to explain this all to Blaine, who will only become confused by it.

Judy calls me from Roberta's apartment. My mother's helper, Kathy, has called her at work because she found Roberta "not very responsive" in the morning. Judy hurries to Seminary Estates and concludes that Roberta has had a massive stroke. She can't speak more than one or two words at a time before her thought abandons her. Her eyes are bulging out like frogs' eyes.

They call an ambulance and rush her to the ER. Judy calls me on her way there and tells me to stay home. I am grateful for that. I don't know what I could do for her now in the ER, nor do I want to be in a hospital two nights before Christmas. I turn on the Christmas lights in the house and on the porch and outside in the front yard, and I sit in the recliner and take in the silence and the moment of relief from responsibility.

At seven, I walk into the hospital's emergency room. Judy is there with a nurse. My mother is struggling to speak and understand between falling asleep in exhaustion and waking up in confusion. I am sure, as well, that she's had a stroke, and I believe I will never communicate normally again with my mother. I am ashamed that I suddenly feel bathed in release—my own as well as my mother's. I say to myself, "Dear Lord, please take her now."

Judy stays with her for six hours. I stay for four until they take her to the intensive care unit and tell me to leave. No one listens to me anymore when I say, "I don't think Mom will be alive tomorrow," but I say it again and believe it.

I'm wrong again. It is eight in the morning. I'm at the hospital with Judy. My mother can say a few more words now, but her talk sounds insane. She thinks she is in a new residence and that they tore her other room down in order to build the new one and that they moved her here. She's not sure why, but she's heard them talking in soft voices, and she caught just enough of it to know that there is a conspiracy underway, and that it's taking place right here in the motel. What she cannot get straight is why they would tear down the perfectly good building she was in and build this one. We gently try to straighten her out, but it seems to confuse her more since my mother has such a hard time accepting that what's going on in her head at any time is not reality.

The next morning, both the doctor and the nurse have decided that Roberta did not have a stroke. They tell me with shaky conviction that with old people, sometimes infections can cause confusion, and she has pneumonia in both lungs and severe infection there.

That makes some sense to me. It's like a nation (her body) that has only a few hundred aging soldiers left to fight an invading army of thousands of twenty-year olds. Obviously, they'll need to call up the National Guard to help fight, most of which are ninety-three-year old brain cells who will have to temporarily abandon their regular duties (like thinking more or less clearly).

The nurse tells me the doctor wants to perform a bronchoscopy at nine thirty, which is the third one in a year, to clean out my mother's lungs. Obviously, he feels her current situation is life-threatening since he wants to perform a life-threatening procedure upon her. The nurse asks my opinion. I caution her that I am only Roberta's pseudo-physician, but I tell her I think they should do it, and I comment upon how much better my mother felt the other two times.

Roberta seems to remember this, too, which is a testimony to her uncanny memory. She tells me that she doesn't think, however, that they should do the procedure again so soon, but if I think they should, then she will consent to it. I have become accustomed now to making life and death decisions on a dizzyingly frequent basis. "Yes," I tell her. "I think you should."

The nurse who called me wanted my permission, as well. So do another doctor and another staff member. By the time I actually consent in writing to my mother having a life-saving procedure done, I have been unofficially asked for my permission for it by five different people at five different times. I humbly suggest to them that if they could reduce the number of times they had to ask permission, perhaps they would be able to start life-saving procedures more quickly.

Judy leaves. Just then, an army of nurses and assistants wearing surgery attire enters the room, carrying equipment and pushing carts full of tools and tubes. One of them tells me that the bronchoscopy is going to be done right there, now. I look at the clock. It's nine thirty. "What amazing dispatch," I say under my breath. "How rare in the medical world! How Teutonic!"

I tell my mother I'm going to see Dad. She begs me to tell him not to call her like he did last night at ten o'clock, right in the middle of all the commotion. I say I'll return later after she wakes up from the bronchoscopy. I promise her she'll feel a lot better. She takes my hand and smiles tenderly and thanks me again. My mother is always given comfort by knowing how, why, when, and where.

I tell Roberta before I leave the hospital that I'm not going to leave with Judy for Christmas as planned—that I'll watch after her, instead. I assure her that the next time I see her she'll feel much better.

I can sense that my caretaking batteries have only a bit of life left and no quick way to charge them. But for obvious reasons, I need to stay in Galesburg for Christmas, as depressing as it is to contemplate eating Christmas dinner at Seminary Manor or in the hospital.

I go home to rest. It's snowing. I'll need to see Blaine. The poor man's been without contact with his wife for days. Their sixty-ninth wedding anniversary will be December 26, although he will have forgotten that, most likely.

I get to Blaine's room at 4:15 and spend an hour and a half with him, finally walking him down to his dining room. Half of the time is spent talking about his not being able to take two dumps a day and me trying again in vain to explain to him why that is, changing batteries in his five flashlights to get him ready for Christmas Eve, and getting him ready to go to dinner. The other half of the time is spent clarifying the issue of calling Roberta tonight. Basically, I tell him not to call her because she's had a breathing procedure today, and she'll be very tired and possibly not feeling well. He resists understanding that and continues to obfuscate and say, "Pete, would you write that down for me?"

Finally I say, "Dad, here's all you need to remember. Don't call Mom tonight."

"What's tonight?"

"Tonight is Thursday. Christmas Eve."

"*Tonight* is Christmas Eve?"

"Yes."

He looks pleasantly astonished. "Which day of the week is it?"

"It's Thursday."

"Write that down. 'Don't call Roberta tonight—Thursday, Christmas Eve.' What about tomorrow? Should I call her on Christmas?"

"Let's just see how she feels, Dad. Okay?"

"How will I know whether to call her or not?"

"Just don't call her tonight. Period. And don't call her tomorrow either unless I tell you it's okay."

"Would you write all that down, Pete?"

"I just did, Dad. It's right there on the pad." He reads the pad out loud, slowly. I tell him he has to go to dinner.

"Pete, Pete, before we go, I want to get this straight in my mind what I'm supposed to do about not calling Roberta. See, Pete, I'm lonely. I want to talk to my wife of…how many years?"

"Almost sixty-nine."

"Almost sixty-nine years. Pete, when is our anniversary?"

"The day after Christmas."

"When is Christmas?"

"Tomorrow."

He looks stunned. It's *so* complicated.

By the time we get to the dining room, I and the nurse who'll put my father to bed tonight have written so many things on the pad in his pocket—literally several pages of notes—that he will never understand what to do or not to do. But he'll forget it all very soon and ask someone else to tell it all to him again.

"Pete, you have helped me *so* much tonight. I will not call Roberta tonight, and I feel okay about it. I won't call her until you say I can. When will we be talking again so that I can ask you if I can call her?"

"I'll be in touch tomorrow."

"You'll come out? What time?"

"I don't know, Dad. I'll be in touch tomorrow, though. I promise."

My father releases his hold on his walker and stands upright, unassisted, and proud like a new toddler—confident enough to try but not quite confident enough yet to know for sure that he'll succeed. He walks over close to me carefully, walker-less, and then falls into my arms and bows his head against my chest and says, "I love you, Pete."

"I love you too, Dad."

I walk out into the cool winter air in the deserted, circular driveway in front of Seminary Manor where the snow has stopped falling, and the ground is fluffy and welcoming, and the city lights are Christmas-colored everywhere and festive below a nearly full moon in a stray and starry sky. I stand in front of my truck and feel an almost overwhelming sense of delirious freedom overlain with a caretaker's delight at having accomplished the mission of giving proper and wholesome care. It is Christmas Eve, and though I'll be alone tomorrow and without my wife and with no prospect of a jovial optimistic Christmas celebration, I don't care right now. I just want to feel my free will and my liberating abundant health and my mind recalling as it should the suitable ordering of things past and present and things to come and to cherish feeling them properly aligned for as long as it will last.

At 8:15 on Christmas Eve, I return to the Intensive Care Unit of Cottage Hospital. One must either dial the code or call on the intercom to gain access through the locked double doors, and then there is another set of double doors. This is serious business here in intensive care. From what I can see while walking to my mother's room—number seven—there are only one or two other patients here, and they seem to be comatose. It's very quiet. A nurse hurries up to me before I get to Roberta's room and says, "Your mother is using the commode right now. Do you want to wait over there?" There's no waiting room—visitors are not encouraged here because it's so intensive. So I stand at the far end of the long, square nurses' desk and wait.

A long time passes, and then I hear someone say, "Are you through, yet?"

My mother answers, "No, and I can't finish with you hovering over me."

"Well, you have a visitor."

"Oh, I don't *want* any visitors. Who is it?"

"It's your son."

"Tell him to just come in."

The nurse is short and has reddish hair and smiles a sheepish smile as she tells me I can go to my mother's room now and talk to her while she continues to try to have a bowel movement. I reluctantly follow her. Roberta is in her gown that is hiked up to her waist and sitting on the commode. I quickly wonder if I will ever be unembarrassed about having people visit me in a hospital and watching me try to have a bowel movement.

I greet my mother and ask how she's feeling, hoping she'll say, "Marvelous! Never better! You were right!" but she doesn't. She complains first about the iniquity of being interrupted all the time in the midst of a bowel movement by insensitive intensive care nurses. Then she starts again on the conspiracy thing. But I interrupt and ask if she's breathing better. "Well, yes, I am," she says and is surprised and maybe even slightly pleased to have recognized it. She cannot get it straight in her mind what is going on with the condos and the time shares and all of that, and she's very upset with an outburst she claims to have had with one of the nurses.

Apparently my mother needed Depends in the night, and the nurse supposedly told her she was not allowed to use them in the hospital. She corrected the nurse, saying she's used them there many times. She finally threatened to expose the nurse's abuse of her to higher authorities.

The nurse had eventually walked away from her and had told the other nurses she was quitting and stormed out. My mother could hear them all plotting behind the desk, and she had thought they were also probably drinking because it was New Year's Eve. Then, of course, she had to bring up the new construction and why they didn't just leave it the way it was. She grabs hold of her bed railing and shakes it and says, "Look at this, how shaky it is, and it's supposed to be brand new!"

I don't remember ever having spent a more dreary and negative Christmas Eve moment that seemed to foretell no potential for gaiety.

I spend thirty minutes explaining to my mother that she is having hallucinations and that this is the same building she entered two days ago, not a motel; it is the same room she's always been in—number seven. She's confused, I tell her, because of the infection in her lungs and also because of the medication she's taking. I tell her she is in Cottage Hospital where she gave birth to me. I describe all of the corridors and additions until she has a veritable epiphany of understanding and goes slack with life-giving comprehension. I convince her that she's been wrong about all these things and these good people. She happily accepts this from me but keeps insisting that the nurse was abusive to her and that she is going to turn her in to the ombudsman of the hospital.

A tenuous peace has just crossed my mother's face and seems now that it will reside there at least until morning. So it is with regret that I must take this opportunity to tell her what I have just decided this moment in the intensive care unit of Cottage Hospital on this night of Christmas Eve: "Mom," I say, holding her hand and about to leave, "I am going to Royal tomorrow to be with Judy and her family. I haven't been there for a long time, and I want to see them all." Actually, I have to say it in pieces repeatedly until she at least understands the gist of it. She sighs. I knew she would, and I have steeled myself against succumbing to guilt by rigidly convincing myself beforehand that I have a right to experience joy on Christmas even if it's selfish and thereby violates the very spirit of the day. I am sure that I cannot find Christmas cheer there in IC.

To my surprise, she takes my hand and literally pleads with me to stay in Royal for the night. I can see that she genuinely wants me to go, at least for the moment. There are tears in her eyes as I leave, promising her I'll come see her in the morning before I leave.

I drive the few blocks home in the twinkling, colored Christmas Eve lights past the magnificent Victorian and Queen Anne mansions that seem to have been put upon this earth for this night to shine their prismatic glory throughout the eventide and give hope for greater things to those who drive and walk by—the hope of Christmas and its Eve.

I return from Royal to Galesburg midday. It's snowing again, and I drive slowly, not being anxious to return. Just on the other side of Peoria, I remember something vital. I call my father who rarely answers his phone, but this time he does.

"Hi, Dad. It's Pete." He's happy to hear my voice, and we say a few things. He seems to be doing okay.

"Dad, today's the day after Christmas. You know what that means?"

"It is? Christmas was *yesterday*? Where are you now?"

"I'm coming back from Royal. Remember I went to see Judy's family?"

"Yes I do. Did you have a nice time?"

"I did, a wonderful time. I'll tell you why I'm calling, Dad. Today's your sixty-ninth anniversary, and I wanted to remind you to call Mom."

"Oh, Pete, I'm so glad you called to remind me."

"Call her right now, Dad, and wish her happy anniversary right away. She'll be so impressed with you."

"I'll do that, Pete. Right now. You think it's okay to call her now, huh?"

"Yes I do, especially because it's your anniversary. If the first thing you say to her is, 'Happy Anniversary,' she'll be happy you called no matter what else might be wrong."

"Pete, that's a great idea. Thank you so much. I am so glad you called to remind me."

"Okay, Dad, I'll see you tomorrow."

"Wait a minute, Pete, before you go. Do you know what Roberta's number is?"

Judy and I discuss Roberta's options. They aren't many. She refuses to go to Hawthorne Inn. She will not take therapy again; therefore, Bounce Back is out. Kathy cannot spend twenty-four hours a day with her at Seminary Estates, and she recognizes that without Kathy's constant help, she can no longer live there *independently*. So essentially, her choices are two: live in a private room in Seminary Manor or live in Seminary Manor in a room with Blaine. When Judy says, "Your father spends so much time in the bathroom! I don't think they could share a room with only one bathroom," I know that for that reason alone—and there are many other reasons—we must get her a private room even though their funds are shrinking low. My proud and proper, dignified mother would collapse being around my father's severely advanced shenanigans all day long. At least earlier in their marriage, she could require Blaine to confine his antics primarily to Blainie's Carpet Barn. But here, in the same, small, constricted room amidst their equally strong final and selfish resolves to survive at nearly any cost, there would be a constant menagerie of wild things going on around Blaine that would quickly take an even greater toll upon her.

Roberta is sitting on the side of the bed as I enter her hospital room. She smiles at me and offers a harmless greeting. Today we shall take her to Seminary Manor nursing home to her own small private room, which is just down the hall, it turns out, from her husband of sixty-nine years. Amazingly enough, she has decided this on her own. She does not seem to be bitter but is prepared to begin this last chapter of her life in Seminary Manor nursing home. Not once does she complain. On the ride back to Seminary Village, sitting on the seat beside me, she volunteers, "Pete, I need more help than Seminary Estates can offer. I need a place like this where there are people on duty day and night to help me. I just can't live alone anymore."

This is not how I had envisioned it happening, but it will represent a reuniting—my parents, married sixty-nine years now, and having been separated for the last two and a half years, will occupy separate bedrooms just fifty feet apart in the same "home," sharing life together in most principal ways.

My father will be ecstatic when he finds this out. My father will be utterly confused when he finds this out. My father will be renewed when he finds this out. My father will be scared when he finds this out. For days and days, my father will be totally obsessed with trying to apportion the indivisible good and bad of this into separate understandable units. He'll be over-energized and overwhelmed by what's going on here. What does it mean?

I don't want to be the one to try to tell him I understand what I think it means and to have to trudge ponderously and tripping like a drunk through the boggy, snarled network of his twisted and severed cerebral connections.

I pull away from Seminary Manor in the early afternoon alone in Judy's car, and I drive slowly toward home, having told my younger brother Bill and his son Chris and Chris's wife Amber and Roberta's helper Kathy, all of them sensitive and compassionate and compliant souls who've come to help me, that I need to go.

"Would you guys please explain all of this to Dad?"

It must have been the drugs they gave her at the hospital for anxiety that made her compliant. Within one day, after they've worn off, my mother hates Seminary Manor. She has become hostile to Judy, to my brother Bill, who came heroically to help us move, and to everyone else.

Bill has supported us unequivocally and has counseled us that we have to start taking care of ourselves and that no one else could possibly do more for our parents than we've done. He's intervened in vital ways for us and has helped us for four entire days to physically move her numberless personal items that give her identity once again. We have moved her and Blaine so many times that it is hard to remember them all.

There will be no money left for my parents in about another year, and they will have to go on Medicaid and become wards of the state. My mother seems to be in denial about all of this. We are worn out over my mother's endless dissatisfaction with her life now and everyone in it and with my father's tireless needs—physical, material, and emotional—and his instinctive, automatic manipulations.

Now my mother only sleeps. When she wakes up, she gives orders to her helper, Kathy, whom she's hired to sit with her for four hours a day seven days a week. Often she sleeps the entire four hours while Kathy reads or watches television. She constantly haggles with Kathy, which is sometimes in an unpleasant guilt-engendering way, to have her come for more hours or for split shifts—two hours in the morning, two in the afternoon, and several more at night. This, in effect, means Kathy has no life of her own. It is amazing to me how skillful my gravely sick mother is, through the use of her personal power, at getting what she wants.

Blaine is barely in the picture now. Although he lives only about one hundred feet from his wife and stops in her room to see her fairly often but only briefly, going to or coming from the dining room, she gets little comfort from him and is mainly distracted by his presence. She never goes to see him or requests that he visit her. They do not eat at the same table in the dining room, but they are within sight of each other.

It was said by Charles Darwin that more important for survival than intelligence or even strength is the ability to adapt. Next to the definition of *survivor* in any dictionary should be a picture of Blaine. He is not bitter that his wife of sixty-nine years no longer accepts him in her room or that she doesn't eat at the same table with him or share with him her woes or her happiness—which is rare now. He is not angry that where he is now seems to be an improper reward for a life well lived in accordance with religious and ethical principles. Rather, he considers it a rare and wonderful gift that he was given ninety-five years of life. He does not feel embarrassed or shamed or belittled that his principal powers have vanished and he is now dependent upon others. He was always glad to be dependent upon others. He is indeed sad, but it's not a sadness that could infect his entire outlook or the life that remains to him or that could cause him to become immobilized by depression. Rather, he has adapted, in an elastic Darwinian sense. Whenever his name is mentioned by anyone—a nurse, an aide, a doctor, another resident, or even another resident's visitors—it is followed by statements of praise and love and amazement. Everyone is inspired by him and is given hope for their own old age. He is truly a template that everyone seems to want to be like in a similar situation that they probably fear will befall them sooner or later. Blaine has not surrendered or given up his power—only apparently. He has found new applications for it; he has adapted. He has not become imprisoned by his situation. He has fit it to his new set of circumstances. I'm not sure you can teach someone how to do that. I think it's a power my father had at birth that made him a great salesman of carpet and of everything else imaginable. Basically, Seminary Manor has become for my father Blainie's Carpet Barn II.

My brother Mike is here to help me with various legal and financial details. His visit also relieves me emotionally by his automatically stepping into a primary leadership position of responsibility, which I gladly surrender to him for the duration of his visit. During our long and detailed discussions of any and all things relevant to my parents' conditions, one subject comes up that we had never even thought of. Its new emergence into the light of relevance seems to foretell finality—funeral services and expenses.

Our parents' money is dwindling. In their lifetime they achieved almost unbelievable financial success, considering that they both grew up in the Depression and were both from relatively modest, working class, uneducated families. However, the money they made was not enough to provide for them both to live to be nearly a century old.

Mike is here to help me determine what lies ahead for our parents. It is not realistic for them to maintain two separate private rooms at the nursing home and for my mother to continue to employ a helper for up to forty hours a week to essentially duplicate the services of the nursing home. However, it's their money. Or rather at this point, it's *her* money since my father has dissociated himself entirely from pecuniary concerns.

Mike and I have slightly different perspectives about all of this—his being generally more compassionate but mine being sometimes existentially more accurate.

I tell my brother that the funeral expenses for each of our parents will be approximately $10,000 in my opinion. And I tell him this should be deducted from the money they have left. Otherwise, we shall inherit these costs. This will mean that our parents will have to give up their private rooms a few months sooner than they would have had to anyway. Then they will have to choose either to live together in a single room or to each have a roommate. At first my brother is against even bringing this up to my mother and tells me he will pay the $20,000 himself if he has to. That's noble of him. And it might be considered ignoble of me to refuse to do so.

The funeral director whom we meet with suggests that it is permissible by the IRS for us to prepay the funeral expenses from our parents' remaining funds. He says without hesitation that this is what people almost always do, even suggesting that it is ethically and morally incumbent upon people to pay these expenses themselves while they can rather than burdening their heirs with them. This changes Mike's view to mine, and he decides firmly that we need to discuss this with our mother, too, and to present it to her as a further deduction from her funds remaining. He is not of the opinion that we should strongly encourage her to get rid of her helper Kathy, however. While not sharing his opinion entirely, feeling instead that all choices are simply no longer available to our mother, I finally agree with Mike's opinion that the solace that Kathy gives her is vital at this time of her life. This makes compassionate sense to me even if it results in both of our parents becoming wards of the state sooner. I am also of the opinion, however, that without Kathy to align with, our mother would bond sooner with the good helpers at Seminary Manor.

Roberta has agreed to meet with us late Sunday morning to discuss these financial matters. My brother has offered to be in charge of the meeting. He is a natural diplomat, uncommonly fair minded, and willing to adjust to suggestions that are amenable to the conjugation of fairness, compassion, and reason. So his skills will be called upon.

Our mother's room is too hot as usual. I boldly walk to the wall heater and turn it off, which is something I could not have gotten away with doing even a few days ago. But now, she is not aware of the real world.

"Something is happening," my father had said prophetically a few days ago, and then his voice had trailed off, not because, I suspect, he had forgotten his thought, but more likely because he had not been willing to put it forth out loud and make its possibility real to himself.

Judy stands up like a commander and points a clear direction, saying to my mother, "Roberta, let's wash your hands, okay?" My mother makes a slight almost indiscernible nod of acknowledgment, which probably anyone other than a commander would be afraid to assume with my mother is a nod of approval. Roberta's face is blank and unreadable. There is no longer anger or criticism or even pain from it except the pain that comes to a clear and exact person when she's been overridden by uncertainty.

Judy walks to the sink and runs the water a long time until it gets hot and then wrings out the washcloth and walks it quickly to the opposite side of my mother's bed before it cools off. She picks up Roberta's left hand decisively but gingerly, with the strength that she simply has innately and through which she is able to transmit confidence magically. My mother complies and surrenders her hand to Judy's. The hand now has no extra flesh whatsoever—just the microscopically thin, Saran-like epidermis that covers her bones that barely is able any longer to protect her against even slight assaults from her environment. And yet the hand is still beautiful and a composition of long, elegant, slow, blue lines of gentle and patient wisdom. (She used to play the piano.) She lays her hand trustingly on the altar of my wife's palm. The two hands touch each other tenderly for the second time in mutually allowable sensuousness.

The first time was last night. It was a different circumstance then (they change so dramatically now). Last night my mother was positive that she was going to die. She was telling everyone good-bye and that she loved them: Antonio, her wonderful nurse; Kathy, her faithful helper; and all of the attendants who came by to see how she was doing, knowing she was fading out. Last night her face was radiant as if she'd seen a vision. But tonight it's different.

Earlier this afternoon, she had said to Judy, distressed, "Have they told you?" Judy had said no and had asked her what it was. "They told everybody. Everybody here knows now. They're going to put me in an insane asylum." Judy assured her that it wasn't true and that she was only dreaming. Then she asked Roberta if she wanted her hands washed with hand cleaner. Judy had cleaned them then for the first time, which was a symbolic act of obedient service.

Judy rubs my mother's hand gently on the front and the back sides with the warm washcloth while holding Roberta's hand in hers. My mother's eyes begin to close upon the peaceful feeling Judy has administered to her. I can't remember the last time I have seen such serenity cross my mother's face and stay.

Judy finishes the left hand and places it down softly on my mother's lap. Roberta looks at her and smiles a bit with thankfulness and pleasure. Then Judy gets up and walks to the sink again and runs the water hot and wrings out the cloth and returns to my mother's far bedside. She picks up Roberta's other hand and performs the same service. By now my mother's eyes are closed completely in glorious relief. I am so enthralled that I cannot even blink and lose a tenth of a second of this stalwart performance that is bringing about some kind of conclusive self-forgiveness.

Judy starts to put my mother's right hand down next to her other hand, but Roberta doesn't want to let it go, and so they silently agree to hold hands a moment longer a few inches above my mother's lap. Then Judy stands up and goes back to the sink and runs hot water one more time and then returns to my mother's side. She says, "Okay, Roberta, let's do your face now," and she gently caresses my mother's transparent skin with an intuitive pressure just enough to create pleasure without causing pain. Perhaps no one has ever been allowed to show my mother such tenderness before.

At the end of the washing, there is a radiance upon my mother's face I've not seen for years. We talk to Blaine who is sitting quietly in the corner on the recliner, watching intensely like me. He appears ready to fall asleep from partaking vicariously of the luxurious pleasure given by my wife, taken by my mother, who is now sound asleep in ecstasy.

"She's not doing very well, is she, Dad?"

"No," is all he says.

"We're going to go now, Blaine," Judy says.

"So am I," he says and instantly struggles to get up.

I walk next to my mother and take her tiny, bony, purple forearm. Her eyes come open, and she looks at me. "Hi, Mom, it's Pete."

"Oh, my goodness!" she says with unexpected pleasure and surprise. "Are you Pete *Gorham*?"

She can't be serious. "Yes, Mom, it's me, Pete Gorham. I'm your son." Her expression changes to something else, like confusion, and her lips speak a word or two I can't understand. I don't probe her more. "We're going, Mom." She says something. "We're going home."

She's trying to understand. "I'm home," she says.

"Yes, you're home," I echo. I'm not sure if we've communicated anything, but I hope so.

Then I stroke her forehead tenderly. I feel her thin, gray hair around the outside of my hand, and I put my hand into the midst of it upon her head and lean down and kiss her on her forehead. Her hair is silky and baby soft but still wiry like her mother's, whose people were from the Madeira Islands, which is part of Portugal but is closer to Africa. I've always suspected that someone in her family ventured off to Morocco by ship and met an African there and that they had children who show up in my family now and then with kinky, curly hair.

"It's okay, Mom," I whisper to her.

Spring 2010

I have written this e-mail to Dr. Carl Strauch:

Carl,

I am getting very worried about my mother. She is out of it—in a permanent way now, I think—over and beyond the drugs she's taking (Ativan, steroid, antibiotics, whatever). Once again she is in a downward cycle of partial "recovery," which will lead again, no doubt, to her return to Seminary Manor (or simply staying lonely and lost endlessly in the hospital) and then, I would think, to her quick decline again. I am not capable of knowing what to do next. If it were up to me, I'd put her on continuous morphine, which would take her consciousness and her pain away permanently and soon her life, too, which is now awful. She's afraid, confused (clarity has always been my mother's lifeboat!), and panicked. Judy and I ourselves are wearing out from this intense situation. Mom does not want to live anymore and keeps telling everyone that. If we were able in this country to treat people truly compassionately at this point in their lives—when there should be some sort of "gathering" at the end—rather than making the end be a nightmare of unthinkable proportions, it could be a benign and even pleasant passing. Whatever you can do in this regard to keep her from what I see will be the inevitable scene at the end of her life—gasping desperately for air and suffocating to death—I beseech you to do it.

Blaine is sitting in Roberta's room in the corner in her recliner. There are no lights on—only light from the hallway. Antonio comes in to remind my father to continue his journey to the dining room. "Okay, old buddy," Blaine says and reaches for Antonio's hand. Antonio takes Blaine's hand gently in both of his and drops to the floor on his knee in front of Blaine and leans forward with his face close to my father's. (This is a good and compassionate man, being genuine in his concern for old people and artistic in his care giving.)

"Blaine, Roberta's not here right now, remember? She's in the hospital."

"Oh, she is?" Blaine says, maybe not because he's forgotten but because he would never say, "Yes, I know."

"I stop by here on my way to meals just to be near her," he says to Antonio.

"I know you do, Blaine, but it's almost twelve thirty, and they'll close the dining room soon, so let's go on up there and eat, okay Blaine?"

"Okay, old buddy," Blaine says while struggling to get out of the recliner, being pulled up by Antonio's hand, which he's still holding. "I sit here in the recliner, and I say, 'Dear Lord, just let her return so I can see her one more time.'"

He stops halfway upright and chuckles and looks Antonio in the eye and clasps his other hand around Antonio's wrist in a gesture of trust and says to Antonio, "I've bartered with the Lord my whole life, but now I've got nothing left to give Him, so I just have to ask if He'll do me one last favor."

"I think she'll come back, Blaine. Don't worry. But now you have to go to lunch. Come on."

"Do you think so?"

"Yes, she'll come back."

"Okay, old friend, that gives me a reason to eat again. Let's go."

Judy visits Roberta in the hospital. She is asleep as she usually is now most of the time. She is down to eighty pounds in weight and is taking prednisone and an antibiotic for the chronic bad infection she has in her left lung from pneumonia, probably the same pneumonia she had at Christmas, which never goes away now. She's also taking a serious pain pill and sometimes

Ativan. One or both of them are causing her to have hallucinations in addition to the natural hallucinatory characteristic of dying. When I visited her the day after she was admitted, she saw a giant spider running across her ceiling and asked me if I could see it, too. I said I could. Then she pointed to the corner and said, "And over there, look at all those reptiles. Those crocodiles!" I'd promised her I wouldn't let them bother her. She'd laughed a little at that.

She commonly waves her hand slowly in front of herself gently and gracefully as if conducting an invisible orchestra. Her hands are swollen and a ghastly blue bruised color. When she's not asleep, she's detached or only semi-rational or angry or in pain or confused or scared, sometimes gasping for breath. She would like a family member or Kathy to be with her all of the time. When I arrived early one morning after having been with her the night before, she was livid, saying, "Where have you *been?* I need you here *all* the time!"

The best thing to do, Judy's discovered, when sitting with her—rather than trying to communicate—is to hold her hand. That soothes her and puts her into calm sleep. When she wakes up intermittently she looks over and smiles at the one clasped to her and then falls asleep again. Wholesome energy sparks across the synapses between the touching fingers—the laying on of hands. My mother's hand twitches constantly now as do various other muscles and tendons in her upper body. This is probably because they are crying for oxygen, which only one lung cannot provide now but which it heroically tries to do. She occasionally squeezes down hard on the visitor's hand, displaying an uncanny muscular strength still. It is a reassuring squeeze, which seems to say, "Please don't let go!"

But finally Judy must go. At the right moment, as my mother sleeps, Judy slides her hand away imperceptibly from Roberta's. My mother is soothed enough not to notice, and Judy leaves the room and the hospital and drives to Seminary Manor.

At three p.m., Blaine is asleep. But his eyes are half-open, which is a sign that he can be or is prepared to be aroused easily from his sleep. Judy speaks his name. "Who is it?"

"Happy Saint Patrick's Day, Blaine."

"Is this Saint Patrick's Day?"

"Yup. You're Irish, aren't you, Blaine?"

"Well, honey, I married an Irish woman. Does that count?"

"Yes, it does, and it also allows you to listen to the Irish music I've brought for you. So you just lie back and close your eyes, and I'll put it on."

"What day *is* it?"

"It's Saint Patrick's Day. It's Wednesday, March 17."

"This is *March*?"

"March 17, Blaine. Saint Patrick's Day."

"The winter's over, isn't it?"

"'Tis, laddie!"

Judy walks to my father's open closet and retrieves the CD player that Roberta gave him several Christmases ago, which he's never used himself. She plugs it into the wall beside the recliner and holds it upon her lap. The CD she puts on is "The Long Journey Home." It was taken from the television series by that title and is a beautiful, heart-wrenching tale of the Irish migration to America during the potato famine.

The first song is "Shenandoah," sung poignantly by Van Morrison. It grabs Blaine's attention.

"Oh Shenandoah, I love your daughter…Oh Shenandoah, I'll be your lover…Oh Shenandoah, I'm bound to leave you."

In the great Irish mass starvation between 1845 and 1852, which was caused by a potato blight, a million people died, and another million left Ireland—Skibbereen. One was my mother's paternal grandmother, Mary, then just a girl.

Oh father dear I oft times heard you talk of Erin's Isle.

Her lofty scene and her valleys green, her mountains rude and wild.

They say it is a pretty place wherein a prince might dwell.

Oh why did you abandon it, the reason to me tell?

One-third of the Irish population was entirely dependent upon the potato for food. Twenty-five percent of them left their homeland to escape starving to death and to find a better life.

Oh dear, I loved my native land with energy and pride,

'Til a blight came over on my crops, my sheep and cattle died.

The rent and taxes were so high, I could not them redeem.

And that's the cruel reason why I left old Skibbereen.

My mother's grandmother was named "Mary Delaney." She sailed across the sea to America in the belly of a ship in "steerage," the lowest deck, the cheapest fare, the most wretched conditions, next to the control lines of the rudder. Those in steerage were crammed together like cattle going to slaughter and forced to stand in the abominable stench of neglect and disrespect with no air or sunlight and miserable food from a common cauldron. The trip took three months. Many didn't survive the journey to America, but Mary Delaney did.

"*Oh, my Mary, long we wait here, while the hunter combs the mountain high, and the soft wind whispers 'Guard her,' Though as hunters we must die.*"

"That's just beautiful, Judy. Did you say this was Saint Patrick's Day?" my father asks.

"That it is, laddie!"

"Judy, this is so nice of you to bring this music here on Saint Patrick's Day. You knew Roberta was Irish, didn't you?"

"Of course, Blaine. That's why I brought you this Irish music."

"And did you know her grandmother came to this country from Ireland, and that she came over here by ship, in 'steerage'?"

"I did."

"Can you believe the determination and the strength it took to do that?"

"Is that where Roberta gets hers from?"

"Yes, I think so."

"Oh, the dawn is long time coming, and the long night clings with care, but they shall not find with their chains to bind my Mary, pure and fair."

"Judy? Do you think Roberta will come back here?"

"Yes, I think so, Blaine. She's like her grandmother Mary. She'll make it across the sea."

"You're right, Judy. Thank you."

So I had to leave from my country of birth.

And for each child grown tall another lies in the earth.

And for every rail we laid in the loam.

There's a thousand miles of the long journey home.

At the end of the last song, Blaine is spellbound and at peace and falls to sleep easily.

Blaine is asleep in Roberta's recliner. Contrary to my fears, it was a painless transfer of my mother from the hospital back to her room at Seminary Manor. She looks relatively peaceful, asleep again. I turn to Blaine, and he wakes up, and we talk in whispers. He is distressed, I can see. I say, "Isn't it great to have Mom back, Dad?"

"Yes it is, Pete. But she won't talk to me."

"Well, Dad, she's tired. She's just made a long journey home."

I turn to my mother and take her tiny wrist in my left hand, and I stroke her forehead gently and put my face close to hers. She opens her eyes, and they suddenly look astounded with ecstasy. "Hi, Mommy. It's Pete, your son." She smiles a smile I don't remember ever having seen come across her lips. It's a pure smile without any inhibition at all...like a child's. Her eyes are sparkling and focused on some essence of me I'm happy to be able to reflect somehow.

She says in a voice of glee that's understandable, "Is it *Pete*? Pete *Gorham*?"

"Yes, Mom, it's me, Pete Gorham. Your son." Her face is aglow in ecstasy as if she's entered Heaven and I'm greeting her as Saint Peter. I turn toward my father and point to him and say, "And look over there, Mom. There's Blaine."

She looks in his direction, and he waves and calls her name and she says, like a school girl fallen in love for the first time with a boy in her class, "Oh, I just *love* Blaine!"

"Mike's coming back tomorrow, Mom, to see you."

"Where is he?"

"He lives in Colorado, remember?" She looks blank, maybe because she is now living in a time of memory in another place, and maybe there in her mind, Mike, her oldest son, is still living with us in our childhoods.

In no time, my mother falls back into a deep sleep, and I tell Blaine I'm tired and going home. "But first I'll walk you to your room," I say.

At his room, my father convinces me to talk a moment. I can see that he is troubled. He lies on the bed and closes his eye and covers himself with the quilt, leaving his tennis-shoe-covered feet outside the covers. I sit in the recliner in the corner. We're silent a long while. Then Blaine says, "Tell me, Pete, what's going on?"

"What do you mean, Dad?"

"I mean, why is everyone rushing toward climax?"

"What does that mean?"

"I mean, why are Mike and his family coming back here all of a sudden?"

I give him an anemic and harmless response about them wanting to see Mom. "I know what's happening here, Pete. We're all waiting for *Godot*, aren't we?"

✳ ✳ ✳ ✳ ✳

Judy and I meet with the nurse from hospice in the Green Room, the lounge where we had Blaine's ninety-fifth birthday. She has copious brochures and policy guidelines and handouts to explain and to give to us. She also has copious patience and wisdom and gentle humor and compassion and all of the things one would hope from hospice. At one point I say, "We would like to leave this in your hands now to decide what to do at each stage of her death. I am not qualified any longer to make those decisions. Frankly, my last decision—to put her in the hospital—would not have been my choice, but it was borne of urgency—she was gasping for air. No one here knew what to do and relied upon me, who didn't know what to do, either. She wants to die, and I want to let her now, and I trust you will make it be an experience as painless as possible."

My brother Mike and his wife Mary have been here for two days, from Colorado, offering to help us. This offer of theirs is merciful and timely and relieves us of great burden, but still we cannot fail to visit my mother daily.

I am in the country at a beautiful, peaceful farm owned by a friend to whom I have just delivered a package. My cell phone rings as I'm talking to her just outside of her spectacular barn.

It's Judy, who's with my mother. The hospice nurse Amy is there beside her exactly as I'd hoped she'd be in the event of an emergency. She has asked Judy to call me, the medical power of attorney for my parents, to authorize beginning to give morphine to my mother, who is in great pain and whose breathing has suddenly gotten worse. I authorize it over the phone and then drive to Seminary Manor.

My brother and sister-in-law and Judy and Amy are all there in my mother's room. Amy is explaining the procedure and that the morphine, a very small amount at this initial stage that is administered orally and rubbed on the inside of her cheek, will not only help to take away her pain but also to improve her breathing. Amy is young but decisive and has profound compassion, which seems to be the most essential part of hospice, whose purpose it is to provide the maximum possible comfort—physical, mental, and spiritual—to people who are dying.

Amy also decides to remove Roberta from most of her medicines except the heart medicines and the antibiotic, saying that, "It doesn't make sense at this point to load her down with medicines designed for long-term effects, does it?"

When Amy leaves the room while my mother sleeps, Judy and I decide to visit Blaine. He is sleeping when we enter his room, but Judy speaks his name, and he wakes up in a daze. He thanks Judy over and over for bringing the music the other day, which was "absolutely wonderful and soothing." The next thing he says is, "How's Roberta?"

I am tired and have closed my eyes already, having selfishly taken the recliner in the corner not only for comfort but for detachment. I don't answer, but Judy does. She is able to honestly hint at being concerned about Roberta while clothing her statement of concern in a pleasing attire of hopefulness. So when Blaine asks if his wife is dying, Judy's skill at presenting potentially unpleasant possibilities benignly is just what's needed at that moment, and I am pleased to be left silent in the corner and out of the discussion, until Blaine says, "What do *you* think, Pete? Is she dying?"

I could only answer that question one way, and so instead I say, "You know, I don't think I have anything to say that would do anything but detract from the discussion you've already had." I have told my father on at least one other occasion in the last month that, yes, I thought Roberta was dying. He had asked me because he knew I would speak frankly, which I did. But now the way Judy speaks should prevail. There is no need to belabor the somewhat cold factual nature of what is occurring now to my mother.

"I don't want to say anything that would insult you in any way," my father says, "but I think you are keeping things from me to protect me from the truth. However, I think that now is the time of the Ostrich." He continues misquoting from Lewis Carroll's *The Walrus and the Carpenter* and mismatching and commingling images of birds flying into the boiling sea and cabbages and kings and oysters and pigs with wings. But he is nonetheless quite remarkably still able to remember the gist of the long poem, which to him has always signaled the *end*. "The time has come, the ostrich said, to talk of many things…"

"Dad, I think that was the walrus, not the ostrich."

"Yes, the time has come, the walrus said, to talk of many things."

Judy appropriately re-enters the conversation before the actual subject of my mother's death is dwelt upon and puts closure to it by talking euphemistically and hopefully and non-conclusively, which Blaine seems happy to accept in that form and without the final seal he'd asked for.

We part on that good note.

Judy and I and Mike and Mary all gather in Blaine's room to discuss his requested but unnamed subject.

Our father lies on his bed and stares up at the ceiling. We have opened his draperies, and the afternoon light is pouring into his room from the courtyard and bathing us in a good feeling of timeliness. The four of us are sitting on metal chairs surrounding the foot of his bed, except for Judy who is sitting in the corner in the recliner.

In a rare instance of bluntness, Blaine says directly to no one in particular and therefore to everyone or to anyone who'll answer, "Is Roberta dying?" No one answers right away as if we are all paying deference to each other's privately held opinion. Finally I assume priority since I have been, by default, the primary caregiver. I answer in a manner as uncharacteristically diplomatic for me, even evasive, as Blaine's question is uncharacteristically blunt. The room is silent again.

Then Blaine repeats exactly the same question. Mike answers it this time, only a little less evasively than my answer.

Blaine asks the same question again, but this time his voice is more plaintive than before, trying to tell us, perhaps, that this subject must be addressed fully truthfully right now in all of its dreadful certainty and its cold, steely facticity—in a way that Blaine has *no* natural ability at nor any comfort level with—since he himself has seen the truth of Roberta's situation and needs to know if we will confirm what he's seen.

Mary, Mike's wife, speaks next. She is a devout Christian who often provides spiritual comfort and acceptance to those who are facing death either directly or in regard to the death of someone they love. It is she, more than any of us, who knows what to say to Blaine now.

Her voice is strong and unwavering but tender. It also has a sense of finality about it, implying that it will resolve the question that won't need to be asked again, at least not in the same way. "Yes, Blaine, Roberta is dying. We just don't know when." Mike and I have said something similar but more ambiguously, lacquering it with hedges. However, Mary, for the first time, says it unequivocally.

Whatever leaves a body and a consciousness as it dies—the theories vary but not the accurate observation of it—for the most part has already, it seems clear, begun to take leave of Roberta. Something remains, but it appears to be the body still alive and still soldiering onward as long as her soul's shadow will partly inhabit it.

Mary adds this comforting thought for Blaine, gesturing around her upper body with both of her swirling arms toward an invisible canopy surrounding her, "I should correct myself, Blaine. Roberta's body is dying. This tent, Blaine, that surrounds her soul, is dying."

Mike and I go early to Seminary Manor. A thin, young, new nurse named Julie is standing over our mother, taking "vitals." Her extreme youth is at once reassuring and alarming to me. Her body language speaks concern.

We sit down. Julie doesn't speak to us yet. Her body's been blocking my mother's face, but finally I look around it, thinking Roberta is conscious, but she's not. In fact, she is not just totally unaware but is slack and leaning like a rag doll the way someone might be who'd passed out from exhaustion. She looks very different from just yesterday. Her eyes are sunken, and her mouth is a circle that is pulling in air delicately. Her nose seems longer and thinner, and her eyes are pacific and have surrendered. She has literally turned into someone else overnight. She looks now a lot like her own mother did at her end.

When Julie is finished with her testing, we ask how Roberta is doing. Without offering a conclusion, she says, "We took her off morphine this morning because her blood pressure had gone to eighty over forty, and her respiration was low."

"How low?" I ask, knowing I'll immediately have to ask next, "What's considered normal?"

"It was down to five this morning."

"What's considered normal?" I ask Julie.

"Between fifteen and twenty."

"Is that five breaths per minute?"

"Yes."

Reflecting for just an instant upon my own breathing, it is hard to imagine sustaining myself with just five breaths per minute, especially five shallow, volume-less breaths like my mother is taking as we speak.

"That's not good, is it?"

"No. That's why we took her off the morphine. We called hospice first, of course, and they agreed. She doesn't seem to be in any pain."

My first reaction is a minor form of anger, which I don't share with anyone, of course, because they might consider it insensitive. Had they left her on the morphine, she would probably die soon or be dead already. That's what she wants, and she has begged us for it fifty times. It's what I want, too. The indignity of her situation is enough in itself to have shorn her of the will to live—to say nothing of the pain and suffering, both physical and mental, or of her imprisonment in eighty square feet of a nursing home.

Like all professionals, Julie seems genuinely honored that we are interested in her chosen profession and that we obviously know more than an average person about medicine and are articulate enough to pose relevant questions to her and acknowledge her expertise. So she explains to us in great detail what is going on. Her language points toward the imminent end of our mother's life and what to look for as signs of that. Roberta has many of these signs present. To take her off the morphine does not reverse the process; it only slows it down.

When Julie leaves, I walk beside my mother's bed and take her hand. It is cool now, which is one sign that life is holding on to its last moments by gathering in the campfires of warmth from whatever outlying cantonments can be sacrificed, so that the last remaining executive soldiers—the brain—can dispatch the battle a little longer from one last fortification. It is heroism at its finest—to fight for life until no soldier remains standing, until they've all willingly sacrificed themselves for the cause.

I speak my name to her softly as the hospice literature advises me to do. There seems to be a slight upturn in my mother's eyebrows and a perceptible curling of her lip, which I need to imagine is a smile. So I speak it again, but there is nothing more. The hospice literature advises also that the patient can often hear you even if she doesn't acknowledge that she's heard. I wonder if this is true even if the patient is deaf. I say to my mother that I love her, with nothing but a sense of true and honest genuineness, which, although I've thought it and said it before, this time feels different. Perhaps for the first time ever, I say, "I love you," to my mother in a way a parent would say, "I love you," to a child of theirs—that is, without qualification. I hold her cool, blue hand, which I remember many times thinking displayed spontaneously a startling grace and sensitivity and fluidity, which had always made me wonder if there was a dancer or an artist inside of her whom she had never allowed to come out completely.

I squeeze her palm slightly, and I think she is squeezing my palm back. I put my hand on her forehead, which has been warm when I've done it before, but it's cool, too. Now the air all around Central Command is cooling down, and the fuel of battle will soon be expired, and then even the commandants will shiver and shudder in front of the last dying embers of the last winter morning of my mother's life.

I tell Mike I'm going to go find Blaine and see how he's doing.

Blaine is the last one in the dining room as always. "The last dog hung," he describes himself. The kitchen crew is cleaning the table all around him, and each time one of them walks by his table, he says, "You can take most of this stuff now, honey. I'm all done."

And the woman says to him this day, with a slight smile of tenderness, what she says to him every other day with the same tenderness, "That's okay, Blaine, take your time."

"No, honey. I mean it. I'm done with all of it, except for this glass, which he picks up to distinguish it from the rest of the incredible array of breakfast foods they put before him each morning and all of the other residents there too, most of which are left uneaten.

I sit down, and my father puts his hand out for me to shake, which I do, and I ask him how he's doing. "Not well, Pete. Let me ask you something. Is Roberta dying?"

"Dad, we talked about this yesterday, remember?"

"Yes, I remember," he says. And then he bursts into crying, and tears flow like small, unblocked streams down his face into his lap. "But now I am able to say the words—'Roberta is dying'—and believe them." I put my hand under the table on his leg and squeeze it and tell him I'm sorry. He takes my hand in his. He recovers, and we talk about it more. Fifteen minutes later, I say, "I'm going back to Mom's room. When you finish up eating, you walk down there too, okay?

We finally disperse. Aaron, my brother Bill's son, upon being told that Roberta was in bad shape, drove all the way from Chicago with his wife Amber to be with his grandmother and then with Blaine before finally arriving at our house long after dark.

The six of us have talked about Blaine and Roberta until finally it is time to shut down the discussion and go home. We all hug in the living room, and Aaron and Amber leave first. Then Mike and Mary start out the door. Mary turns to Judy and me and says, "I'm going to spend the night with Roberta. I think it's important that someone be with her tonight."

* * * * *

I sleep with rare purity, only waking one time in the night and then falling back to sleep and sleeping soundly again until five a.m.

I arise and make tea and wonder happily why the phone didn't wake me up. Then I realize that my mother once again miraculously has dodged a certain bullet aimed truly at her heart. I go upstairs in the dark to spend my first two sacred hours of the morning alone in my office on the third floor, drinking tea, listening to music, writing, and thinking.

At seven o'clock, just as the sun is rising, the phone rings. It's my brother. He tells me that Mary, who slept beside my mother the entire night in the nursing home, has just called him to say that Roberta is dead. She died at 5:57 in the morning.

The bullet has finally found its mark. My mother is gone.

Roberta is lying dead in her bed at Seminary Manor. There has never been a moment of my life before when my mother was not alive on the earth with me. Seeing her dead body inspires in me an odd mixture of shock and curiosity. I feel some part of me melting away, which I'm certain I will never be able to identify positively but only as a loss.

It seems that I can still perceive tiny movements of my mother's skin and lips, and her nose seems to twitch just a little. It's not verifiable (the scientific method is irrelevant here in mapping details of the heart), but I'm perceiving it nonetheless. Is this because her body has never been without life before and that I am feeling a type of kinesthesia associated with sixty-four years of experiencing her movement?

I am suddenly aware for the first time ever—because it is the flesh from which my own flesh originated—of the peculiar phenomenon of a body without consciousness. It is impossible to grasp. I reach forward and uncover my mother's arms. Her hands are supinely resting on top of each other as if they were put there together warmly by her in a conscious final act sometime before she'd died, to show repose. I take her right hand at the wrist and pick it up. I have read about the repulsive quality of dead flesh, of its being cold and lifeless and hard. So I am moved that my mother's skin is warm—and still soft—warmer than when I'd touched it yesterday, in fact. I pick up her tiny wrist for the last time, and she lets me without resistance. I hold her hand. It's warm, too. I am very happy about this and am glad that I can warmly resurrect last feelings for the touch of my mother who is dead but who in other ways, besides the fact of it, seems still to be living. But her expression doesn't change. Her mouth is locked into an amiable circle as if she's coquettishly blowing a smoke ring in a bar in a younger day. Her nose, which I see from the bottom, is crooked like a broken nose. I'd never noticed that before, but I'd never looked up at the bottom of her nose as an adult.

I keep holding her hand, adding my warmth to hers, while I stand up and place the palm of my left hand against her forehead as I've done at least five other times in the last month like a doctor searching for a fever. She always smiled. Her forehead is warm, too. I am able now to examine her face up close. It is alarming that, despite the other lively sensations of my mother that I've discovered or have created, illusory or real, her face is the deadest part of her now, which will absolutely never show affection and will never smile again. It was always the liveliest part of her, the part which looked into my heart with fierce honesty and into whose countenance I could look with my entire range of emotions: fear, joy, happiness, deception, pride, anger, sadness, regret, guilt, triumph. The overall summation of her whole being had always seemed to start with the nucleus of her face. But now her face is the same every instant that I look at it. It never changes. It's not her. It's her body. It has no consciousness anymore. It's the part of her that was really her, and which is now gone. Forever.

"How will my father possibly be able to adjust to that, ever?" I ask myself as I hear his walker strain and scrape as he picks it up and drags a fast right turn with it into my mother's doorway behind me.

Part Three

Summer 2010

The phone rings. My father answers it.

"Hello, this is the Peoria Journal Star calling."

It's a young woman's voice, which I can hear clearly even though she's speaking into my father's ear and not mine. She is speaking so fast that the words run together as one long one.

"Could-I-interest-you-in-the-special-one-year-subscription-which-we're-offering-for-this-week-only-at-a-fifty-percent-reduction?"

"Hello?"

My father says this word back into the receiver with a stunned, dull, monotonous voice that sounds out of touch—perhaps permanently.

"Hi-this-is-the-Peoria-Journal-Star. Could-I-interest-you-in-our-one-year-subscription-we're-offering-for-this-week-only-at-a-fifty-percent-reduction?"

"*Hello?*"

My father repeats the word in the same faltering bovine-like fashion as before, only louder, designed—I'm sure of it—to portray a lower intelligence unable to grasp the situation. Or unable to hear. Or both. If I were the caller, I would hang up instantly.

I look over at him, thinking that maybe he's put the wrong end of the phone to his ear and actually *cannot* hear anything. But no, that's not it. He has devised on the spot another ruse, even still at the age of nearly ninety-six, to make life's pace slow down by gently torturing into compliance the caller who's trying to speed it up.

My father would *never* say anything insulting to a telemarketer or tell them he wasn't interested in them or in their product. He would never tell them not to call back again, nor would he have malice in his heart toward them or toward their actions. In fact, if he were alone, he might just engage them for as long as they'd permit it. One way or the other, though, he would conquer them with absurdity. He'd blow their minds with incomprehensible deliberation and with apparently never-ending time waste. The best of them would eventually understand his mission, though, as being really rather endearing, if not actually funny, and eventually also, in some way, enlightening. The rest, like this caller, will just guess they've run into an imbecile.

The young woman tries again.

"Hi, this is the Peoria Journal Star. Could I interest you in our one-year subscription we're offering for this week only at a fifty percent reduction?"

"*Hellooo!*"

She hangs up.

My father pulls the phone away from his lips and looks at me and smiles and says with mock shame for his behavior, "And just think of it. I used to be a newspaper man."

When my mother died, Antonio took me aside and said, "Peter, you need to keep a close eye on your father now. This will be very hard on him." Others said that, too.

Three times Seminary Manor has called for an ambulance to take Blaine to the emergency room. One time they thought he'd had a massive stroke, and so did I when I saw him because he could not answer any questions with anything but a monotonous grunt. Another time he insisted that he needed to see the doctor—at nine p.m.—because something was wrong with him. He couldn't say what it was. Finally, we decided he was terribly sad and empty and was experiencing emotions foreign to him, which he could only conceptualize as illness.

Seminary Manor respectfully called me each time for my permission to call an ambulance, and each time I went to Seminary Manor first to see him before the ambulance arrived. Then I followed it to the hospital and stayed with him until they admitted him or didn't. If they didn't, then I'd drive him home.

These midnight emergencies have diminished. There may not be another one because he has reached a place of peace. I believe this comes from his awareness that a huge burden has been lifted from him. My very sick and very sad and often angry mother had become estranged from her husband of nearly seventy years for reasons that none of us, especially Blaine, could fully understand. He kept trying to, futilely.

Now she is gone, and it's over. Now there's no possibility of ever understanding what couldn't be understood when she was alive. With each day, she fades further and further away from my father's also-fading memory. There is something merciful about this.

I brought this up to him once—his new sense of peace—and he readily agreed with me and seemed happy I'd articulated his feelings. But then he said, "I just wait. And in the air I feel her hovering above me, and then I sing, *Abide with me; fast falls the eventide; the darkness deepens; Lord, with me abide; When other helpers fail and comforts flee, Help of the helpless, oh, abide with me.*" And while he sings, tears roll down his face, and his voice wails slightly.

I believe more and more that my father himself will eventually just fade out quietly in the night like his own sweet father did because the show is over, and it's time to go home.

Fall 2010

About ten years ago, my father and I began taking an annual trip together back to Olds, Iowa, his hometown. It became a generalized trip to any of the towns in eastern Iowa my father had spent time in, including Olds, Winfield, New London, Mt. Pleasant, Fairfield, Morning Sun, and others. It was rural wandering around country roads. "That's the creek where my dog Peggy and I would trap muskrats," or, "There's the farmhouse my mother lived in as a kid."

We wandered around for a whole day, knocking on doors he hadn't knocked on for decades and often surprising people from his past. We aroused many a heartfelt reunion that way.

The trips were only partially planned out by him. When we started out, he would loosely discuss an itinerary or sometimes just point in a direction. Invariably, the day would unfold serendipitously upon nuggets of wonder neither of us had anticipated.

Once we ended up in Olds in the afternoon. It was early October, and so the late afternoon sun had an orange, peaceful memory-evoking ability that made the day even more poignant. We'd been at a big farmhouse of a friend of my father's father where the woman was still living alone.

She was beautiful—with hair still dark—vivacious, and with a lovely, intelligent, and gently humorous personality. The sun was near the horizon, coming in her bay window on the south of a huge parlor room with very high ceilings where we were sitting drinking coffee. Her husband had been named Blaine, and my grandparents had named their son, my father, after him. Mrs. DeYarman gave us delicious cookies she'd made to go with our coffee. She didn't want us to leave, and when we did, I knew it was the last time my father would ever see her alive. Her farmhouse was magnificent, huge, with many outbuildings and ancient trees in the front yard right on the old two-lane road into town.

Just down the street was the high school, where we went next. It was an old, two-story, dark-brick building. My father and I walked around outside of the school lot, and he told me stories about himself and his friends. It was around four o'clock in the afternoon and getting cold. We went into the school to look around. My father showed me various administrative rooms of the school, the gym, and even the bathroom, all of which held memories for him. Even though school was still in session, we hadn't really seen anyone as we started up the granite stairway to the second floor.

A bell rang, and all at once students began flooding the hallways. It was the end of the school day. We felt like salmon swimming upstream, fighting to reach the top of the stairs with torrents of students flooding over us, loud and joyous to be moving toward their freedom outside. We finally made it to the top of the stairs and saw a teacher come out of the first door on the right. He looked stern and a bit annoyed to see us going in the wrong direction, and he said to my father, "Is there something I can help you find?"

My father took him by the hand and held onto it and looked him gently in the eyes a long time and then said, "Yes, sir, there is. Can you help me find my youth?"

My father's body brace, which he's worn dutifully night and day, inextricably—and, I've believed, needlessly—since Dr. Amit prescribed it several years ago, hangs neatly now on a towel rack next to the toilet. His never-to-be-removed toe brace and his blue knee support, also inseparable parts of his body for as long as he's been in Seminary Manor, are lying on the table beside his bed. He doesn't ask me anymore to check his flashlight batteries. His omnipresent watch is off his wrist, lying away from him on the other side of the table next to the urinal with a half inch or so of extremely dark urine in it.

There are no Kleenex boxes nearby. My father's walker hasn't been moved for days. The delicate, beautiful, big, pastel-yellow butterfly that Judy bought my mother that she'd hung from her Seminary Estates window and Blaine had taken when she'd died and had hung from his, is pointed downward toward the ground…on a collision course, perhaps. "Happy Birthday" is curling off the wall behind him.

"Nineteen fourteen," Blaine says softly. "Nineteen *fourteen*," he repeats with a bit more emphasis upon the "fourteen." "Nineteen *fourteen*," he says loudly. "*Nineteen fourteen!*" he practically yells until Amy, the hospice nurse, finally acknowledges that he'd meant 1914 when he had said, "Nineteen eighteen," in response to her question, "What year were you born?" She also asks him where he was born, and he doesn't know but is happy when I say, "Winfield."

"Yes! Winfield, Iowa," he mumbles boldly but barely understandable.

All day long nurses and attendants check my father's room to see how he's doing. They hug him and kiss him and call him "babe" and "honey" while tears flow down their cheeks and they sob with their faces buried in his. He says over and over the one declaration they *can* understand, "I love you."

They all answer, "I love you, too, Blaine."

They keep vigil behind me as I hold my father's hand, which is growing colder. Almost nothing of what he struggles intermittently to communicate is intelligible, but now and then the one question that he asks off and on stands out, "Am I dying?"

No one ever answers it honestly—"Yes!"—but instead evades it with one trite response or another— "We're all dying, aren't we?" or, "You're getting weak, Blaine."

One time while Lori was giving him a swab of morphine under his tongue, he said, "Am I dying?"

And she said, "No, I'm just giving you medicine."

And he said, "To make me die?" and she laughed.

I go home again at eight p.m. to eat, and after dinner I fall asleep on the couch, exhausted. I'm awakened by a call from Seminary Manor—a "status report," they call it. Essentially, Blaine's breathing is more labored. I want to say, "Is he dying?" but I'm afraid they'll say, "We're all dying."

Against my will—I have been there all day for three days and am weary of it—I return to Seminary Manor at 9:15 p.m. The room is full of nurses and aides, still crying, hugging my father, attending to every need they seem able to discern or infer from his plaintive voice that is no longer able to make clear words but somehow, as my father could always do, can rally people to his cause.

At ten thirty the shifts change. All of the staff members of Seminary Manor who have become dear friends of mine over these long years of pathos laced with humor are leaving to go home. Blaine has said, "I love you," to most of them an uncountable number of times. Some of them, perhaps, are people who had never been told this by anyone until Blaine. They are thereby bonded to him emotionally, inextricably, in a bizarre, shared, almost connubial but somehow permissible way, irrespective of vast age differences (twenty-six and ninety-six, say). They are there again, crying and laughing nervously, generally agitated to be serving him some form of his last rites. They make a seat for me in the front row beside him, and I take hold of his cold, bony, bluish hand again. My presence, as his more dignified but similar heir, stills the unrest, and we all sit silently and watch him breathing like an exhausted runner at the end of the race. His eyes are off focus onto some spot in the near distance, probably heaven, in a relatively peaceful pose except for now and then when he tries to request something and everyone goes blank and apprehensive with lack of understanding until at last Blaine fades back into silence again.

Finally, sometime later in the night, they all leave to go home long after their shift ends. Danishie is the last to leave. I stand up and hug her and say, "Thank you for caring for my father the way you have." She sobs on my shoulder and can't let go of me, but when she does, there is a wet spot of her tears on my shirt.

The room is empty—just Blaine and me. I hold his hand and whisper again for him to let go now, let himself pass on, and that it's going to be all right, a peaceful, beautiful place with no pain or no sorrow; that he has no other business here on earth and that no one needs him to stay, that he has no responsibilities anymore, that Mom needs him in Heaven, and that he'll see his mother, Gladys, and his father, Ralph, and his sister, Lois. He seems to agree happily with all of these glad prospects, and he repeatedly appears to thank me and seems enthusiastically assured that we can handle the rest of life here on earth without him.

His forehead is cold now, and his cheeks are too. His tendons are shaking without control, and his muscles are going into tiny spasms the way my mother's did too. I can feel them in my hand. I can see his pulse beat erratically fast between his thumb and index finger.

Nurse Antonio comes in with his coat on to bid one last farewell to Blaine. He kisses him on the forehead, saying, "Okay, buddy, I am leaving now. I'll see you later, okay?" Blaine mumbles things poignant on his tongue, none of which Tony can understand. Like all of us, though, Tony answers what he thinks Blaine has asked, but Blaine sighs soundlessly, disappointed not to have been understood. A less determined man than my father would give up trying.

Antonio turns to me and is shocked at how cool Blaine's face is already. He whispers, very honestly, as no one else quite can do, "He is passing now. He may not make it through the night. Everything is shutting down." Then he rubs my neck as if to say, "Carry on, soldier, the last battle is almost over," and hugs me and walks out the door.

In a few minutes, I say to Blaine, "I think we should turn the light off now and take a nap together, don't you?" to which he heartily agrees with affirmative noises, confirming the essence of our relationship of the last several months.

We haven't talked much during those months— what more was left to say and with what memory to enact it? When I'd visit, we would nap together. At first he'd felt guilty for not conversing with me and would say—when he could still talk—"Are you okay with just taking a nap together? Are there things you expect me to say?" and I'd approved our nap as a worthy, single-shared purpose, which was a perfect form of fellowship in his eyes. He would always say, "You'll wake me up before you go, won't you?" and I'd say yes, and we'd close our eyes and start our nap. Then he'd say, "Pete? You'll wake me up before you go, won't you?" and I'd say yes again. And then we'd nap together in a sacred silence in his own created space that housed his whole being now.

When I would leave, I'd wake him up and would tell him, "I'm leaving now, Dad." He wouldn't beg me to stay as before but would just say, "Okay, Pete, thanks for coming. I love you," and would fall back asleep.

So now we do it again for the last time ever. The room is dark except for the night light. It feels peaceful here as it always has. Judy's decorations and pictures and other memorabilia are hung everywhere on the walls, denoting stages of his life there mainly of joy and happiness and camaraderie. There's hardly a spot on the wall left vacant.

Finally he falls asleep, being wholly peaceful for the first time all day, with no one else around him now to mourn or fear or delay his coming passing and cajole him into staying on earth a little longer. Eventually, I can tell that he is in a deep sleep. I stand up and look over at him, and he doesn't move. His amazingly quick attention, which ordinarily could have discerned from within sleep a disturbance in the room that signaled someone coming in or leaving, is now focused inward. There is no pain. There are no unanswered questions.

He has not asked me to wake him up before I leave. It is the last entry in his life log before the final exit. *Now* is the time of the Walrus. *Godot* has finally come.

I put my sweater on and then my coat. I stare at him a long while with just a hidden night light illuminating his face in reflected light, enough to find it in the dark. He looks like his sweet father, Rusty.

"I love you, Dad," I say.

He doesn't answer. His lamps are out. The night watchman can go home now. It's almost midnight.

I arise at three thirty a.m. and realize at once that I should return to Seminary Manor. I put my clothes on from yesterday and brush my teeth and go downstairs into the kitchen in which the only light is the yellow one flashing on the telephone, indicating someone's called. I listen to the message that says to call Michelle at Seminary Manor. There's a message after that, but I don't listen to it. I call Michelle. She seems relieved but desperate at the same time.

"We've been trying to get you. Your father passed away in the night."

It's the start of Thanksgiving Day.

Even such is Time, which takes in trust
Our youth, our joys, and all we have,
Who in the dark and silent grave,
When we have wandered all our ways,
Shuts up the story of our days:
And from which earth, and grave, and dust,
The Lord shall raise me up, I trust.

—Sir Walter Raleigh

"The present lives brighter as a memory."

Collage #1: Portrait of Blaine by Lonnie Stewart (31" X 41");
Galesburg's first 3-color ad (1976); Gorhams' First
Presbyterian Church.

Collage #2: Blaine and Roberta's 50th Wedding Anniversary;
In their home at Lake Bracken; Wearing antlers at
Christmas; In Minnesota home; Blaine loved Indian
wisdom and history.

Collage #3: Will (Peter and Judy's son) spiking Grandpa's hair;
Peter on Blaine's lap on fishing trip; Extended family
at Minnesota house; Judy and Blaine, Christmas.

Collage #4: Blaine in Peter's tuxedo; 94th birthday party, blowing
out (two) candles; Beating a drum, as always; Sittin'
on the dock of the bay; Christmas in the hospital.